PENGUIN BOOKS

BIOENERGETICS

Dr. Alexander Lowen is the creator of bioenergetics, which he has defined as "a therapeutic technique to help a person get back together with his body and to help him enjoy to the fullest degree possible the life of the body." Incorporating direct work on the body into the psychoanalytic process, Dr. Lowen practices psychiatry in New York and Connecticut and is the executive director of the Institute of Bioenergetic Analysis. He is married and lives in New Canaan, Connecticut, with his wife and son.

By Alexander Lowen, M.D.

LOVE AND ORGASM
THE BETRAYAL OF THE BODY
PLEASURE
THE LANGUAGE OF THE BODY
DEPRESSION AND THE BODY
FEARS OF LIFE

Bioenergetics

ALEXANDER LOWEN, M.D.

PENGUIN BOOKS

PENGUIN BOOKS

Published by the Penguin Group
27 Wrights Lane, London W8 5TZ, England
Viking Penguin Inc., 40 West 23rd Street, New York, New York 10010, USA
Penguin Books Australia Ltd, Ringwood, Victoria, Australia
Penguin Books Canada Ltd, 2801 John Street, Markham, Ontario, Canada L3R 1B4
Penguin Books (NZ) Ltd, 182–190 Wairau Road, Auckland 10, New Zealand

Penguin Books Ltd, Registered Offices: Harmondsworth, Middlesex, England

First published in the United States of America
by Coward, McCann & Geoghegan, Inc., 1975
First published in Great Britain by Coventure Ltd 1976
Published in Penguin Books 1976
Reprinted 1977 (twice), 1978 (twice), 1980, 1981 (twice), 1983 (twice),
1984, 1985, 1986, 1988

ISBN 0 14 00.4322 5
Library of Congress catalog card number: 76-16442

Printed and bound in Great Britain by
Cox & Wyman Ltd, Reading
Set in Baskerville

For permission to quote from copyrighted material,
the author makes grateful acknowledgment to Simon & Schuster, Inc.,
for an excerpt from *Report to Greco* by Nikos Kazantzakis,
copyright © Simon & Schuster, Inc., 1965.
Reprinted by permission of the publisher.

To My Parents
whose devotion to me made it possible for me to confront and work through the conflicts in my personality

Contents

Three kinds of souls, three prayers:

I am a bow in your hands, lord.
Draw me, lest I rot.

Do not overdraw me, Lord, I shall break.

Overdraw me, Lord, and who cares if I break.

—Nikos Kazantzakis, *Report to Greco*

BIOENERGETICS

I. From Reich to Bioenergetics

Reichian Therapy, 1940–1945

Bioenergetics is based on the work of Wilhelm Reich. He was my teacher from 1940 to 1952 and my analyst from 1942 to 1945. I met Reich in 1940 at the New School for Social Research in New York, where he was giving a course on Character Analysis. I was intrigued by the catalogue description of this course in which reference was made to the functional identity of a person's character with his bodily attitude or muscular armoring. Armoring refers to the total pattern of chronic muscular tensions in the body. They are defined as an armor because they serve to protect an individual against painful and threatening emotional experiences. They shield him from dangerous impulses within his own personality as well as from attacks by others.

For a number of years prior to my meeting Reich, I had been pursuing an investigation into the mind-body relationship. This interest grew out of my personal experience with physical activity in sports and calisthenics. During the 1930's I had been an athletic director at several summer camps, and had found that a regular program of physical activity not only improved my physical health but also had a positive effect on my mental state. In the course of my investigations I looked into the ideas of Emile Jacques-Dalcroze called Eurythmics, and Edmund Jacobson's concept of Progressive Relaxation and Yoga. These studies confirmed my strong feeling that one could influence mental attitudes by working with the body, but their approach did not entirely satisfy me.

Reich captured my imagination with his first lecture. He introduced the course with a discussion of the problem of hysteria. Psychoanalysis, Reich pointed out, had been able to elucidate the historical factor in the hysterical conversion syndrome. This factor proved to be a sexual trauma that the person had experienced in early childhood and that in later years had been completely repressed and forgotten. The repression and the subsequent conversion of the repressed ideas and feelings into the symptom constituted the dynamic factor in the illness. Although the concepts of repression and conversion were at that time well-established tenets of psychoanalytic theory, the process by which a repressed idea was converted into a physical symptom was not at all understood. What was lacking in psychoanalytic theory, according to Reich, was an understanding of the time factor. "Why," Reich asked, "did the symptom develop when it did and not sooner or later?" To answer this question, one had to know what was going on in the life of the patient during those interim years. How was he dealing with his sexual feelings during this period? Reich believed that the *repression* of the original trauma was maintained by the *suppression* of sexual feeling. This suppression constituted the predisposition to the hysterical symptom, which was triggered into manifestation by a later sexual incident. For Reich the suppression of sexual feeling together with the characterological attitude that accompanied it constituted the true neurosis; the symptom itself was only its overt expression.

The consideration of this element—namely, the behavior and attitude of the patient to sexuality—introduced an "economic" factor into the problem of neurosis. The term "economic" refers to the forces that predispose an individual to the development of neurotic symptoms.

I was greatly impressed by Reich's perspicacity. Having read a number of Freud's books, I was generally familiar with psychoanalytic thinking, but I did not recall that this factor had been discussed. I sensed Reich was introducing me to a new way of thinking about human problems, and I was immediately excited. The full significance of this new approach dawned on me only gradually as Reich expanded his ideas during the course. I realized that the economic factor was an important key to the understanding of personality, for it dealt with how a person handles his sexual energy or his energy in general. How much energy does a person have, and how much does he discharge in sexual activity? One's energy economy or sexual economy refers to the balance one maintains between energy charge and discharge or between sexual excitement and sexual release. Only when this economy or balance is upset does the hysterical conversion symptom develop. Muscular armoring or chronic muscular tensions serve to maintain this balanced economy by binding the energy that cannot be discharged.

My interest in Reich grew as he proceeded to unfold his thinking and observations. The difference between a healthy sexual economy and a neurotic economy was not in the question of balance. At this time Reich was speaking of sex economy rather than energy economy; however, the terms were synonymous in his mind. A neurotic individual maintains a balance by binding his energy in muscular tensions and limiting his sexual excitement. A healthy individual has no limitation, and his energy is not bound in muscular armoring. All his energy is, therefore, available for sexual pleasure or any other creative expression. His energy economy functions at a high level. A low-level energy economy is characteristic of most people and is responsible for the tendency to depression which is endemic in our culture.*

Although Reich presented his ideas clearly and logically, I remained slightly skeptical during the first half of the course. This attitude, I have since learned, is typical of me. To it I credit much of my ability to think things out for myself. My skepticism of Reich focused on his apparent overemphasis of the role of sex in emotional problems. *Sex is not the full answer,* I thought. Then, without my being aware of it, this skepticism suddenly vanished. During the balance of the course I felt completely convinced of the validity of Reich's position.

The reason for this change became clear to me about two years later, after I had myself been in therapy with Reich for a short time. It occurred to me that I had not completed my reading of one of the books listed by Reich in the bibliography for his course, Freud's *Three Essays on the Theory of Sexuality.* I had got halfway into the second essay, entitled "Infantile Sexuality," when I stopped reading. I realized, then, that this essay had touched my unconscious anxiety about my own infantile sexuality, and while I was unprepared to face that anxiety, I could no longer maintain my skepticism about the importance of sexuality.

Reich's course on character analysis ended in January, 1941. In the period that intervened between the termination of the course and the start of my own therapy, I remained in touch with him. I attended a number of meetings at his house in Forest Hills where we discussed the social implications of his sex-economic concepts and evolved a project for implementing these concepts in a program of community mental health. In Europe Reich had been a pioneer in this area. (This aspect of his work and my relationshp to it will be explored more fully in a subsequent book about Reich.)

I began my personal therapy with Reich in the spring of

*Alexander Lowen, *Depression and the Body* (New York, Coward, McCann & Geoghegan, Inc., 1972).

1942. During the preceding year I had been a fairly frequent visitor at Reich's laboratory. He showed me some of the work he was doing with bio preparations and cancerous tissue. Then, one day, he said to me, "Lowen, if you are interested in this work, there is only one way to get into it, and that is by going into therapy." His statement startled me, for I had not contemplated this move. I told him, "I am interested, but what I want is to become famous." Reich took this remark seriously, for he replied, "I will make you famous." Over the years I have regarded Reich's statement as a prophecy. It was the push I needed to overcome my resistance and to launch me into my lifework.

My first therapeutic session with Reich was an experience I will never forget. I went with the naïve assumption that there was nothing wrong with me. It was to be purely a training analysis. I lay down on the bed wearing a pair of bathing trunks. Reich did not use a couch since this was a body-oriented therapy. I was told to bend my knees, relax and breathe with my mouth open and my jaw relaxed. I followed these intructions and waited to see what would happen. After some time Reich said, "Lowen, you're not breathing." I answered, "Of course I'm breathing; otherwise I'd be dead. He then remarked, "Your chest isn't moving. Feel my chest." I placed my hand on his chest and noticed that it was rising and falling with each breath. Mine clearly was not.

I lay back again and resumed breathing, this time with my chest moving outward on inspiration and inward on expiration. Nothing happened. My breathing proceeded easily and deeply. After a while Reich said, "Lowen, drop your head back and open your eyes wide." I did as I was told and . . . a scream burst from my throat.

It was a beautiful day in early spring, and the windows of the room opened onto the street. To avoid any embarrassment with his neighbors, Dr. Reich asked me to straighten my head, which stopped the scream. I resumed my deep breathing. Strangely, the scream had not disturbed me. I was not connected to it emotionally. I did not feel any fear. After I had breathed again for a while, Dr. Reich asked me to repeat the procedure: Put my head back and open my eyes wide. Again the scream came out. I hesitate to say that I screamed because I did not seem to do it. The scream happened to me. Again I was detached from it, but I left the session with the feeling that I was not as all right as I thought. There were "things" (images, emotions) in my personality that were hidden from consciousness, and I knew then that they would have to come out.

At that time Reich called his therapy Character Analytic Vegetotherapy. Character analysis had been his great contribution to psychoanalytic theory, one for which he was highly regarded by all analysts. Vegetotherapy referred to the mobilization of feeling through breathing and other body techniques that activated the vegetative centers (the ganglia of the autonomic nervous system) and liberated "vegetative" energies.

Vegetotherapy represented a breakthrough from a purely verbal analysis to direct work with the body. It had occurred some nine years earlier in the course of an analytic session. Reich described it as follows:

> "In Copenhagen, 1933, I treated a man who put up especially strong resistance against the uncovering of his passive-homosexual phantasies. This resistance was manifested in an extreme attitude of stiffness of the neck ("stiff-necked"). After an energetic attack upon his resistance, he suddenly gave in, but in an alarming manner. The color of his face kept changing rapidly from white to yellow or blue; the skin was mottled and of various hues; he had severe pains in the in the neck and in the occiput; he had diarrhea, felt worn out, and seemed to have lost hold.*

*Wilhelm Reich, *The Function of the Orgasm* (New York, Orgone Institute Press, 1942), pp. 239-240.

The "'energetic attack" was only verbal, but it was directed at the patient's "stiff-necked" attitude. *"Affects had broken through somatically after the patient had yielded in a psychic defense attitude."* Reich realized then that "energy can be bound by chronic muscular tension."* From that time Reich studied the bodily attitudes of his patients. He observed: "There is no neurotic individual who does not show a tension in the abdomen."† He noted the common tendency of patients to hold their breath and inhibit exhalation as a means of controlling their feelings. He concluded that holding the breath served to diminish the organism's energy by reducing its metabolic activities, which in turn decreased the production of anxiety.

For Reich, then, the first step in the therapeutic procedure was to get the patient to breathe easily and deeply. The second was to mobilize whatever emotional expression was most evident in the patient's face or manner. In my case this expression was fear. We have seen what a powerful effect this procedure had on me.

Succeeding sessions followed the same general pattern. I would lie on the bed and breathe as freely as I could, trying to allow a deep expiration to occur. I was directed to give in to my body and not control any expression or impulse that emerged. A number of things happened that gradually brought me into contact with early memories and experiences. At first the deeper breathing to which I was not accustomed produced strong, tingling sensations in my hands which, on two occasions, developed into a severe carpopedal spasm, severely cramping the hands. This reaction disappeared as my body accommodated to the increased energy the deeper breathing produced. Tremors developed in my legs when I moved my knees gently together and apart and in my lips when I followed an impulse to reach out with them.

Several breakthroughs of feeling and associated memories followed. On one occasion, as I was lying on the bed breathing,

**Ibid.*, p. 240.
†*Ibid.*, p. 273.

my body started to rock involuntarily. The rocking increased until I sat up. Then, without my seeming to do so, I got off the bed, turned to face it, and started to pound it with both fists. As I was doing this, my father's face appeared on the bedsheet, and I suddenly knew I was hitting him for a spanking he had given me when I was a young boy. Some years later I asked my father about this incident. He said it was the only spanking he had ever given me. He explained that I had come home very late and my mother was upset and worried. He had spanked me so that I would not do that again. The interesting part of this experience, as of the scream, was its completely spontaneous and involuntary nature. I was moved to strike the bed as I was to scream, not by any conscious thought but by a force within that had taken over and possessed me.

On another occasion, while lying on the bed breathing, I began to get an erection. I had an impulse to touch my penis, but I inhibited it. Then I recalled an interesting episode out of childhood. I saw myself as a boy of five walking through the apartment where I lived, urinating on the floor. My parents were out. I knew I was doing it to get back at my father, who had scolded me the day before for holding my penis.

It took about nine months of therapy for me to find out what had caused the scream in that first session. I had not screamed since then. As time went on, I thought I had the distinct impression that there was an image I was afraid to see. Contemplating the ceiling from my position on the bed, I sensed it would appear one day. Then it did, and it was my mother's face looking down at me with an expression of intense anger in her eyes. I knew immediately that this was the face that had frightened me. I relived the experience as if it were occurring in the present. I was a baby about nine months of age, lying in a carriage outside the door of my home. I had been crying loudly for my mother. She was obviously busy in the house, and my persistent crying had upset her. She came out, furious at me. Lying there on Reich's bed at the age of thirty-three, I looked at her image and, using words I could not have known as a baby, I said, "Why are you so angry with me? I am only crying because I want you."

In those days Reich used another technique to implement the therapy. At the beginning of each session he asked his patients to tell him all the negative thoughts they had about him. He believed that all patients had a negative transference to him as well as a positive one, and he did not trust the positive unless negative thoughts and ideas were expressed first. I found this extremely difficult to do. Having made a commitment to Reich and to the therapy, I had banished all negative thoughts from my mind. I felt I had nothing to complain about. Reich had been very generous with me, and I had no doubt about his sincerity, his integrity or the validity of his concepts. Characteristically, I was determined to make the therapy succeed, and it was not until it almost failed that I opened up my feelings to Reich.

Following the experience of fear when I saw my mother's face, I went through a long stretch of several months during which I made no progress. I was seeing Reich three times a week then, but I was blocked because I couldn't tell Reich my feelings about him. I wanted him to take a fatherly interest in me, not merely a therapeutic one, but knowing this was an unreasonable request, I couldn't express it. Struggling inwardly with the problem, I got nowhere. Reich seemed unaware of my conflict. Try as hard as I could to let my breathing become deeper and fuller, it just didn't work.

I had been in therapy for about a year when this impasse developed. When it seemed to go on indefinitely, Reich suggested I quit. "Lowen," he said, "you are unable to give in to your feelings. Why don't you give up?" His words were a sentence of doom. To give up meant the failure of all my dreams. I broke down and cried deeply. It was the first time I had sobbed since I was a child. I could no longer hold back my feelings. I told Reich what I wanted from him, and he listened sympathetically.

I do not know if Reich had intended to end the therapy or

whether his suggestion that I terminate treatment was a maneuver to break through my resistance, but I had the strong impression that he meant it. In either case, his action produced the desired result. I began to move again in the therapy.

For Reich the goal of therapy was the development by the patient of the capacity to give in fully to the spontaneous and involuntary movements of the body that were part of the respiratory process. Thus the emphasis was on letting the breathing take place fully and deeply. If this was done, the respiratory waves produced an undulating movement of the body that Reich called the orgasm reflex.

In the course of his earlier psychoanalytic work Reich had come to the conclusion that emotional health was related to the capacity for full surrender in the sexual act or what he called orgastic potency. Reich had found there was no neurotic individual who had this capacity. A neurosis not only blocked surrender, but by binding energy in chronic muscular tensions prevented that energy from being available for sexual release. Reich had also found that patients who gained the ability to achieve full orgastic satisfaction in the sexual act became and remained free of any neurotic behavior or attitude. The full orgasm, according to Reich, discharged all of the organism's excess energy, and consequently, there was no energy to support or maintain the neurotic symptom or behavior.

It is important to understand that Reich defined orgasm as different from an ejaculation or a climax. It represented an involuntary response of the *total* body, manifested in rhythmic, convulsive movements. The same type of movement can also occur when the breathing is completely free and the person surrenders to his body. In such case there is no climax or discharge of sexual excitement since there has been no buildup of such excitement. What happens is that the pelvis moves spontaneously forward with each exhalation and backward with each inhalation. These movements are produced by the respiratory wave as it travels down or up the body with expiration and inspiration. At the same time the head executes movements similar to the pelvis' except that it moves backward in the expiratory phase and then forward in the inspiratory phase. Theoretically, a patient whose body was free enough to have this reflex during the therapy session would also be capable of experiencing the full orgasm in intercourse. Such a patient could be considered emotionally healthy.

For many people who read Reich's *The Function of the Orgasm** these ideas may have seemed the fanciful imaginings of a sex-obsessed mind. They were first expressed, however, when Reich was already a highly regarded training psychoanalyst whose formulation of the character analytic concept and technique was considered one of the major contributions to analytic theory. Yet they were not accepted by most psychoanalysts, and even today they are unknown or ignored by most researchers in sex. Reich's concepts take on a convincing reality, however, when one experiences their validity in one's own body as I did. This conviction based on personal experience accounts for the fact that many of the psychiatrists and others who worked with Reich became, at least for a time, his enthusiastic followers.

Following the breakthrough of crying and the expression of my feelings for Reich, my breathing became easier and freer, my sexual responsiveness deeper and fuller. A number of changes occurred in my life. I married the girl I was in love with. Commitment to marriage was a big step for me. Also, I was actively preparing to become a Reichian therapist. During this year I attended a clinical seminar on character analysis conducted by Dr. Theodore P. Wolfe, who was Reich's closest associate in the United States and translator of Reich's first English-language publications. I had recently completed my premedical studies, and I was applying for the second time to a number of medical schools. My therapy progressed steadily but

*These ideas were first published in an earlier book, *Die Funktion des Orgasmus* (Internationaler Psychoanalytischer Verlag, 1927.)

slowly. Although there were no dramatic breakthroughs of feeling or memories in the sessions, I felt I was getting closer to the ability to surrender to my sexual feelings. I also felt closer to Reich.

Reich took a long summer vacation. He ended the year in June and resumed in mid-September. As this year's therapy drew to a close, Reich suggested we interrupt the treatment for a year. I was not finished, though. The orgasm reflex did not develop consistently although I felt very close to it. I had tried hard, but it was precisely this trying that was the stumbling block. The idea of a vacation seemed a good one, and I accepted Reich's suggestion. There were personal reasons, too, for my decision. Unable to get into a medical school at that time, I took a course in gross human anatomy at New York University in the fall of 1944.

My therapy with Reich was resumed in the fall of 1945 with sessions once a week. Within a short time the orgasm reflex came through consistently. There were several reasons for this positive development. During the year's leave of absence from therapy, striving to please Reich and gain sexual health was in abeyance, and I was able to assimilate and integrate my previous work with Reich. At this time, too, I saw my first patient as a Reichian therapist, which gave my spirit a tremendous boost. I felt I had come home and was aware of feeling very secure about my life. Surrender to my body, which also meant a surrender to Reich, became very easy. In a few months it was obvious to both of us that my therapy had come to a successful conclusion by his criteria. Years later I realized, however, that I had not resolved many of my major personality problems. My fear of asking for what I wanted even if it was unreasonable had not been fully discussed. My fear of failure and my need to succeed had not been worked through. My inability to cry unless I was pushed to the wall had not been explored. These problems were finally resolved many years later through bioenergetics.

I do not wish to say that the therapy with Reich was ineffective. If it did not fully resolve all my problems, it made me more aware of them. More important, however, it opened a way for me to self-realization and helped me advance toward that goal. It deepened and strengthened my commitment to the body as the basis of the personality. And it gave me a positive identification with my sexuality which has proved to be the cornerstone of my life.

Work as a Reichian Therapist, 1945–1953

In the fall of 1945 I saw my first patient. Although I had not yet gone to medical school, Reich encouraged this move on the basis of my educational background and my training with him, including my personal therapy. This training involved continued participation in the clinical seminars on character analytic vegetotherapy under the direction of Dr. Theodore Wolfe and in seminars Reich gave at his home in which he discussed the theoretical foundations of his approach, emphasizing the biological and energetic concepts that explained his work with the body.

Interest in Reichian therapy was steadily growing, as more people became acquainted with his ideas. The publication of *The Function of the Orgasm* in 1941 accelerated this development, although the book did not meet with a favorable critical response or gain a wide distribution. Reich had formed his own publishing company, the Orgone Institute Press, which had no salesmen and did no advertising. The promotion of his ideas and the book, then, was solely by word of mouth. Nevertheless, his ideas did spread, albeit slowly, and the demand for Reichian therapy increased. There were, however, very few trained character analysts available, and it was this, as much as my own personal readiness, that was responsible for my starting to do therapy.

For two years before leaving for Switzerland, I was a practicing Reichian therapist. In September, 1947, I left New York with my wife to enter the medical school of the University of Geneva from which I was graduated in June, 1951, with an MD degree. While in Switzerland, I also did a limited amount of therapy with some Swiss who had heard of Reich's work and were anxious to take advantage of this new therapeutic approach. Like so many young therapists, I began with the naïve assumption that I knew something about the emotional problems of people and with an assurance based more on enthusiasm than experience. Looking back on those years, I can see my limitations in both understanding and skill. Nevertheless, I believe I did help some people. My enthusiasm was a positive force, and the emphasis on breathing and "giving in" was a positive direction.

Prior to my leaving for Switzerland, an important development occurred in Reichian therapy—the use of direct contact with the patient's body to release muscular tensions which blocked his ability to give in to his feelings and allow the orgasm reflex to take place. During his work with me Reich occasionally applied pressure with his hands to some of the tense muscles in my body to help them relax. Usually, with me and with others, he applied such pressure to the jaw. In most people the jaw muscles are extremely tense—the jaw held tightly in an attitude of determination often verging on grimness or thrust forward defiantly or abnormally retracted. In all these cases it is not fully mobile, and its fixed position denotes a structured attitude. Under pressure jaw muscles become tired and "let go." As a result, the breathing becomes freer and deeper, and often involuntary tremors occur in the body and the legs. Other areas of muscular tension to which pressure was applied were the back of the neck, the lower back and the adductor muscles of the thighs. In all cases pressure was applied selectively only to those areas in which chronic muscular spasticity could be palpated.

The laying on of hands constituted an important deviation from traditional analytic practice. In Freudian analysis any physical contact between analyst and patient was strictly forbidden. The analyst sat behind the patient, unseen, and functioned ostensibly as a screen upon which the patient would project his thoughts. He was not completely inactive, since his guttural responses to and spoken interpretations of the patient's expressed ideas constituted an important influence on the patient's thinking. Reich made the analyst a more direct force in the therapeutic proceeding. He sat facing the patient where he could be seen and made physical contact with him when that was necessary or advisable. Reich was a big man with soft brown eyes, as I recall them in the sessions, and strong, warm hands.

We do not appreciate today the revolutionary advance that this therapy represented then or the suspicions and hostility it evoked. Because of its strong focus on sexuality and its use of physical contact between therapist and patient, practitioners of Reichian therapy were accused of using sexual stimulation to promote orgastic potency.

It was said Reich masturbated his patients. Nothing was further from the truth. The slander reveals the degree of fear surrounding sexuality and physical contact in those days. Fortunately the atmosphere has changed greatly in the past thirty years, with regard to both sexuality and touching. The importance of touching is becoming recognized as a *primary form* of contact,* and its value in the therapeutic situation is not questioned. Of course any physical contact between therapist and patient places a great responsibility on the therapist to respect the therapeutic relationship and to avoid any sexual involvement with the patient.

I might add, here, that in bioenergetics therapists are trained

*Ashley Montagu, *Touching: The Human Significance of the Skin* (New York, Columbia University Press, 1971).

to use their hands to palpate and sense muscular spasticities or blocks; to apply the necessary pressure to release or reduce the muscular contraction with sensitivity to the patient's tolerance for pain; and to establish contact through a gentle and reassuring touch that provides support and warmth. It is difficult to realize now what a big step Reich took in 1943.

The use of physical pressure facilitated the breakthrough of feeling and the corresponding recovery of memories. And it served to speed up the therapeutic process, an acceleration necessary when therapy sessions were reduced in frequency to once a week. By this time Reich had developed great skill in reading the body and knowing how to apply pressure that would release muscular tensions, promoting the flow of sensation through the body that he called streamings. By 1947 Reich was able in some patients to bring about the orgasm reflex within a period of six months. One can appreciate this achievement by comparing it with the fact that I had been in therapy with Reich for close to three years with sessions three times a week before the orgasm reflex became established.

The orgasm reflex is not, let me emphasize, an orgasm. The genital apparatus is not involved; there is no buildup and, therefore, no discharge of sexual excitation. It denotes that the way is open for such a discharge if the giving in or surrender can be transposed to a sexual situation. But this transfer does not necessarily occur. The two situations, the sexual one and the therapeutic one, are different; the former is much more charged emotionally and energetically. Also, in the therapeutic situation a person has the benefit of his therapist's support, which, as in the case of a man like Reich with a very strong personality, can be a powerful factor. However, in the absence of the orgasm reflex it is unlikely that a person will allow the involuntary pelvic movements to occur at the climax of the sexual act. These movements are the basis of a full orgastic response. We must remember that in Reich's theory it is the orgastic response in sex, not the orgasm reflex, that is the criterion of emotional health.

Nevertheless, the orgasm reflex does have some positive effects on the personality. Even though it occurs in the supportive atmosphere of the therapeutic situation, it is experienced as exhilarating and liberating. The person senses what it feels like to be free of inhibitions. At the same time he feels connected and integrated—with his body and, through his body, with his environment. He has a sense of well-being and an inner peace. He gains the knowledge that the life of the body resides in its involuntary aspect. I can attest to this reaction from personal experience, as well as from the comments of patients over the years.

Unfortunately these beautiful feelings do not always hold up under the stress of daily living in our modern culture. The pace, the pressure and the philosophy of our times are antithetical to life. Too often the reflex itself may be lost if the patient hasn't learned how to handle his life stresses without recourse to his neurotic patterns of behavior. This is what happened to two of the patients Reich treated at this time. Several months after the apparently successful termination of their therapy, they asked me for additional therapy since they had not been able to hold the gains they achieved with Reich. I realized then there could be no shortcut to emotional health and that the consistent working through of all of one's problems was the only way to assure optimum functioning. However, I was still convinced that sexuality was the key to the solution of the neurotic problems of the individual.

It is easy to criticize Reich for his emphasis on the central importance of sexuality, but I would not do so. Sexuality was and is the key issue in all emotional problems, but the disturbances in sexual functioning can be understood only within the framework of the total personality, on the one hand, and the conditions of social living, on the other. Over the years I have reluctantly come to the conclusion that there is no single key that will unlock the mystery of the human condition. My reluctance stemmed from a deep wish to believe that there is an answer. Now I think in terms of polarities with their inevitable conflicts and temporary resolutions. A view of personality that sees sex as the sole key to personality is too narrow, but to ignore the role of the sexual drive in shaping the individual personality is to disregard one of the most important forces in nature.

In one of his early formulations, prior to the concept of the death instinct, Freud had postulated an antithesis between the ego instincts and the sexual instinct. The former seeks the preservation of the individual; the latter aims at the preservation of the species. This implies a conflict between the individual and society which we know is true for our culture. Another conflict inherent in this antithesis is the one between the striving for power (an ego drive) and the striving for pleasure (the sexual drive). The overemphasis on power in our culture sets the ego against the body and its sexuality and creates an antagonism between drives which should ideally support and reinforce each other. Nevertheless, one cannot go to the opposite extreme of focusing solely on sexuality. This became clear to me after I had unsuccessfully pursued the single goal of sexual fulfillment for my patients, as Reich had. The ego exists as a powerful force in Western man that cannot be dismissed or denied. The therapeutic goal is to integrate the ego with the body and its striving for pleasure and sexual fulfillment.

Only after many years of hard work and not without my share of errors did I learn this truth. No one is exempt from the rule that learning occurs through the recognition of error. However, without a determined pursuit of the goal of sexual satisfaction and orgastic potency, I would not have understood the energy dynamics of the personality. And without the criterion of the orgasm reflex one cannot comprehend the involuntary movements and responses of the human organism.

There are still many mysterious elements in human behavior and functioning that the rational mind cannot grasp. For example, for about a year before I left New York I treated a young man who had many serious problems. He suffered from severe anxiety every time he approached a girl. He felt inferior, inadequate and had many masochistic tendencies. At times he had the hallucination that the devil was leering at him from a corner. In the course of his therapy he made some progress with his symptoms, but they were by no means resolved. He had, however, developed a steady relationship with a girl, though he experienced little pleasure in the sexual climax.

I saw him again five years later after my return to this country. He told me a fascinating story. After my departure he was without a therapist, so he decided to continue therapy on his own. This involved doing the basic breathing exercises we had used in the therapy. He went home after work each day, lay down on a bed, and let himself breathe deeply and easily as he had done with me. Then, one day, the miracle happened. All his anxiety disappeared. He felt sure of himself, and his self-deprecation ended. Most important, however, was the emergence of a full degree of orgastic potency in the sexual act. His orgasms were full and satisfying. He was a different person.

Sadly he told me, "It only lasted a month." Just as suddenly as the change occurred, it vanished, and he was plunged back into his old misery. He saw another Reichian therapist with whom he then worked for several years, again making only slight progress. When I resumed my practice, he came back for more therapy with me. I worked with him for about three more years and helped him overcome many of his handicaps. But the miracle never recurred. He never reached the height, sexually and otherwise, that he had achieved during the brief period following my departure.

How can we explain the unexpected breakthrough of health that seemed to happen by itself and its subsequent loss? My patient's experience reminded me of James Hilton's *Lost Horizon* which was popular at that time. In this story the hero, Conway, is abducted together with some fellow passengers on a plane and carried to a secret valley high in the Himalayan mountains called Shangri-La, a remote mountain fastness literally "out of this world." For those who live in this valley, old age and death are seemingly postponed or suspended. The governing principle is moderation which is also not "of this world." Conway is tempted to remain in Shangri-La; he finds its serene and rational mode of life extremely agreeable. He is offered the leadership of the valley community but he allows his brother to persuade him that it is all a fantasy. His brother who has fallen in love with a young Chinese girl induces Conway to escape with them to "reality." They leave, but once outside the valley, Conway is horrified to see the young Chinese girl turn into an old woman and die. Which reality is the more valid? Conway decides to return to Shangri-La, and at the end of the story we learn that he is wandering in the mountains seeking his "Lost Horizon."

The sudden transformation that occurred in my patient can be accounted for by assuming a change in a person's sense of reality. For a month, my patient, too, had stepped "out of this world" and, in doing so, had left behind all the anxieties, guilts and inhibitions associated with his living in this world. Many factors undoubtedly contributed to produce this effect. There was a mood of euphoria and excitement among the people involved with Reich's work at this time, both as students and patients. It was felt that Reich had proclaimed a basic truth about human beings and their sexuality. His ideas had a revolutionary appeal. I am sure my patient inhaled this atmosphere, which, together with his deeper breathing, could have produced the remarkable effect described above.

Stepping out of one's world or out of one's habitual self is a transcendental experience. Many people have had similar ones of longer or shorter duration. Common to all is the feeling of release, the sense of liberation and the discovery of a self fully alive and spontaneously responsive. Such transformations, however, happen unexpectedly and cannot be planned or programmed. Unfortunately they are often reversed just as rapidly as they occur, and the glittering carriage becomes, overnight, the pumpkin it originally was. We are then left with a sense of wonder—which is the true reality of our being? Why *can't* we remain in the liberated state?

Most of my patients have had some transcendental experiences in the course of therapy. Each discloses a horizon previously obscured by a thick fog and suddenly clearly perceived. Though the fog closes in again, the memory remains and provides a motivation for a continued commitment to change and growth.

If we seek transcendence, we may have many visions, but we will surely end where we started. If we opt for growth, we may have our moments of transcendence, but they will be peak experiences along the steady road to à richer and more secure self.

Life itself is a process of growth that starts with the growth of the body and its organs, moves through the development of motor skills, the acquisition of knowledge, the extension of relationships, and ends in the summation of experience that we call wisdom. These aspects of growth overlap, since life and growth take place in a natural, cultural and social environment. And though the growth process is continuous, it is never even. There are periods of leveling off when the assimilation of experience occurs, preparing the organism for a new ascent. Each ascent leads to a new high or summit and creates what we call a peak experience. Each peak experience, in turn, must be integrated into the personality for new growth to occur and for the individual to end in a state of wisdom. I once mentioned to Reich that I had a definition of happiness. He raised his brows, looked at me quizzically and asked what it was. I replied, "Happiness is the consciousness of growth." His brows came down as he commented, "Not bad."

If my definition has validity, it suggests that most people come to therapy because they sense their growth has been arrested. Certainly many patients look to therapy to reinstitute the growth process. A therapy can do this if it provides new experiences and helps remove or reduce the blocks and obstacles preventing the assimilation of experience. These blocks are structured patterns of behavior that represent an unsatisfactory resolution, a compromise of childhood conflicts. They create the neurotic and limited self from which one seeks to escape or be liberated. By working backward into his past, a patient in therapy uncovers the original conflicts and finds new ways to handle the life-denying and life-threatening situations that forced him to become "armored" as a means of survival. It is only by making the past become alive again for a person that true growth in the present is facilitated. If the past is cut off, the future does not exist.

Growth is a natural process; we can't make it happen. Its law is common to all living things. A tree, for example, grows upward only as its roots go deeper into the earth. We learn by studying the past. So a person can grow only by strengthening his roots in his own past. And a person's past is his body.

As I look back on those years of enthusiasm and excitement, I realize it was naïve to expect that the deeply structured problems of the modern person could be easily resolved by any technique. I do not mean to say that Reich had any illusions about the immense task he faced. He was well aware of the situation. His search for more effective ways to deal with these problems stemmed directly from this awareness.

The search left him to investigate the nature of the energy at work in living organisms. He claimed, as is known, to have discovered a new energy, which he called orgone, a word he derived from organic and organism. He invented an apparatus that could accumulate this energy and charge the body of anyone sitting in it. I have built these "accumulators" myself and used them personally. For some conditions they have proved helpful, but they have no effect on personality problems. On the individual level these problems still require for their resolution a combination of careful analytic work and a physical approach that helps a person release the chronic muscular spasticities that inhibit his freedom and constrict his life. On the social level there has to be an evolutionary change in man's attitudes to himself, to his environment, and to the community of mankind.

On both levels, Reich made great contributions. His elucidation of the nature of character structure and his demonstration of its functional identity with the bodily attitude were important advances in our understanding of human behavior. He introduced the concept of orgastic potency as a criterion of emotional health, which it certainly is, and showed its physical base to be the orgasm reflex of the body. He enlarged our knowledge of bodily processes by discovering the meaning and significance of the body's involuntary responses. And he developed a relatively effective technique for treating disturbances in the emotional (involuntary) life of the individual.

Reich pointed out clearly how the structure of society is reflected in the character structure of its individual members, an insight that clarified the irrational aspects of politics. He saw the possibility of human existence free from the inhibitions and repressions that strangle the living impulse. In my opinion, if this vision is ever to be realized, it will be by following the direction Reich gave us.

For our present purpose Reich's greatest contribution was his delineation of the central role the body must play in any theory of personality. His work provided the foundation on which the edifice of bioenergetics has been built.

The Development of Bioenergetics

People often ask me, "How does bioenergetics differ from Reichian therapy?" The best way to answer this question is to continue with our historical account of the development of bioenergetics.

On completing my internship in 1952, following my return

from Europe the year before, I learned a number of changes had occurred in the attitudes of Reich and his followers. The enthusiasm and excitement so evident in the years 1945 to 1947 had given way to feelings of persecution and dejection. Reich had stopped doing any personal therapy and had moved to Rangeley, Maine, where he devoted himself to orgone physics. The term "character-analytic vegetotherapy" was dropped in favor of the name "orgone therapy." This resulted in a loss of interest in the art of character analysis and a greater emphasis on the application of orgone energy through the use of the accumulator.

The feeling of persecution was engendered in part by the critical attitude of the medical and scientific communities to Reich's ideas, in part by the overt hostility of many psychoanalysts, some of whom let it be known they were out to get Reich, and in third part by anxieties within Reich and his followers. The feeling of dejection stemmed from the collapse of an experiment Reich conducted in his laboratory in Maine involving the interaction of orgone energy and radioactivity. The experiment had a negative effect; Reich and his assistants became ill and had to abandon the laboratory for a time. In addition, the collapse of the hope for a relatively quick and effective therapy of the neuroses contributed to the mood of discouragement.

I did not share these feelings. My isolation for five years from Reich and his struggles allowed me to retain the excitement and enthusiasm of those earlier years. And my medical school education, plus the experience of my internship, convinced me more than ever of the general validity of Reich's ideas. I was reluctant, therefore, to identify myself fully with the group of orgone therapists—a reluctance further increased by my awareness that Reich's followers had developed an almost fanatical devotion to him and his work. It was considered presumptuous, if not heretical, to question any of his statements or modify his concepts in the light of one's own experience. It was clear to me that such an attitude would stifle any original or creative work. These considerations dictated that I maintain an independent position.

While I was in this frame of mind, a discussion with another Reichian therapist, Dr. Pelletier, who was outside the official circles opened my eyes to the possibility of modifying or extending Reich's technical procedures. Throughout all my work with Reich he had stressed that my jaw should hang loose in an attitude of letting go or surrender to the body. In my years as a Reichian therapist I, too, had stressed this position. In the discussion Dr. Louis G. Pelletier observed that he had found it helpful to have patients stick their jaws out in an attitude of defiance. Mobilizing this aggressive expression released some of the tension in the contracted jaw muscles. Of course, I realized, it would work either way, and suddenly I felt free to question or change what Reich did. It turned out that both positions work best when used alternately. Mobilizing and encouraging a patient's aggression facilitates his "giving in" or surrender to tender sexual feelings. On the other hand, if one starts with an attitude of "giving in," it often ends in feelings and expressions of sadness and anger because of the pain and frustration that are experienced in the body.

In 1953 I became associated with Dr. John C. Pierrakos who had just completed his psychiatric residency at Kings County Hospital. Dr. Pierrakos had himself been in Reichian therapy and was a follower of Reich. At this time we still considered ourselves Reichian therapists, though no longer officially connected with the organization of Reichian doctors. Within a year we were joined by Dr. William B. Walling, whose background was similar to Dr. Pierrakos. The two had been classmates at medical school. The initial result of this association was a program of clinical seminars at which we would personally present our patients with the aims of seeking a deeper understanding of their problems, while at the same time teaching other therapists the underlying concepts of the body approach. In 1956 the Institute for Bioenergetic Analysis was formally launched as a nonprofit trust to carry out these aims.

In the meantime Reich had got into difficulty with the law. As if to vindicate his feeling of persecution, the Food and Drug Administration had brought an action in federal court to enjoin Reich from selling or shipping orgone accumulators in interstate commerce on the ground that there was no such thing as orgone energy and that, therefore, their sale was fraudulent. Reich refused to contest or defend this action, claiming that his scientific theories could not be argued in a court of law. The FDA won a sweeping injunction by default. Reich was advised to ignore the injunction, and his violation of its terms was soon discovered by FDA agents. Reich was tried for contempt of court, convicted and sentenced to two years in a federal penitentiary. He died in Lewisburg Prison in November 1957.

The tragedy of Reich's death proved to me that man cannot be saved against himself. However, what about the individual who is sincerely committed to his own personal salvation? If by "salvation" one means freedom from the inhibitions and restraints imposed by one's upbringing, I could not claim that I had achieved this state of grace. Despite my having successfully completed Reichian therapy, I was aware that I still had many chronic muscular tensions in my body that prevented me from experiencing the joyfulness I longed for. I could feel their restrictive influence on my personality. And I wanted a still richer and fuller sexual experience—an experience I knew was possible.

My solution was to start therapy again. However, I could not go back to Reich, and I had no faith in the other Reichian therapists. I was convinced it had to be a body approach, so I elected to work with my associate John Pierrakos as a joint venture, since I was his senior in both age and experience. It was out of this joint work on my own body that bioenergetics was conceived. The basic exercises we use were first tried and tested on me, so I knew from personal experience how they work and what they can do. In all the years since, I have made it a practice to try out on myself everything I ask my patients to do, since I do not believe one has a right to demand of others what one is unprepared to ask of one's self. Conversely, I don't believe one can do for others what one cannot do for one's self.

My therapy with Pierrakos lasted close to three years. It had an entirely different quality from my work with Reich. There were fewer of the spontaneously moving experiences I described above. This was mainly because I largely directed the body work, but also because it was focused more on the release of muscular tension than on giving in to sexual feelings. I was very conscious of not wanting to try anymore. I wanted someone to take over and do it for me. Trying and controlling are aspects of my neurotic character, and it was not easy for me to surrender. I had been able to do this with Reich because of my respect for his knowledge and authority, but my surrender was limited to that relationship. The conflict was resolved by a compromise. In the first half of the session I worked with myself, describing my bodily sensations to Pierrakos. In the second half he dug in on my tight muscles with his strong, warm hands, kneeding and relaxing them so that the streamings would occur.

Working on myself, I developed the basic positions and exercises which are now standard in bioenergetics. I sensed a need to get more fully into my legs and so I began in a standing position rather than the prone one Reich used. I spread my legs, turned my toes inward, bent my knees and arched my back in an attempt to mobilize the lower half of my body. I would hold the position for several minutes, sensing that it enabled me to feel closer to the ground. It had the added effect of getting me to breathe deeper into my abdomen. Since this position produced some strain in my lower back, I reversed it by bending forward and touching the floor lightly with my fingertips, keeping my knees slightly bent. Now the feeling in my legs increased, and they began to vibrate.

These two simple exercises came to be the concept of grounding—a concept unique to bioenergetics. It developed slowly over the years as it became evident that all patients lacked a sense of having their feet firmly planted on the floor. This lack corresponded to their being "up in the air" and out of touch with reality. Grounding or getting a patient in touch with reality, the ground he stands on, his body and his sexuality, has become one of the cornerstones of bioenergetics. A full elaboration of the concept of grounding in relation to reality and illusion occurs in Chapter VI. Many of the exercises used to achieve grounding are described in there.

One of the other innovations we developed in the course of this work was the use of a breathing stool. Breathing is as crucial to bioenergetics as it is to Reichian therapy. However, it has always been a problem to get patients to breathe deeply and fully. It is even more difficult to have such breathing become free and spontaneous. The idea of the breathing stool arose from people's common tendency to arch over the back of a chair when, after sitting at a desk for some time, they need to stretch and breathe. I had been in the habit of doing this myself while working with patients. Sitting in an armchair tended to depress my breathing, and I used to arch backward and stretch to get my breathing going more deeply again. The first stool we used was a wooden kitchen stepladder, two feet high, on which a tightly rolled blanket was strapped.* Lying with one's back on this stool had the effect of stimulating the breathing in all patients without the need to do breathing exercises. I personally explored the use of the stool during my therapy with Pierrakos and have continued to use it regularly since.

The results from my second period of therapy were markedly

*Alexander Lowen, *Pleasure* (New York, Coward-McCann, Inc., N.Y., 1970).

different. I made contact with more sadness and anger than I had experienced previously, especially in relation to my mother. The release of these feelings had an exhilarating effect. There were occasions when my heart opened up and I felt radiant and glowing. More significant, though, was the sustained sense of well-being that I often had. My body gradually became more relaxed and stronger. I recall losing the feeling of brittleness. I sensed that though I could be hurt, *I would not break.* I also lost my irrational fear of pain. Pain, I learned, was tension, and I found that when I gave in to the pain, I could understand the tension that produced it, and this invariably brought about its release.

During this therapy, the orgasm reflex broke through only occasionally. I was not concerned by its absence because I was concentrating on my muscular tensions, and this intensive work took the focus away from giving in to sexual feelings. A tendency I had to premature ejaculation that had persisted despite the apparent success of my therapy with Reich diminished greatly, and my response at climax became more satisfying. This development led to the realization that the most effective approach to a patient's sexual difficulties lies in working through the personality problems, problems necessarily including sexual guilts and anxieties. The focus on sexuality that Reich employed, though theoretically valid, generally failed to yield results that could be sustained under the conditions of modern living.

As an analyst Reich had emphasized the importance of character analysis. In his treatment of me this aspect of the therapy was somewhat minimized. It was further diminished when character-analytic vegetotherapy became orgone therapy. Though character-analytic work takes much time and patience, it seemed to me that it was indispensable to a solid result. I decided then that no matter how much importance we placed on the work with muscular tensions, the careful analysis of a person's habitual mode of being and behavior merited equal attention. I made an intensive study of character types, correlating the psychological and the physical dynamics of behavior patterns. This was published in 1958 under the title *The Physical Dynamics of Character Structure.** Though not fully complete as a compendium of character types, it is the foundation for all character work done in bioenergetics.

I had ended my therapy with Pierrakos several years earlier feeling very good about what had been accomplished. However, if someone had asked me, "Have you resolved all your problems, completed your growth, realized your full potential as a person or released all your muscular tensions?" my answer would still have been "No." There comes a point where one no longer feels it necessary or desirable to continue in therapy, and so one quits. If the therapy has been successful, the person feels able to take upon himself the full responsibility for his well-being and continued growth. Something in my personality has always inclined me in this direction anyway. Leaving therapy did not mean I stopped working with my body. I have continued to do the bioenergetic exercises I use with my patients both alone or with others in a group setting. I believe this commitment to my body is partly responsible for the fact that many positive changes have continued to occur in my personality. These changes have generally been preceded by a deeper understanding of myself, both in terms of my past and in terms of my body.

It is now more than thirty-four years since I met Reich and more than thirty-two years since I began my therapy with him. I have worked with patients for more than twenty-seven years. Working, thinking and writing about my personal experiences and those of my patients have led me to one conclusion: *The life of an individual is the life of his body.* Since the living body includes the mind, the spirit and the soul, to live the life of the

*Alexander Lowen, *The Physical Dynamics of Character Structure* (New York, Grune & Stratton, 1958). Available in paperback under the title, *The Language of the Body* (New York, Macmillan, 1971).

body fully is to be mindful, spiritual and soulful. If we are deficient in these aspects of our being, it is because we are not fully in or with our bodies. We treat the body as an instrument or machine. We know that if it breaks down, we are in trouble. But the same could be said of the automobile on which we so much depend. We are not identified with our body; in fact, we have betrayed it, as I pointed out in a previous book.* All our personal difficulties stem from this betrayal, and I believe that most of our social problems have a similar origin.

Bioenergetics is a therapeutic technique to help a person get back together with his body and to help him enjoy to the fullest degree possible the life of the body. This emphasis on the body includes sexuality, which is one of its basic functions. But it also includes the even more basic functions of breathing, moving, feeling and self-expression. A person who doesn't breathe deeply reduces the life of his body. If he doesn't move freely, he restricts the life of his body. If he doesn't feel fully, he narrows the life of his body. And if his self-expression is constricted, he limits the life of his body.

True, these restrictions on living are not voluntarily self-imposed. They develop as a means of survival in a home environment and culture that denies body values in favor of power, prestige and possessions. Nevertheless, we accept these restrictions on our lives by failing to question them, and thus, we betray our bodies. In the process we also subvert the natural environment our bodies depend on for their well-being. It is equally true that most people are unconscious of the bodily handicaps under which they labor—handicaps that have become second nature to them, part of their habitual way of being in the world. In effect, most people go through life on a limited budget of energy and feeling.

The goal of bioenergetics is to help people regain their primary nature, which is the condition of being free, the state

*Alexander Lowen, *The Betrayal of the Body* (New York, Macmillan, 1967).

of being graceful and the quality of being beautiful. Freedom, grace and beauty are the natural attributes of every animal organism. Freedom is the absence of inner restraint to the flow of feeling, grace is the expression of this flow in movement, while beauty is a manifestation of the inner harmony such a flow engenders. They denote a healthy body and also, therefore, a healthy mind.

The primary nature of every human being is to be open to life and love. Being guarded, armored, distrustful and enclosed is second nature in our culture. It is the means we adopt to protect ourselves against being hurt, but when such attitudes become characterological or structured in the personality, they constitute a more severe hurt and create a greater crippling than the one originally suffered.

Bioenergetics aims to help a person open his heart to life and love. This is no easy task. The heart is well protected in its bony cage, and the approaches to it are strongly defended both psychologically and physically. These defenses must be understood and worked through if our aim is to be achieved. But if the objective is not gained, the result is tragic. To go through life with a closed heart is like taking an ocean voyage locked in the hold of the ship. The meaning, the adventure, the excitement and the glory of living are beyond one's vision and reach.

Bioenergetics is an adventure in self-discovery. It differs from similar explorations into the nature of the self by attempting to understand the human personality in terms of the human body. Most previous explorations focused their investigations on the mind. Much valuable information was gained through these inquiries, but it seems to me they left untouched the most important domain of personality—namely, its base in bodily processes. We would readily acknowledge that what goes on in the body necessarily affects the mind, but that is not new. My position is that the energetic processes of the body determine what goes on in the mind just as they determine what goes on in the body.

II. The Energy Concept

Charge, Discharge, Flow and Movement

Bioenergetics is, as I have emphasized, the study of the human personality in terms of the energetic processes of the body. The term is also used in biochemistry to define an area of research that deals with energy processes on the molecular and sub-molecular levels. As Albert Szent-Gyorgyi pointed out,* it takes energy to move the machine of life. In fact, energy is involved in the movement of all things, both living and nonliving. In current scientific thinking this energy is regarded as electrical in nature. There are, however, other views of its nature, especially as it applies to living organisms. Reich postulated the basic cosmic energy he called orgone which was nonelectrical in nature. Chinese philosophy postulates two energies in a polar relationship to each other, yin and yang. These energies form the basis of the Chinese medical practice called acupuncture some of whose results have astounded Western doctors.

I do not think it is important for this study to determine

*Albert Szent-Gyorgyi, *Bioenergetics* (New York, Academic Press, 1957).

what the energy of life actually is. There is some validity to all these points of view and I have not been able to reconcile the differences between them. We can, however, accept the fundamental proposition that energy is involved in all the processes of life—in moving, feeling and thinking—and that these processes would come to a stop if the supply of energy to the organism were seriously interrupted. For example, a lack of food would deplete an organism's energy so severely that death would occur, or cutting off necessary oxygen by interfering with respiration could lead to death. Poisons that block the body's metabolic activities and so reduce its energy will also have this effect.

It is commonly accepted that the energy of an animal organism comes from the combustion of food. Plants, on the other hand, have the capacity to capture and use the energy of the sun for their life processes, binding and transforming it into the tissues of the plant, thus making it available as food for herbivorous animals. Changing the food back into free energy the animal can use for its own life needs is a complex chemical procedure that ultimately involves the use of oxygen. The combustion of food is not unlike the combustion that occurs in a wood fire which also requires oxygen to maintain the process. In both cases the rate of combustion is related to the amount of available oxygen.

This simple analogy does not explain the complicated phenomenon of life. A simple fire burns itself out when the fuel supply is exhausted; it also burns indiscriminately with no regard for the energy liberated by the combustion. In contrast, the living organism is a self-contained, self-regulating and self-perpetuating fire. How it is enabled to perform this miracle—that is, to burn without burning up or burning out—is still the great mystery. While we cannot solve the riddle yet, it is important to try to understand some of the factors involved, for all of us want to keep the flame of life burning brightly and continuously within.

We are not accustomed to thinking of personality in terms of energy, yet the two cannot be dissociated. How much energy an individual has and how he uses it must determine and be reflected in his personality. Some people have more energy than others; some are more contained. An impulsive person, for example, cannot contain any increase in his level of excitement or energy; he must discharge the increased excitation as rapidly as possible. A compulsive person uses his energy differently; he, too, must discharge his excitement, but he does so in rigidly structured patterns of movement and behavior.

The relation of energy to personality is most clearly manifested in a depressed individual. Although the depressive reaction and the depressive tendency result from the interplay of complicated psychological and physical factors,* one thing is abundantly clear. The depressed individual is energetically depressed. Cinematic studies show he makes only about one-half the spontaneous movements usual in the nondepressed individual. In a severe case, he might sit quietly, hardly moving at all, as if he didn't have the energy to move actively. His subjective state often corresponds to this objective picture. He generally feels that he lacks the energy to get moving. He may complain of feeling enervated without, however, being tired. The depression of his level of energy is seen in the decrease of all energetic functions. His breathing is depressed, his appetite is depressed, and his sexual drive is depressed. In this state he could not possibly respond to our exhortations that he interest himself in some pursuit; he literally *doesn't have the energy* to develop an interest.

I have treated many depressed patients, since that is one of the most common problems that brings people to therapy. After listening to a person's story, reviewing his history and evaluating his condition, I try to help him build up his energy.

*Lowen, *Depression and the Body*, *op. cit.*

The most immediate way to do this is to increase his oxygen intake—that is, to get him to breathe more deeply and fully. There are a number of ways a person can be helped to mobilize his respiration which I shall describe in subsequent chapters. I start from the assumption that he cannot do it for himself, or he would not have come to me for help. This means I must use *my* energy to get him started. What this involves is directing him into some simple activities that slowly deepen his breathing and using physical pressure and touch to stimulate it. The important thing is that as one's respiration becomes more active, his energy level rises. When a person becomes charged up, a fine, involuntary tremor or vibration may occur in the legs. This is interpreted as a sign that there is some flow of excitation in the body, specifically in the lower part. The voice may become more resonant since there is more air flowing through the larynx, and the face may brighten. It may not take more than twenty to thirty minutes to accomplish this change and for the patient to feel "lifted up." He *has* been lifted out of his depressive state temporarily.

Although the effect of deeper and fuller breathing is immediately evident and experienced, it is not a cure for the depressive condition. Nor will the effect last, since the person himself cannot maintain this quality of deeper respiration spontaneously. This inability is the core problem of depression, and it cannot be worked through except by a thoroughgoing analysis of all the factors that have operated to produce a relatively deadened body and a depressed personality. But the analysis itself will not help greatly unless it is accompanied by a consistent effort to raise the person's energy level by charging his body energetically.

The concept of energetic charge cannot be discussed without also considering energetic discharge. The living organism can only function if there is a balance between energy charge and discharge. It maintains a level of energy consistent with its needs and opportunities. A growing child will take in more energy than it discharges and use this extra energy for growth. The same is true of convalescence or even of personality growth. Growth takes energy. Apart from this, it is generally true that the amount of energy one will take in will correspond to the amount one can discharge through activity.

All activity requires and uses energy—from the beating of the heart, the peristaltic movement of the intestines, to walking, talking, working and sex. However, no living organism is a machine. Its basic activities are not performed mechanically but are expressions of its being. A person expresses himself in his actions and movements, and when his self-expression is free and appropriate to the reality of the situation, he experiences a sense of satisfaction and pleasure from the discharge of his energy. This pleasure and satisfaction in turn stimulate the organism to increased metabolic activity, which is immediately reflected in deeper and fuller breathing. With pleasure the rhythmic and involuntary activities of life function at an optimal level.

Pleasure and satisfaction are, as I have said, the immediate experience of self-expressive activities. Limit a person's right to express himself, and you limit his opportunities for pleasure and creative living. By the same token, if a person's ability to express himself, his ideas and his feelings, is limited by internal forces (inhibitions or chronic muscular tensions), his capacity for pleasure is reduced. In this case the individual will reduce his energy intake (unconsciously, of course) to maintain an energy balance in his body.

Increasing a person's energy level cannot be accomplished by simply charging him up through breathing. The avenues of self-expression through movement, the voice and the eyes must be opened up, so a greater energy discharge can occur. Not infrequently this happens spontaneously in the course of charging up. A person's breathing may deepen spontaneously as a result of lying over a breathing stool. Suddenly without any conscious intent or awareness, he may begin to cry. He may not know at the moment why he is crying. The deeper breathing opened his throat, charged his body, and activated suppressed emotions with the result that a feeling of sadness erupted and flowed out. Sometimes it is anger that breaks through. Many times, however, nothing happens, for the person may be too afraid to open up and let go of his feelings. In this case he will, however, become aware of his "holding" and of the muscular tensions in his throat and chest that block the expression of feeling. It may be necessary, then, to release the holding by direct physical work on the chronic muscular tension.

Since charge and discharge function as a unit, bioenergetics works with both sides of the equation simultaneously to raise a person's energy level, to open up his self-expression and to restore the flow of feeling in his body. Thus, the emphasis is always on breathing, feeling and movement, coupled with the attempt to relate the present-day energetic functioning of the individual to his life history. This combined approach slowly uncovers the inner forces (conflicts) that prevent a person from functioning at his full energetic potential. Each time one of these inner conflicts is resolved, the person's energy level increases. This means he takes in more energy and discharges more in creative activities that are pleasurable and satisfying.

I do not wish to give the impression that bioenergetics can resolve all buried conflicts, remove all chronic tensions and restore the full and free flow of feeling in a person's body. We may not fully achieve this goal but we do institute a process of growth that leads in that direction. Every therapy is handicapped by the fact that the culture we live in is not oriented toward creative activity and pleasure. As I have pointed out elsewhere,* it is not geared to the values and rhythms of the living body but to those of machines and material productivity. We cannot escape the conclusion that the forces inhibiting self-expression and, therefore, decreasing our energetic functioning derive from this culture and are part of it. Every

*Lowen, *Pleasure, op. cit.*

sensitive person knows that it takes considerable energy to protect one's self from becoming caught up in the frantic pace of modern living with its pressures and tensions, its violence and insecurities.

The concept of flow needs some elaboration. Flow denotes a movement within the organism best exemplified by the flow of blood. As the blood flows through the body, it carries metabolites and oxygen to the tissues, providing them with energy, and it removes the waste products of combustion. But it is more than just a medium; it is the energetically charged fluid of the body. Its arrival at any point of the body adds life, warmth and excitement to that part. It is the representative and carrier of Eros.* Consider what happens at the erogenous zones, the lips, nipples and genitals. When they become suffused with blood (each of these organs is richly endowed with a big vascular network), we become excited, feel warm and loving and seek contact with another person. Sexual excitement is synchronous with increased blood flow to the periphery of the body, especially to the erogenous areas. Whether the excitement brings the blood or the blood carries the excitement is unimportant. The two always go together.

In addition to the blood, there are other energetically charged fluids in the body—lymph, interstitial fluids and intracellular fluids. The flow of excitation is not limited to the blood but travels through all the body fluids. Energetically speaking, the whole body can be viewed as a single cell with the skin as its membrane. Within this cell excitation can spread in all directions or flow in specific directions depending on the nature of our response to a stimulus. This view of the body as a single cell does not deny the fact that within it there are very many specialized tissues, nerves, blood vessels, mucous membranes, muscles, glands, etc., all of which cooperate as parts of the whole to promote the life of the whole.

One can experience the flow of excitation as a feeling or

*Lowen, *The Physical Dynamics of Character Structure, op. cit.*

sensation which often defies anatomical boundaries. Haven't you experienced the surge of anger into the upper part of the body charging the arms, face and eyes? It may vary from a sensation of being "hot under the collar" to an apoplectic engorgement of head and neck with blood. When a person is so angry that he sees red, it indicates to me that the retina of his eyes has become flooded with blood. On the other hand, the feeling of anger may have a white, cold quality and look, owing to a peripheral vasoconstriction that prevents the blood from reaching the surface. There is also a black rage in which the anger is capped by a dark cloud of hate.

The upward flow of blood and excitation can produce an entirely different emotion when it follows different channels and excites different organs. A flow of excitation along the front of the body from the heart to the mouth, eyes and hands will give rise to the feeling of longing expressed in an attitude of opening up and reaching out. The flow of anger is mainly along the back of the body. A downward flow of blood and excitation will produce some interesting sensations. One can experience them riding a roller coaster or during the quick rise and descent of an elevator. These sensations are much sought after by children, who get them by swinging. They are most intense and pleasurable when they occur as melting sensations in the belly accompanying a strong sexual charge. However, the same flow can be coupled with anxiety in which case it is experienced as a sinking sensation in the belly.

When one realizes that 99 percent of the body is composed of water, some of it structured, but much of it fluid, we can picture sensations, feelings and emotions as currents or waves in this liquid body. Sensations, feelings and emotions are the perceptions of internal movements within the relatively fluid body. Nerves mediate these perceptions and coordinate responses, but the underlying impulses and movements are inherent in the body's energetic charge, in its natural rhythms and pulsations. These internal movements represent the body's motility as distinguished from the voluntary motions that are subject to conscious control. They are most evident in the very young. Looking at a baby's body, one can see the constant play of motion like the waves of a lake, only these movements are produced by inner forces. As people get older, their motility tends to decrease. They become more structured and stiffer until finally with death, all motion ceases.

In all our voluntary movements there is also an involuntary component, representing the essential motility of the organism. This involuntary component, which is integrated with the voluntary action, accounts for the aliveness or spontaneity of our actions and movements. When it is absent or reduced, body movements have a mechanical, lifeless quality. Purely voluntary or conscious movements give rise to few sensations other than the kinesthetic sense of displacement in space. The feeling tone of expressive movement comes from their involuntary component—the component not subject to conscious control. The fusion of conscious and unconscious elements or of voluntary and involuntary components gives rise to movements that have an emotional ring, yet are coordinated and effective actions.

A person's emotional life depends on the motility of his body, which in turn is a function of the flow of excitation throughout it. Disturbances of this flow occur as blocks, which are manifested in areas where the body's motility is reduced. In these areas one can also easily palpate, or feel with one's fingers, the spasticity in the musculature. Thus the terms "block," "deadness" and "chronic muscular tension" refer to the same phenomenon. Generally one can infer a block from seeing an area of deadness and sensing or palpating the muscular contraction that maintains it.

Since the body is an energetic system, it is in constant interaction energetically with its environment. Apart from the energy derived from the combustion of food, an individual gets excited or charged by contact with positive forces. A bright and clear day, a beautiful scene, a happy person has a stimulating effect. Dark and heavy days, ugliness or depressed people have a negative impact on our energies, seeming to exert a depressing influence. We all are sensitive to the forces or energies that surround us, but their impact is not equal on all people. A more highly charged person is more resistant to negative influences. At the same time he is a positive influence for others, especially when the flow of excitation in his body is free and full. Such individuals are a joy to be with, and we all sense this intuitively.

You Are Your Body

Bioenergetics rests on the simple proposition that each person is his body. No person exists apart from the living body in which he has his existence and through which he expresses himself and relates to the world around him. It would be foolish to argue against this proposition because one could be challenged to name a part of himself that is not a part of his body. Mind, spirit and soul are aspects of every living body. A dead body has no mind, it has lost its spirit, and its soul has departed.

If you are your body and your body is you then it expresses who you are. It is your way of being in the world. The more alive your body is, the more you are in the world. When your body loses some of its aliveness, as when you are exhausted, for example, you tend to withdraw. Illness has the same effect, producing a state of withdrawal. You may even sense the world as at a distance or see it as through a haze. On the other hand, there are days when you are radiantly alive and the world about you seems brighter, closer, more real. We all would like to be and feel more alive, and bioenergetics can help us toward the achievement of this goal.

Since your body expresses who you are it impresses us with how much you are in the world. It is not accidental that we use such terms as "a nobody" to denote a person who fails to impress us with his being or "a somebody" to indicate a powerful impression. This is simple body language. Similarly, your state of withdrawal is no secret. People sense it as they sense your fatigue or your illness. Your tiredness is expressed in many visual or auditory signs—in a sag of the shoulders, a droop in the skin of the face, a lack of luster in the eyes, a slowness and heaviness in movement and flatness or lack of resonance in the voice. Even the effort to mask the feeling betrays itself, revealing the strain of the forced attempt.

What one feels can also be read from the expression of the body. The emotions are bodily events; they are literally movements or motions within the body that generally result in some outward action. Anger produces a tension and, as we have seen, a charge in the upper half of the body where the main organs of attack, the teeth and the arms, are located. We can recognize the angry person by his flushed face, clenched fists and snarling mouth. In some animals the raising of the hair along back and neck is another manifestation of this emotion. Affection or love produces a softening of all the features, plus a suffusion of warmth in the skin and eyes. Sadness has a melting look, as if the person were about to breakdown into tears.

Far more than this, however, is revealed by the body. A person's attitude toward life or his personal style is reflected in the way he holds himself, his carriage, and in the way he moves. The individual with a so-called noble carriage or regal bearing can be distinguished from an individual whose bent back, rounded shoulders and slightly bowed head indicate submission to burdens weighing heavily on him. Some time ago I treated a young man whose body was big, fat and unshapely. He complained of being so ashamed that he refused to expose himself in swim trunks on a beach. He also felt sexually inadequate. For several years he struggled to overcome his bodily handicaps by dieting and running, but with no success.

In the course of therapy he realized his bodily appearance expressed an aspect of his personality he had previously been unable to accept—namely, that a part of him was identified with being a big, fat slob, and more a baby than a man. This was also expressed by the way he sat sprawled in a chair, and by the sloppiness of his dress. He then realized that being a big, fat, sloppy baby was an unconscious attitude he had adopted to resist his parents' continual demands that he grow up, be a man, and be outstanding. His actual conflicts were deeper than this statement indicates, but they all were epitomized in this bodily attitude. On a conscious or ego level he went along with his parents' demands, but his unconscious or bodily resistance was not effected by any determined effort. A person cannot succeed in life by fighting himself. The effort to overcome the body is doomed to failure.

Both the identity and the difference between psychic and physical processes must be recognized. My patient was not just a big, fat, infantile slob. He was also a man earnestly endeavoring to function on that level. But he was not fully a man, for his unconscious and his body kept him fixated at some childish level. He was a man trying to realize his potential, but failing. His body dramatically revealed both sides of him, for it was big like a man's body but with rolls of fat that made him look like a baby.

Many people are similarly handicapped by an unconscious conflict between different aspects of their personality. The most common is between the unfulfilled needs and demands of the infant in them and the urges and strivings of the adult. Adulthood requires that one be independent (stand on his own feet) and take the responsibility for fulfilling his wants and desires. But in people who have this conflict the effort to be independent and responsible is undermined by unconscious desires to be supported and taken care of. The result is a mixed picture both psychologically and physically. In his behavior such a person may show an exaggerated independence together with a fear of being alone or with an inability to make decisions. One can see the same mixed picture in the person's body. The infantile aspects of his personality may be manifested in small hands and feet, thin, spindly legs that appear to be inadequate supports, or an underdeveloped muscular system that does not have the aggressive potential to get what one needs or wants.

In other cases there is a conflict between the playfulness of the child and the realism of the adult part of the personality. On the surface the person appears serious, often grim, rigid, hardworking and moralistic. Then, when he attempts to let down or let go, he becomes childish. This is especially evident when such people drink. The child also comes through in inappropriate pranks and jokes. The face and body of the person have a tight, hard and drawn quality which makes him look old. Yet one frequently glimpses a boyish expression on the face accompanied by a smile or grin that manifests a feeling of immaturity.

This conflict arises when the natural playfulness of the child is not allowed its full and free expression. The suppression of a child's sexual curiosity and fun-loving proclivities does not eliminate these tendencies. They are buried and removed from consciousness but remain alive in the subterranean layers of the personality, emerging, when the person lets down, as perversions of the natural tendencies. The qualities of the child have not been integrated into the personality but are split off and encapsulated as foreign bodies alien to the ego.

A person is the sum total of his life experiences, each of which is registered in his personality and structured in his body. Just as a woodsman can read the life history of a tree from a cross section of the trunk showing its annual growth rings, so it is possible for a bioenergetic therapist to read a person's life history from his body. Both studies require knowledge and experience, but they are based on the same principles.

As the human organism grows, it adds layers to the personality, each one of which remains alive and functioning in the adult. When they are accessible to the individual, they constitute an integrated personality that is free of conflict. If any layer or for that matter any experience is repressed and unavailable, the personality is in conflict and, therefore, limited. A schematic diagram of the layering is shown in the following figure:

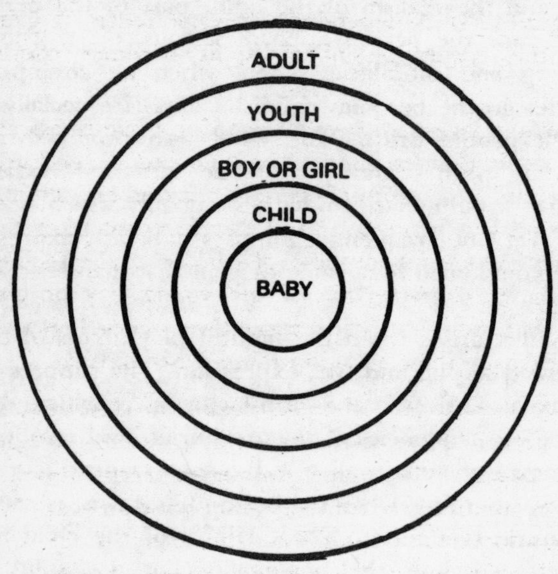

The qualities which each layer adds to life may be summarized as follows:

Baby	= love and pleasure
Child	= creativity and imagination
Boy or girl	= playfulness and fun
Youth	= romance and adventure
Adult	= reality and responsibility

Perhaps it would be best to say when speaking of qualities, that the growth we are considering is the development and expansion of consciousness. Each layer represents, then, a new sense of the self and its potentialities, a new awareness of the self and its relation to the world. Consciousness, however, is not a detached or isolated unit of the personality. It is a function of the organism, an aspect of the living body. It develops in relation to growth of the body physically, emotionally and psychologically. It is dependent on experience; it gains depth through the acquisition of skills; it becomes confirmed in activity.

In equating layers with qualities of consciousness, I do not mean to imply that each new dimension of the self arises fully formed within a certain age period. Playfulness actually begins in childhood but reaches its full development after this phase has passed. The consciousness of play and the feeling of joy are, I believe, characteristic of the young boy or girl rather than of the child. A fuller exposition of each layer and its quality will make their equation more meaningful:

The baby is characterized by its desire for closeness, especially with its mother. It wants to be held, caressed, welcomed and accepted. Love, as I pointed out in an earlier book, may be defined as the desire for an intimate closeness. When the need for closeness is fulfilled, the baby is in a state of pleasure. Deprivation of this needed closeness results in a painful state.

Every feeling of love in an adult stems from this layer in his personality. The feeling of love isn't essentially different in an adult from that in a baby although its form of expression may vary. The desire for an intimate closeness underlies all feelings of love. The individual who is in touch with the baby he was which is still part of him, knows the feeling of love. He is also in touch with his heart. To the degree that one is cut off from his heart or his babyhood he is blocked from experiencing the fullness of love.

Childhood adds a new dimension and a new quality to life. The need for a continuous closeness gives way to the new need to explore the world—a need facilitated by the child's increasing motor coordination. Through this exploration of persons and things, space and time, the child creates the world in its mind. Since it is not encumbered by a structured sense of reality, its imagination is free. During this phase it also creates on a conscious level its sense of self—in the course of which it explores imaginatively the possibility of being other selves, like its mother, for example.

I believe that childhood may be said to end when the person gains a coherent picture of his personal world and personal self. Having achieved this step the *boy or girl* challenges its personal world in its play. The increasing mastery of motor skills and the games with other children constitute a form of playing that is joyful because it is free and richly rewarding. There is a higher degree of excitement in the play of boys or girls than in that of younger children, which also accounts for the feelings of joy that one experiences during this phase of life. There is also a greater sense of freedom deriving from an independence not yet burdened with responsibilities.

Youth is marked by a still further increase in the level of possible excitement related to the emerging interest in the opposite sex and the growing intensity of the sexual urge. Ideally, youth is the time for romance and adventure, combining the deep pleasure of closeness to another, the imagination and mental creativity of the child and the challenge and playfulness of the youngster. When possible consequences have a serious reality and one assumes a responsibility for them, the stage of adulthood is reached.

An adult is a person who is aware of the consequences of his behavior and assumes responsibility for them. However, if he loses touch with the feelings of love and closeness he knew as a baby, with the creative imagination of the child, with the playfulness and joy of his boyhood and with the spirit of adventure and sense of romance that marked his youth, he will be a sterile, hidebound and rigid person. A healthy adult is a baby, a child, a boy or girl and a youth. His sense of reality and responsibility includes the need and desire for closeness and love, the ability to be creative, the freedom to be joyful, and the spirit to be adventurous. He is an integrated and fully conscious human being.

To understand the living body, we must discard mechanical concepts. The mechanisms of the bodily functioning are important, but they do not explain that functioning. An eye, for instance, is not just a camera; it is a sense organ for perceiving and an expressive organ for reacting. A heart is not just a pump; it is an organ for feeling which a pump cannot do. We are sentient beings, which means we have the power to sense or perceive and to experience sensation or feeling. Perception is a function of the mind, which is an aspect of the body. The living body has a mind, possesses a spirit and contains a soul. How are these concepts understood bioenergetically?

Mind, Spirit and Soul

Today we are fond of saying that the mind-body dichotomy is a product of man's thinking, that mind and body are really one. For too long we have regarded them as separate entities, influencing each other but not directly related. This attitude has not fully changed. Our educational process is still split between mental education and physical education, which have nothing to do with each other. Few teachers of physical education believe they can affect a child's learning capacity by their gymnastic or athletic programs. And, in fact, they rarely do. Yet if mind and body are one, a true physical education should at the same time be a proper mental education and vice versa.

I think the trouble is due to the fact that we pay lip service to the concept of unity but fail to apply it in our daily life. We assume that one can educate a child's mind without paying attention to his body. Under threat of failure or punishment we can cram some information into his head. Unfortunately information does not become knowledge unless it has relevance to experience. We constantly overlook the fact that experience is a bodily phenomenon. One only experiences that which takes place in the body. To the degree that the body is alive, one's experience is vivid or dull. When events in the external world affect the body, one experiences them, but what one actually experiences is their effect on the body.

The weakness of psychoanalytic technique is that it ignores the body in its attempt to help the patient work through his emotional conflicts. Since it fails to provide any significant body experience, the ideas that emerge in the course of treatment remain impotent to produce any major changes in personality. Too often I have seen patients who through years of psychoanalysis had gained much information and some knowledge of their condition but whose basic problems had remained untouched. Knowledge becomes understanding when it is coupled with feeling. Only a deep understanding, charged with strong feeling, is capable of modifying structured patterns of behavior.

In previous books I explored the mind-body problem in some depth. Here I would like to point out certain mental functions that have an important bearing on bioenergetics. First, the mind has a directive function with respect to the body. Through his mind a person can direct his attention to different parts of the body and so bring those areas into sharper focus. Let me suggest a simple experiment. Hold your hand straight out in front of you, keeping your arm relaxed, and focus all your attention on your hand. Keep the focus on your hand for about a minute, while you breathe easily, and you may experience your hand differently. You may sense a streaming into your hand, which now feels charged and tingling. It may begin to vibrate or shake a little. If you sense this, you may realize that you have directed a stream of excitation or energy into your hand.

In bioenergetic workshops I use a variation of this experiment to make the experience more intense.

I ask people to press the spread fingers of one hand against the fingers of the other hand, holding the palms and heels of the hands as much apart as possible. Now keeping the same contact, turn the hands inward so that they point toward the chest, and move the hands forward without breaking their contact. One holds them in this position of hyperextension for a minute while breathing easily. At the end of the minute the hands are relaxed and held out loosely. One may again experience the streaming, the charging, the tingling and the vibration. If you do this body-experience exercise, you may also note that your attention is focused on your hands because of the increased charge in them. Your hands are in a state of increased tension or charge which may be translated as they are attention. If you bring the two hands slowly toward each other until the palms are about two to three inches apart in their fully relaxed state while they are still charged, you may sense a charge between them as if it had substance and body.

The mind can direct a person's attention either inward or outward, toward the body or toward external objects. In effect, one focuses one's energy either on the self or on the external world. A healthy person can alternate these two points of focus easily and rapidly so that almost at the same time one is aware of one's bodily self and of the environment. Such a person is mindful of what is happening to himself, as well as what is happening to others. But not everyone has this ability. Some people become too mindful of themselves and develop an

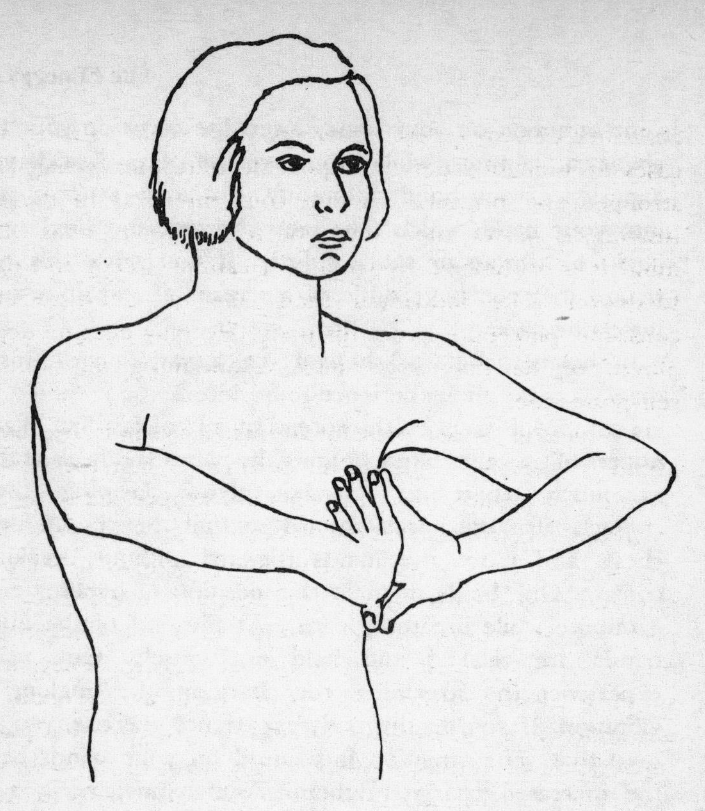

embarrassing self-consciousness. Others are so mindful of what is going on around them that they lose consciousness of the self. This is frequently true of hypersensitive individuals.

To mind your body is one of the tenets of bioenergetics, for only in that way do you know who you are—that is, do you know your own mind. In this connection the mind functions as a perceptive and reflective organ, sensing and defining one's mood, feelings, desires, etc. To know your mind really is to know what you want or what you feel. If you have no feeling, there is nothing to mind (pay attention to), and so one doesn't have a mind. When a person's actions are influenced by other people and not by his own feelings, he doesn't have a mind of his own.

When a person can't make up his mind, it denotes that he is

conscious of two opposing feelings, each equally strong. In such cases decision is generally impossible until one feeling becomes stronger and prevails. To lose your mind, as in the case of insanity, is not to know what you feel. This happens when the mind is overwhelmed by feelings it cannot accept and dare not focus on. The individual then cuts off or dissociates his conscious perception from his body. He may become depersonalized, or he may run amok, abandoning all attempts at self-possession.

If a person is not mindful of his body, it is because he is afraid to perceive or sense his feelings. When feelings have a threatening quality, they are generally suppressed. This is done by developing chronic muscular tensions that do not allow any flow of excitation or spontaneous movement to develop in the relevant areas. People often suppress their fear because it has a paralyzing effect, their rage because it is too dangerous, and their despair because it is too discouraging. They will also suppress their awareness of pain, such as the pain of an unfulfilled longing, because they cannot support that pain. The suppression of feeling diminishes the state of excitation in the body and decreases the ability of the mind to focus. It is the prime cause for the loss of mind power. Mostly our minds are preoccupied with the need to be in control at the expense of being and feeling more alive.

Mind and spirit are also connected. The amount of spirit a person has is determined by how alive and vibrant he is, literally by how much energy he has. The connection between energy and spirit is immediate. When a person becomes excited and his energy increases, his spirits rise. It is in this sense that we speak of a spirited person or a spirited horse. I would define spirit, therefore, as the life force within an organism manifested in the self-expression of the individual.* The quality of a person's spirit characterizes him as an individual, and when it is strong, it makes him stand out from others of his kind.

*See Lowen, *Depression and the Body, op cit.*, for a fuller exposition of this concept.

The life force or spirit of an organism has been associated with the breath. In the Bible it is stated that God breathed His spirit into a lump of clay, giving it life. In theology, the Spirit of God or the Holy Ghost is called the pneuma, which the dictionary defines as "the vital soul or the spirit." The word "pneuma" comes from the Greek, where it means wind, breath or spirit, and is akin to the Greek *phein* which means to blow, breathe. Many Oriental religions place a special emphasis on breathing as a means of communion with the universal. Breathing plays an important role in bioenergetics, because only through breathing deeply and fully can one summon the energy for a more spirited and spiritual life.

Soul is a more difficult concept to work with than either mind or spirit. Its primary meaning is "the principle of life, feeling, thought, and action in man regarded as a distinct entity separate from the body."* It is associated with a life after death, with heaven and hell, ideas sophisticated people today reject. In fact, the very mention of the word in a book like this, which claims to have an objective validity, can put some people off. They cannot reconcile the idea of an entity separate from the body with the concept of unity bioenergetics represents. But, then, neither can I achieve such a reconciliation. Fortunately, everyone regards the soul as being in the body until death. What happens to it at death and afterward I do not know. The question doesn't trouble me since my main interest is with the body in life or the living body.

Does the living body have a soul? That depends on how one defines the term "soul." *The Random House Dictionary* gives a fourth meaning of the word: "the emotional part of man's nature; the seat of feelings or sentiment." Its synonyms are spirit, heart. This doesn't help much, for one could simply dispense with the term then. The word has an entirely different

**The Random House Dictionary of the English Language,* unabridged ed. (New York, 1970).

meaning for me, one that aids my understanding of human beings.

I regard soul as the sense or feeling in a person of being part of a larger or universal order. Such a feeling must arise from the actual experience of being part of or connected in some vital or spiritual way to the universe. I use the word "spiritual," not in its abstract or mental connotation, but as spirit, pneuma or energy. I believe the energy in our bodies is in contact and interacts with the energy around us in the world and in the universe. We are not an isolated phenomenon. However, not everyone feels the connection or the contact. My impression of people is that the person who is isolated, alienated and unconnected lacks the quality of soulfulness that I sense is present in people who feel themselves part of something bigger than themselves.

We are born connected, though that most visible connection the umbilical cord is severed at birth. As long as that cord functioned, the baby was in one sense still part of its mother. Though it begins to lead a fully independent existence after birth, it is still connected to its mother energetically and emotionally. It responds to her excitement and is affected by her moods. I have no doubt that the baby senses its connection and belonging to its mother. It has a soul, and its eyes often have that deep look we call soulful.

Growth is expansion on many levels. New connections are made and experienced. The first is to other members of the family. Once this connection is made, there is an energetic interchange between the baby and each person in the family, plus one with the family as a group. People become a part of its world just as it becomes part of theirs.

As consciousness grows and contacts increase, the person develops widening circles of relationships. There is the world of plants and animals he takes in and also identifies with. There is the community he lives in, which becomes his community just as he becomes its member. And so it continues with increasing age. If one doesn't get cut off, he will sense his belonging to the great natural order of our earth. As he belongs to it, so it belongs to him. On another level of thinking the small community becomes extended to include the nation and then the world of humanity. Farthest out are the stars and the universe. The eyes of older people sometimes have a distant look, as if their vision were focused on the heavens. It seems as if toward the end of life the soul makes contact with its final resting place.

In the following diagram the expanding relationships of a person are shown as a set of concentric circles. This diagram is similar to the one in the preceding section which illustrates, in a different context, the levels of development in an individual's consciousness. As consciousness expands, it incorporates more of the external world into the psyche and personality of the individual. Both energetically and psychically the newborn organism is like a flower which slowly unfolds and opens to the world. In this sense the soul is present at birth but inchoately. As an aspect of the organism it, too, undergoes the natural process of growth and maturation, at the end of which it becomes fully identified with the cosmos and loses its individualistic quality. We can conceive the possibility that at death the free energy of the organism leaves the body to merge with the universal or cosmic energy. We say that the soul departs the body at death.

Life comes into the world as being = be-ing, but just being seems to lack the sense of fulfillment. One of my patients made this clear to me when she said, "Being is not enough. I want to belong [be-long], and I don't feel I do." The extension of being into the world through identifications and relationships gives rise to the *sense* of belonging. Being *longs* for this extension, to belong. The feeling of longing, one of the most important feelings in the organism, reflects its need for contact with its environment and the world. Through belonging the soul escapes the narrow limitation of the self, without losing the sense of self or *being* that is our individual existence.

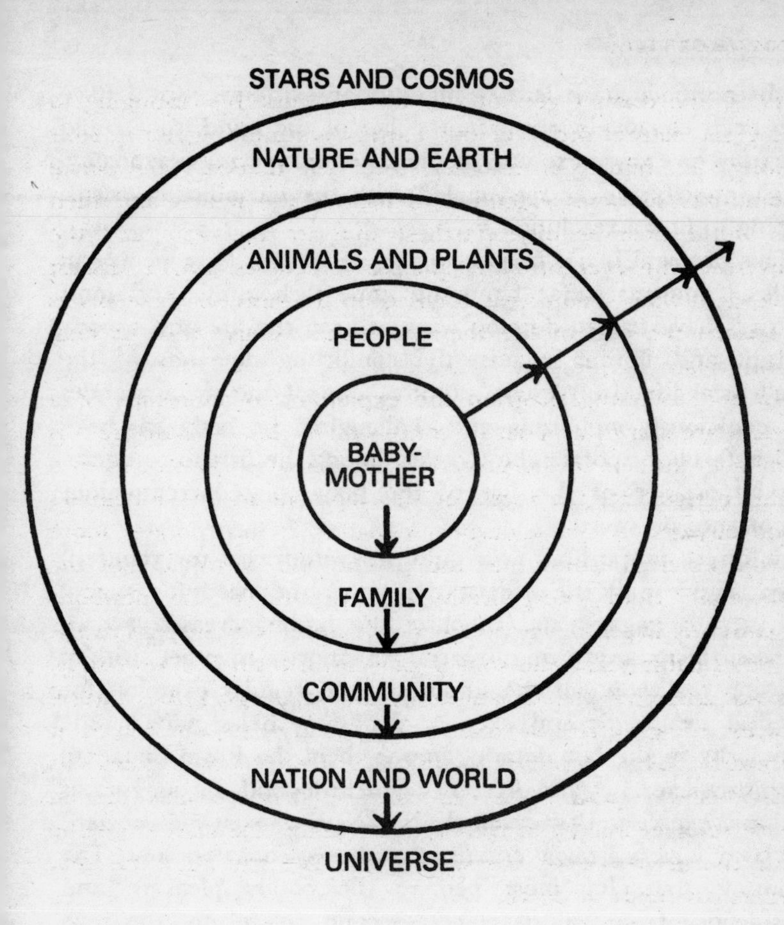

The Life of the Body: The Bioenergetic Exercise

In the first chapter I mentioned that prior to my meeting with Reich I was involved with sports and calisthenics. The life of the body has always had a special appeal for me—one that might normally have led to an outdoor existence. But I have also been equally involved in the life of the mind, so I could not fully give myself to one or the other side of my personality. I felt myself split and struggled with these conflicting needs, hoping to find a resolution.

This problem is not unique to me, of course. Most people in civilized cultures suffer from the same dichotomy. And most cultures have had to develop ways to keep the life of the body vibrant and flowing against the conflicting demands of the intellectual life. In Western cultures one of the main avenues for consciously mobilizing and challenging the body has been and is through sports. The Greeks, among the first to recognize the importance of the life of the body, placed tremendous importance on sports.

In direct proportion to a culture's withdrawal (or removal) from nature and the life of the body, the need for special activities to engage and mobilize the body increases. So we witness today a growing interest in sports, together with a growing realization of the importance of regular exercises for physical health. Several exercise programs have gained wide popularity in the last decade, among them the Royal Canadian Air Force exercises and Aerobics which depends on jogging as its basic exercise. Unfortunately the American attitude toward the body is very heavily encrusted with ego considerations. The result is that, for most people, the bodily pleasure and satisfaction from sports takes second place to the ego satisfaction of winning. The focus on winning often adds a degree of tension to the activity that directly negates its value in stimulating and freeing the body. We all are familiar with the golfer whose morning is ruined by a poor putt. The same ego drives to succeed and to keep up with the fashion also infuse our exercise programs. We do them to promote our looks, to further our image of health or to develop our muscles. Our ideal body has the qualities of a race horse, sleek, trim—and ready to win.

The life of the body is feeling: feeling alive, vibrant, good, excited, angry, sad, joyous and finally contented. It is the lack of feeling or a confusion about feeling that brings people to therapy. I have found that athletes, dancers and exercise addicts suffer from this lack and confusion just as intensely as others. And so did I, despite my involvement with sports and exercises. Through therapy I was able to reach and open up my feelings and so regain some of the life of my body. Both Reichian and bioenergetic therapy aim at this goal.

But a problem remained. How does one keep the life of the body flowing and vibrant after the therapy ceases? Our life-denying culture provides no help in this need. This was a question that Reich never considered. He believed a person finds fulfillment by directing his energies outward. His philosophy was expressed in the dictum "Love, work and knowledge are the wellsprings of life. They should also govern it." This statement leaves only sexual activity as the main avenue for the expression of the life of the body—a path altogether too narrow and restrictive.

My personal solution was to use the bioenergetic exercises, developed to promote the therapy, as a regular routine at home. I have now been doing them for about twenty years. Not only have they enabled me to keep in touch with my body and to maintain its life, but they have also furthered the growth that therapy instituted. I found them so helpful that I encouraged my patients to do them at home as a supplement to the therapy. Their value has been confirmed by all who do them. And we have now instituted regular bioenergetic exercise classes for patients and others who are committed to the life of the body. Since the commitment to the body is lifelong, we expect that a person will make a similar commitment to the exercises.

The disenchantment with the antilife attitude of Western culture has led many people to an interest in Eastern religion, philosophy and disciplines. Most of these recognize the importance of some program of bodily exercise as essential to spiritual development. The widespread interest in yoga is a dramatic demonstration. I had looked into yoga before I met Reich, but it did not appeal to my Western mind. Yet throughout my work with Reich I was aware of some similarity between the practice of yoga and Reichian therapy. In both systems the main emphasis is on the importance of breathing. The difference between the two schools of thought was in their direction. In yoga the direction is inward, toward spiritual development; in Reichian therapy it is outward, toward creativity and joy. A reconciliation of these two views is surely needed, and it is my hope that bioenergetics can help. Several of the foremost yoga teachers in this country have expressed their personal appreciation for the understanding of the body that bioenergetics provides—an understanding that has enabled them to adapt yoga techniques to Western needs.

More recently other Oriental body disciplines have become popular in this country. Foremost is the *t'ai chi ch'uan* exercises the Chinese use. Both yoga and *t'ai chi* emphasize the importance of sensing the body, the achievement of coordination and grace and the attainment of spiritual feeling through an identification with the body. In this they contrast strongly with Western exercise programs which aim at power and control.

Where do the bioenergetic exercises fit into this picture? They represent an integration of both Eastern and Western attitudes. Like the Eastern disciplines, they eschew power and control in favor of grace, coordination and the spirituality of the body. But they also aim to promote self-expression and sexuality. Thus, they serve to open up the inner life of the body, as well as to aid the extension of that life into the world. And they are uniquely designed to help a person get in touch with the tensions that inhibit the body's life. But like the Eastern practices, they will work if they become a discipline, not to be done mechanically or compulsively, but with a feeling of pleasure and a sense of meaning.

I cannot present here the full repertory of exercises we use in bioenergetics. I hope to be able to do this in another book. I might add that they are not formalized and can be improvised on to suit one's need and one's situation. However, I will describe a considerable number of these exercises as we explore the basic tenets to show their purpose. One of the basic exercises was one I developed early to help me get more into my legs and feet and become more grounded. It is called the arch or the bow and is also referred to as the fundamental stress position.

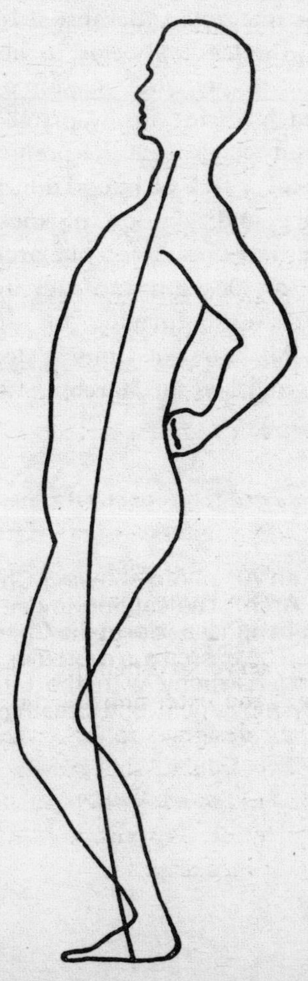

The line superimposed on the figure shows the correct arc or bowing of the body. The center point of the shoulders is directly above the center point of the feet, and the line joining these points is almost a perfect arch passing through the central point of the hip joint.

When a body is in this position, its parts are perfectly balanced. Dynamically, the bow is drawn and ready for action. Energetically the body is charged from feet to head. This means there is a flow of excitation through the body. One feels his feet on the ground and his head in the air, and one also feels fully connected or integrated. Because it is an energetically charged stress position, the legs will begin to vibrate.

We use this position to give the person a sense of being connected or integrated, of being firmly planted in his feet and holding his head up. But we also use the position diagnostically, for it immediately reveals a lack of integration in the body, and it pinpoints the nature and location of the main muscular tensions. I will describe how these affect the arch in a moment.

We had been using this position and exercise for more than eighteen years in our work. Imagine my surprise when a patient showed me an AP photo of Chinese doing precisely the same exercise. (It was published on March 4, 1972.)

→

This is a drawing of an AP photo showing Chinese doing what is called the "Taoist Arch." The caption under the photo states "Three residents of Shanghai perform the Chinese calisthenic of Taichichuan recently. The exercise is rooted in Taoist philosophy and aims at attaining harmony with the universe through a combination of body movement and breathing technique."

The caption and the comment were most interesting. *Tao* means the way. The way of the *tao* is through harmony both within the self and with the environment and the universe. The outer harmony actually depends on the inner harmony which can be achieved through the "combination of body movement and breathing technique." Bioenergetics aims at the same harmony by the same means. Many of our patients have used the various *t'ai chi* exercises concomitantly with bioenergetics.

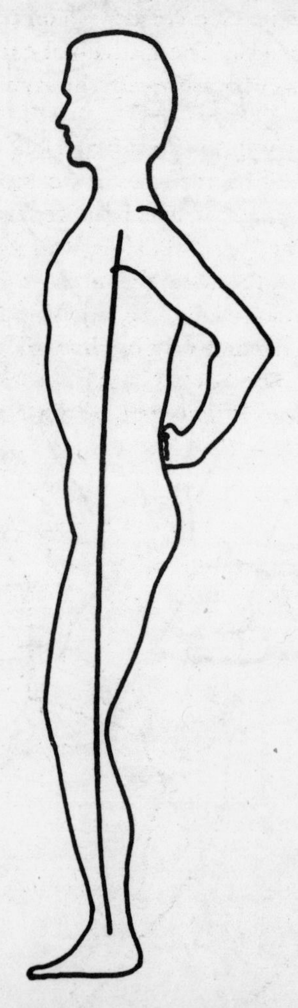

The Chinese, however, start with the assumption that their people have no major body disturbances that prevent them from doing the exercise correctly. This assumption cannot be made of Westerners. And whether it is true of present-day Chinese is questionable.

A common problem I encounter in people is an overall body rigidity that doesn't let the person arch his body. The line joining the midpoint of the shoulder and the midpoint of the foot is a straight line. (See illustration on p. 76.) There is noticeable inflexibility of the legs. The individual cannot fully flex his ankle. Tension in the lower back prevents its arching. The pelvis is slightly retracted.

The opposite condition is a hyperflexibility of the back which bends too much. This denotes a weakness in the back muscles that I relate to a lack of backbone feeling. While the rigid body and personality are too inflexible, this body and personality are too pliable. In both cases the arch is improperly executed so that there is no sense of integration and flow and no feeling of inner or outer harmony. The line of the bow is bent to the breaking point. The lower back is not serving to support the body; that function is assumed by the abdominal muscles, which are very contracted. (See below.)

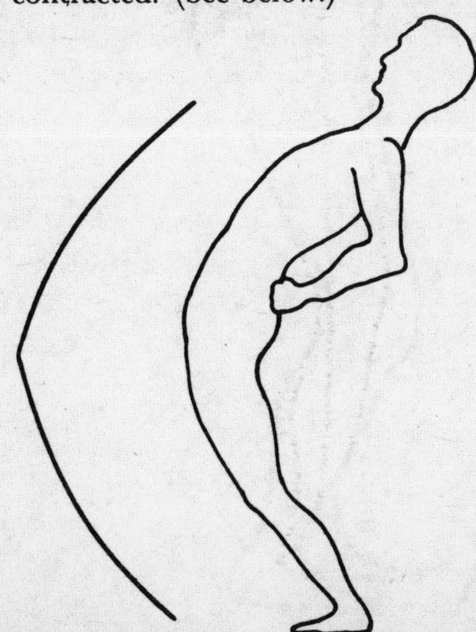

Another common disturbance is a break in the bow line owing to a severe retraction of the pelvis. This contrasts with the preceding condition where the pelvis is pushed too far forward. This disturbance is shown in the following figure:

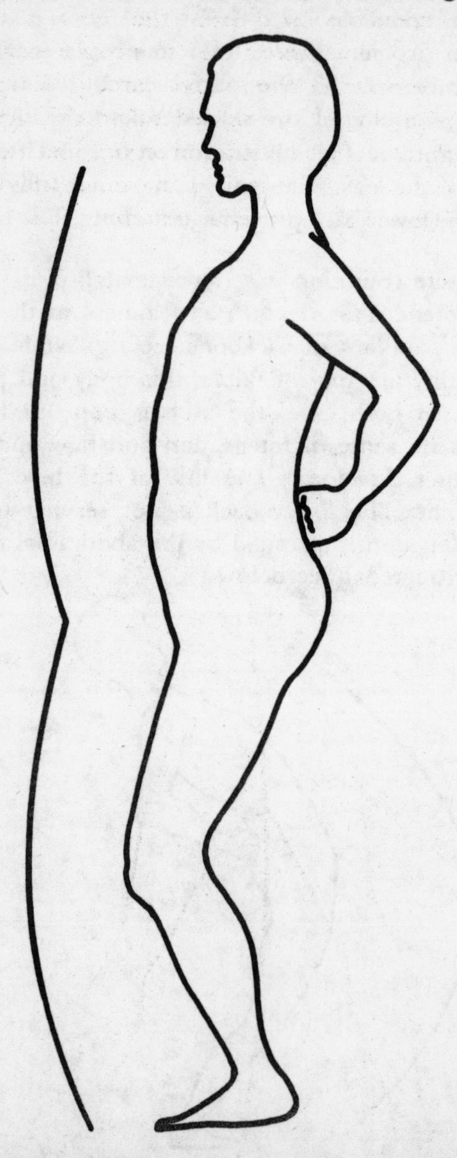

In this condition if the person pushes his pelvis forward, his knees straighten up. He can bend his knees only by pulling his ass back. There is marked tension in the lower back, as well as along the back of the legs.

When the body is viewed from the front, a splitting of the body segments is sometimes clear. The major parts of the body, the head and neck, the trunk, and the legs, simply do not line up. The head and neck are angled off to the right or left. The trunk is angled in the opposite direction, and the legs are also angled opposite to the trunk. I have sketched this position below with a line showing the angulations.

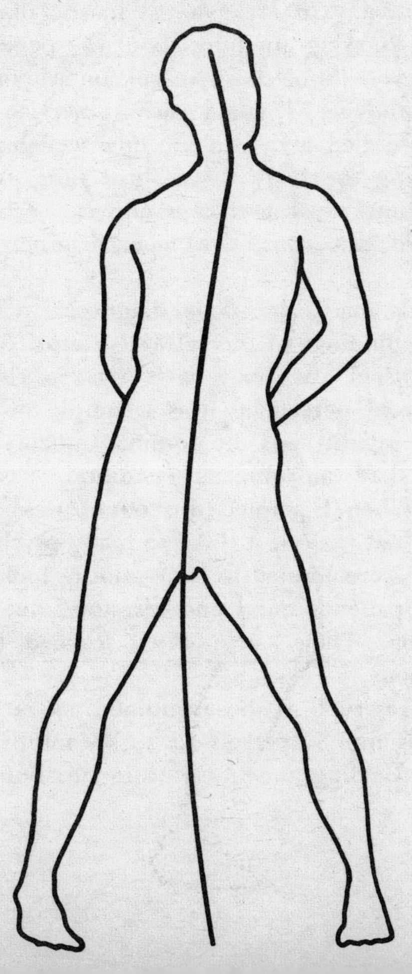

These angulations reveal that the body does not flow together. They represent a fragmentation of the integrity of the personality typical of a schizoid or schizophrenic personality. Schizoid means split. If the splitting exists in the personality, it must also exist in the body on an energetic level. The person is his body.

A number of years ago my associates and I were invited to give a talk and demonstration of bioenergetics to a group of doctors and students at the National Institute of Mental Health. My talk discussed the intimate relationship between the body and the personality. After the talk we were asked to demonstrate our ability to make a psychiatric diagnosis from the body without knowing anything about the person. We were presented with several subjects in succession whom the people at NIMH were studying. I asked each subject to assume the stress position described above to see how well his body lined up. After observing the body for a short time, my associates and I were put into separate rooms and called out one at a time so we could not consult with each other—to offer a diagnosis.

Each one of us made the same diagnoses, diagnoses that accorded with the findings of the NIMH groups. In two of the cases, the splitting of the body lines was so clear that the diagnosis of schizoid personality was a simple matter. In the third an excessive rigidity was the dominant quality. One of the schizoid subjects had an unusual condition. His eyes were different colors. When I pointed this out, I was surprised no one in the room had noticed it. Like so many psychologists and psychiatrists, they were trained to hear—not to look. They were interested in the patient's mind and his story, not in his body and its expression. They had not yet learned to read the language of the body.

Body disturbances such as those outlined above underlie the symptoms that prompt a person to seek therapy. The rigid person will be unyielding and ungiving in situations calling for softness and tenderness. The individual whose back is too soft and pliable will lack aggression where that is called for. All patients feel out of harmony with themselves and the world. For them, doing the arch exercise will not restore this harmony since they cannot do it properly. It will, however, help them sense the tensions in their bodies which prevent its proper execution. These tensions can be released through other bioenergetic exercises, some of which will be described in the later chapters of this book.

When I say that a person who does the arch properly is in harmony with the universe, I have neither hesitation nor reservation, because I have never seen a person with a major emotional problem able to do it correctly. It is not a matter of practice, for this position cannot be learned. It is not a static position. One is required to breathe deeply and fully while in it. One has to be able to maintain the functioning and integrity of the body under stress. Doing the exercise regularly helps greatly, however. It helps a person get in touch with his body, sense its disturbances and tensions and understand their meaning. It also helps him retain the feeling of harmony with the universal once he *has* achieved it. This is no small challenge in a technological culture.

III. The Language of the Body

The Heart of Life: The Heart of the Matter

The language of the body or body language has two parts. One deals with body signs and expressions that convey information about a person; the second deals with verbal expressions that refer for their meaning to body functions. In this chapter I will discuss both parts of what is called body language, starting with the second. For example, the expression "stand on your own feet" is body language. It means, of course, to be independent and derives from our common experience. When we were babies and dependent, we were held or supported. As we grow up, we learn to stand on our own feet and be independent. Many such expressions are part of our everyday language. We may say of a person that he is "stiff-necked" meaning stubborn, "tight-fisted" meaning stingy and gives little or "tight-mouthed" to denote that he says little. We speak of "shouldering our responsibilities," "holding our head high" and "standing firm" to express our psychological attitudes.

Sandor Rado has suggested that language has its roots in proprioceptive sensation—that is, the basis of all language is body language. I believe that this is a valid proposition since communication is primarily a sharing of experience, which in turn is a bodily response to situations and events. In a world, however, where there are other relevant frames of reference, language will incorporate terms from these systems. For instance, the expression "moving in high gear" derives from our experience with automotive machines and has meaning only for people who are familiar with such systems. A second instance is the expression "a full head of steam," which refers to the operation of steam engines. Such expressions might be called machine language. How many of these have become part of our way of speaking and, therefore, of thinking, I do not know. We can anticipate that our advancing technology will introduce many new terms into our vocabulary that are far removed from body language.

All machines are in one sense extensions of the human body and function on principles that operate within the body. This is easy to see in the simple tools such as the pitchfork which is an extension of the hand and fingers, the shovel extending the cupped hand, and the sledgehammer, extending the fist. But even complicated machines bear this relation to the body; the telescope is an extension of the eyes, the computer, of the brain. However, we often lose sight of this fact and tend to think of the body as operating on the principles of the machine rather than the other way around. We identify ourselves with the machine, which in its limited function is a more powerful instrument than the body. We end by seeing the body as a machine and then lose touch with its vital and sentient aspects.

Bioenergetics does not see the body as a machine, not even as the most complex and beautiful machine ever created. It is true that one can compare certain *aspects* of bodily function to a machine; the heart, for example, can be viewed as a pump. Isolated from the body, the heart is a pump, or to put it differently: If the heart were not involved in the total life of the body, it would be only a pump. But it is so involved, and that is what makes it a heart, not a pump. The difference between a machine and the heart is that the machine has a limited function. A pump pumps, nothing more. A heart also pumps, and in that limited operation it functions like a machine. But a heart is also an integral part of the body, and in that aspect of its functioning, it does more than pump blood. It partakes of and contributes to the life of the body. Body language recognizes this difference and that is why it is so important.

The richness of expression involving the word heart shows how important its extramechanical aspects are to people. Here are some of them. In the expression "go to the heart of the matter" we equate the heart with the concept of essence. It also connotes the center or core as in the expression "You have reached my heart," which we assume means a person's deepest, most central aspect. "With all one's heart" indicates total commitment, since it involves the deepest part of the person.

Everyone knows we associate the feeling of love with the heart. "To lose your heart" is to fall in love; "to open your heart" is to take in the love of another person. "To wear your heart on your sleeve" is to look for love. So far it is used largely symbolically. But the heart is not just associated with feeling; it is, according to our language, a feeling organ. When we say, "My heart shrank within me," it conveys a proprioceptive sensation which another person can sense within himself as denoting an extreme of anxiety and disappointment. The heart also expands with joy, and this is a literal statement, not just a figurative one. If that is the case, does the expression "You have broken my heart" denote a real, physical trauma? I tend to believe it does but also that broken hearts often mend themselves. The word "break" does not necessarily mean "break into two or more pieces." It could mean a break in the sense of the connection between the heart and the body's periphery. The feeling of love no longer flows freely from the heart to the world.

Bioenergetics is concerned with how a person handles the feeling of love. Is his heart closed, or does he have an open heart? Open to the world or closed off from the world? His attitude can be determined from the expression of his body, but to make this determination one must understand the language of the body.

The heart is enclosed in a bony cage, the thoracic cage, but this cage can be rigid or soft, immobile or responsive. Its quality can be assessed by palpation, as one notes that the muscles are tight and that the chest wall does not yield to gentle pressure. The mobility of the chest can be seen in respiration. In very many people the chest wall does not move with breathing. In such people the breathing movements are seen to be mainly diaphragmatic but with some slight abdominal involvement. The chest is inflated and held in the inspiratory position. In some people the sternum forms a protuberance as if to keep people away from the person's heart. Sticking out the chest is a form of defiance. If you do it deliberately, you will sense that it says, "I won't let you get close to me."

The primary channel of communication for the heart is through the throat and mouth. It is the infant's first channel, as it reaches with its lips and mouth for the mother's breast. However, a baby doesn't reach with lips and mouth alone, it also reaches with its heart. In the kiss we have retained our awareness of this movement as an expression of love. But a kiss may be a gesture of love or an expression of love; the difference is whether one's heart is in it or not, and that depends on whether the channel of communication between mouth and heart is open or closed. A constricted throat and a tight neck can effectively block any feeling from passing through. In such cases the heart is relatively isolated, closed off.

The heart's second channel of communication is through the arms and hands as they reach out to touch. In this case the image of love is the gentle, tender and caressing touch of a mother's hand. Here, too, if the action is to be an expression of love, the feeling must come from the heart and flow into the hands. Truly loving hands are highly charged with energy. Such hands have a healing quality in the touch. The flow of feeling or energy to the hands can be blocked by shoulder tensions or by spasticities in the muscles of the hand. Shoulder tensions develop when one is afraid to reach out or to strike out. Tensions in the small muscles of the hand are the result of repressed impulses to grasp or seize, to claw or to strangle. I believe such tensions are responsible for rheumatoid arthritis in the hands. In some cases I have found that doing the exercise described in the first chapter, where the hands are pressed together in hyperextension, has helped some people overcome an attack of rheumatoid arthritis in the hands.

A third channel of communication from the heart to the world is downward through the waist and pelvis to the genital organs. Sex is an act of love, but whether it is simply a gesture or an expression of the sincere feeling is, again, a question of whether one's heart is in it. When the feeling of love for one's partner is strong, the sexual experience has an intensity and reaches a level of excitement that makes the climax or orgasm an ecstatic event. I have previously pointed out* that a full and satisfactory orgasm is possible only when one is totally committed. In such a case one can actually feel his heart leap (leap for joy) at the moment of climax. But this channel, too, can be cut off or closed to varying degrees by tensions in the lower half of the body.

Sex without feeling is like a meal eaten without an appetite. Of course, most people have some feeling; the question is how much and how open the channel of communication is. One of the commonest disturbances in the human being is the dissociation of the upper half of the body from the lower half. Sometimes the two halves do not look as if they belong to the same person. In some people the upper half is well developed while the pelvis and legs are small and immature-looking, as if they belonged to a child. In others the pelvis is full and rounded, but the upper half is small, narrow, childlike. In all such cases the feelings of one part are not integrated with the feelings of the other. Sometimes the upper half of the body has a tight, rigid and aggressive quality while the lower half appears soft, passive and masochistic. Wherever a degree of dissociation exists, the natural respiratory movements do not flow freely through the body. Breathing is either thoratic, with little abdominal involvement, or diaphragmatic, with restricted chest movements. If the person is asked to bend his back as in the *t'ai chi*

*Alexander Lowen, *Love and Orgasm* (New York, Macmillan, 1965).

arch described earlier, the line of the body does not form a true bow. The pelvis is either held forward or pulled back, causing a break in the line and in the unity of the body. A lack of unity denotes that head, heart and genitals are not integrated.

The chronic muscular tensions blocking the free flow of excitation and feeling are frequently found in the diaphragm, in the muscles surrounding the pelvis and in the upper legs. Releasing them by using both a physical and a psychological approach makes people begin to feel "connected." That is their word. Head, heart and genitals, or thinking, feeling and sex are no longer separate parts or separate functions. Sex becomes more and more an expression of love with a correspondingly greater pleasure. Invariably, any promiscuous behavior which was previously engaged in ceases.

In women the heart has a direct and immediate connection with the breasts, which respond erotically or glandularly to impulses flowing from the heart. In sexual arousal the nipples become engorged with blood and erect; in nursing the gland secretes milk. Normally, therefore, the act of nursing is one of the clearest expressions of mother love. By the same token it is hard to imagine that a mother's milk would not agree with her child. The infant was conceived and developed in the same milieu from which the milk is produced. However, patients have reported that they experienced their mother's milk as sour. Although I take such statements seriously, I don't believe the milk itself was at fault. More likely, the mother was bitter and resentful at being burdened by the child—a resentment the infant sensed and reacted to. Nursing, like sex, is *more* than a physiological reaction. It is an emotional response, and so it too is subject to the mother's moods and attitude. The flow of feeling from the heart to the breasts can be constructed and reduced.

I have discussed the heart at some length because it is central to all therapy. People come to therapy with various complaints: depression, anxiety, a feeling of inadequacy, a sense of failure, etc. But behind each complaint is a lack of joy and satisfaction in living.

It is popular today to talk of self-realization and the human potential, but such terms are meaningless unless one asks—potential for what? If one wants to live more fully and more richly, it is possible only if one opens his heart to life and to love. Without love—for one's self, for one's fellowman, for nature and for the universe, a person is cold, detached and inhuman. From our hearts flows the warmth uniting us to the world we live in. That warmth is the feeling of love. The goal of all therapy is to help a person increase his capacity to give and receive love—to expand his heart, not just his mind.

Interacting with Life

As we move from the heart to the periphery of the body, we will consider those organs that interact with the environment. Our body language is replete with expressions that derive from the proprioceptive awareness of their functions. These expressions are so rich in imagery and meaning that no student of the human personality can afford to ignore them.

We should start with the face since this is the part of the body that is openly presented to the world. It is also the part first examined when one looks at another person. Just as the word "heart" has come to mean center or core, so the word "face" has been extended to include the outward appearance of objects or situations. Thus, we speak of the face of a building or a landscape. In the remark "These are old problems with new faces" we refer to a change in the outward appearance of situations without a corresponding change in their essence.

The word "face" is also used to refer to a person's image which relates the concept of face to the ego, since the ego in one of its functions is concerned with the image a person projects. "To lose face" is to suffer a blow to one's ego; most people strive, therefore, "to keep face." If one "hides his face," it denotes a sense of shame in which the ego feels humiliated. A person with a strong ego "faces up" to situations, while a weaker person might "face away." Self-expression involves the face, and the kind of face we put on ourselves tells a great deal about who we are and how we feel. There is the smiling face, the depressed face, the bright face, the sad face, etc. Unfortunately most people are unaware of the expression on their faces and to that extent are out of touch with who they are and what they feel.

These considerations allow us to evaluate a person's ego from his face. The face of a schizoid individual generally has a masklike quality, which is one of the diagnostic signs of this condition—an indication of the low state of his ego. As his condition improves through treatment, his face becomes more expressive. A large, full face denotes a strong ego (that is the language of the body), but one sometimes sees a big head and a face on a small body or the reverse, a big body with a small head and face. In these cases, one can presume a degree of dissociation between the ego and the body.

Another interesting observation is the tendency for many long-haired boys and girls to hide their faces behind their hair. This seems to me an expression of their unwillingness to face the world. It may also be interpreted as a rejection of our culture's tendency to overvalue the image. Many young people have an anti-ego bias in their personalities; prestige, status, show and the material signs of position and power are repugnant to them. We can understand this attitude as an overreaction to the importance of the outward appearance their parents valued so highly, often at the expense of inner truth and inner values.

Every organ and feature of the face has its own body language. The brow, the eyes, the cheeks, the mouth and the chin are used to denote various qualities or traits. Let us look at some of the expressions involving these parts of the anatomy. A high brow denotes a person of refinement and intellectuality. Its opposite, the low brow, is a coarser fellow. A person is browbeaten when he looks downcast as a result of being intimidated by another's overbearing words or looks. His brows actually droop. When an individual is fresh and imprudent, he is said to have a lot of cheek. His cheeks literally stand out as they become suffused with blood and feeling.

The function of vision is so important to awareness that we equate the verb "seeing" with understanding. The "farsighted person" not only sees farther, but also thinks ahead. Bright eyes are both a sign and a symbol of exuberance. As expressive organs, the eyes play a big role in the language of the body. So much meaning can be conveyed by a look that we often gauge people's responses by their eyes. Referring to the mouth, we use such expressions as "bigmouth," "mealymouth," "closed mouth," etc. The function of the teeth is rich in metaphors. To "get a good bite on something" is a stronger expression than "coming to grips" with it. A person who holds on "by the skin of his teeth" is desperate. We speak of a "toothsome morsel" as one that promises pleasure. Finally, I would mention the English expression "chin up" which means to keep one's spirit up in adversity. Dropping the chin is the initial movement in giving way to sobs. This can be clearly observed in babies whose chins drop and begin to quiver just before they start to cry. In bioenergetic therapy it is sometimes necessary to get a patient to drop his chin before he can let himself give way to crying.

The human voice is man's most expressive medium. Paul J. Moses, in his book *The Voice of Neurosis,* describes the sonic elements in voice and shows their relationship to personality. In a later chapter I will discuss the underlying concepts that enable one to read the personality from the voice. Body language recognizes the significance of the voice. If a person "has no voice" in an affair, it means he doesn't count. He "has no say." Losing one's voice could, therefore, mean a loss of standing.

The functions of shoulders, arms and hands contribute to body language. A person "shoulders his responsibilities" if he carries them. He "elbows his way" if he is aggressive and "arms himself" when he faces a fight. If he "handles himself well," we are proud of him. One's participation in an affair is described as "having a hand in it."

The hand is the primary instrument of touch. It contains more tactile corpuscles than any other part of the body. Touching is, therefore, largely a function of hand contact, but it is not a mechanical operation. In human terms touching is a feeling contact with another person. Thus, the expression "I am touched by you" is another way of saying you have evoked a feeling response in me—a nicer way of saying it, for there is also implied the idea of closeness. "Being in touch" means being aware. This expression indicates the close connection between touching and knowing. Babies learn the qualities of objects by putting them into their mouths where taste is the important sensory modality. Children, however, learn by touching.

The connection between touching and knowing poses an important question for therapy. Can one really know another person without touching him? Or how can you get the feel of a person if you don't touch him? Traditional psychoanalysis with its avoidance of *any* physical contact between patient and analyst, out of fear, I believe, that such contact might arouse sexual feelings, placed a barrier between two people who needed to be in touch with each other more immediately than through words. By touching a patient's body, a therapist can sense many things about him: the softness or hardness of his musculature; the dryness of his skin; the aliveness of his tissues. Through his touch he can convey to the patient the idea that he feels and accepts the patient as a bodily being and that touching is a natural way of being in contact.

For the patient, to be touched physically by the therapist is a sign that the therapist cares. It relates back to the days when being held and touched by one's mother was an expression of her tender, loving care. Most people in our culture suffer from a deprivation of body contact dating back to their infancy. As a result of this deprivation, they want to be touched and held but are afraid to ask or reach for it. They feel a taboo against physical contact because it is too closely associated in their minds and bodies with sexuality. Since a taboo of this kind makes it difficult for people to be really in touch with each other,* it is therapeutically important to eliminate

*Montagu, *Touching, op. cit.* The importance of touching is fully explored in this study by Montagu.

it. It is incumbent on a therapist, therefore, to show he is not afraid to touch or be in touch with his patient.

But if a therapist lays hands on a patient, it raises the question of the quality of the touch. One can touch a person, especially of the opposite sex, in such a way that the touch is sexual and the physical contact erotic. Such touching confirms the patient's deepest anxiety about physical contact and reinforces the taboo on a deep level, despite the therapist's assurance that it is all right. It isn't all right. Any sexual involvement of the therapist is a betrayal of trust in the therapeutic relationship that subjects the patient to the same trauma he experienced in the parent-child relationship. If the betrayal is accepted as normal, it leads to a pattern of sexual acting out which hides the inability to make a *real* contact through touch.

A therapist's touch has to be warm, friendly, dependable and free of any personal interest to inspire confidence in touching. But since a therapist is a human being, too, his personal feelings may get in the way at times. When this happens, he shouldn't touch the patient. Therefore, a therapist has to know himself, to be in touch with himself before he can be in touch with his patient. Going through one's own therapy is the basic condition for doing therapy with others. One should expect a therapist to know the quality of a touch, to recognize the difference between a sensual touch, a supportive one, between a firm touch and a hard one, and between touching that is mechanical and that which has feeling.

A patient has a great need to touch his therapist since it is the patient's taboo against touching that is the cause of his feeling of isolation. To overcome this taboo, I often ask a patient to touch my face while he is lying on the bed. I use this procedure after I have opened up some of the patient's fears. Bending over him, I am in the position of a mother or father looking at the patient as a child. The hesitation, the tentative gesture, the anxiety this maneuver evoked was surprising to me at first. Many patients touched my face only with their fingertips, as if afraid to make full contact with their hands. Some said they were afraid of being rejected; others said they felt they had no right to touch me. Without encouragement few felt they could bring my face close to theirs, although this was what they wanted to do. In all cases this procedure went to the depths of a problem that could not be reached by words alone.

In some cases the patient's touch has an exploratory quality. The individual will let his fingers wander over my face just like a baby investigating the facial features of a parent. Sometimes a patient will push my face away, returning the rejection he once experienced. However, if the patient gives in to his longing for physical contact, he will pull me to him, hold me tight and feel my body with his hands. As I experience his longing, he feels my acceptance. Getting in touch with me enables him to get more in touch with himself, which is the goal of the therapeutic endeavor.

A third major area of interaction is in a person's relationship to the ground. Every position we take, every step we make involves this relationship. Unlike the birds or the fish, we are most at home on terra firma. And unlike the other mammals, we stand and move on two legs. This posture frees our arms by shifting the weight-bearing function to the vertebral column and the legs. The change to an erect stance places a stress on the muscles of the back which is focused in the lumbosacral region. I shall discuss the nature of this stress and its relation to lower-back disturbances in a subsequent chapter. We are interested here in the relation of the functions of the lower extremities to personality as they are reflected in our body language.

We can, for example, describe an individual as having "standing" or "no standing" in a community. In the latter case, he doesn't count as a person. We can also ask, "How do you stand?" in a situation. Your stance would denote your position. One can "stand for" a proposition or against it. If one doesn't "take a stand," one "stands off." If one does, one may "stand firm," in which case one "stands his ground." There is a concept of strength in standing. This is evident in such statements as "to stand up well" against attack, destruction or decay or to "stand criticism."

The opposite of "to stand" as a verb is not to sit, which is a different type of action, but to slouch, slump or shift. A "shifty" person doesn't take a stand, a person who "slumps" can't hold a stand, and a person who "slouches" forgoes a stand. These terms are metaphors when used to describe behavior; however, when applied to personality, they have a literal significance. There are people whose bodies show an habitual slouch, others whose bodies slump or manifest some degree of collapse. Some people are unable to stand without shifting their weight from one foot to the other. When such terms describe a typical attitude of the body, they describe the person.

How a person stands in life—that is, his basic stance as a human being—is dramatically revealed by his body. Let us take, as a common example, the tendency of many people to stand with locked knees. The effect of this posture is to transform the leg into a rigid support at the expense of its flexibility (knee action). It is not the natural stance, and its use indicates that the individual feels the need for extra support. This stance informs us, therefore, that there is some sense of insecurity in the personality (else why the need for the extra support?) whether the feeling of insecurity is conscious or not. Asking this person to stand with knees slightly flexed will often induce a vibration in the legs which may evoke the feeling "My legs won't hold me up."

To have a good standing, one must be grounded. The feet should be fairly flat on the floor with the foot arches relaxed but not collapsed. What we normally call flatfeet are collapsed arches, as a result of which the weight is shifted to the inside of the feet. A high arch, on the other hand, is a sign of spasticity or contraction in the muscles of the foot. The high arch diminishes the contact between foot and ground and denotes that the person's feet are not well planted. It is interesting to note that a high arch has long been regarded as a healthier and superior quality. Most of us can recall when a policeman was called a flatfoot because, I suppose, his feet were assumed to be flat from "pounding the beat" as we still say. "Flatfoot" was a derogatory expression and denoted a lower position in the social scale.

When I was young, my mother constantly worried about my

flatfeet. She put up a fierce resistance against my wearing sneakers because she was afraid they would increase my tendency to flatfeet. I wanted sneakers badly because they were ideal for running and for the ball games we played. All the other kids wore them, so I put up a strong fight, and in the end I got my sneakers. My mother insisted, however, that I have arch supports in my shoes which were a torture, and it took me some time to free myself from that affliction. The torture was real because all through my childhood I suffered from corns owing to tight, hard shoes. I never did have flatfeet, although I did not have the high arch that would have made my mother happy. In fact, my feet weren't flat enough, and throughout the years that I have worked on myself bioenergetically I have tried to get my feet more fully in contact with the ground by flattening them out. I am sure that as a result of this work, I haven't had a corn, callus, bunion or other disturbance in my feet since then.

The relation of the foot to standing and social position is illustrated by the former Chinese custom of binding the feet of female children so that they would remain small and relatively useless. There were two reasons for this practice. Small feet were a sign of higher social rank; all women of nobility in China had small feet. It meant they didn't have to do hard work or walk very far, but were instead carried in a palanquin. Peasant women who couldn't afford this luxury were left with big, broad flatfeet. The other reason for hobbling women's feet was to tie them to the home and take away their independence. Since the practice was class-limited, however, it must be regarded as a reflection of the cultural and social views of the Chinese. The study of how cultural attitudes are manifested in body expression is called kinesics. In bioenergetics we study the effect of culture on the body itself.

For years we had a cartoon on the bulletin board of the Institute for Bioenergetic Analysis depicting a professor of anatomy standing before a chart of the human foot with a pointer in his hand and facing a medical school class. In the caption he says, "I am sure that those of you who are planning to become psychiatrists are not the least bit interested in what I am going to say." Perhaps what he would say about the foot would be irrelevant to psychiatry. We in bioenergetics have always believed that the feet of a person tell us as much about his personality as his head. Before I make a diagnosis of a personality problem, I like to see how a person stands. To do this, I look at his feet.

A well-balanced person is well balanced on his feet, his weight evenly distributed between the heels and the balls of the feet. When a person's weight is on his heels, which happens if he stands with locked knees, he is off-balance. A slight push against his chest can easily topple him backward, especially if he isn't prepared to resist. I have demonstrated this many times in the course of our workshops. It may be said of such a person that he is a "pushover." The stance is a passive one. Shifting the weight to the balls of the feet prepares one for forward movement and is an aggressive stance. Since balance is not a static phenomenon, to be balanced requires a constant adjustment of one's position and necessitates an awareness of the feet.

The remark that "a person has both feet on the ground" can be taken literally only in the sense that there is a feeling contact between the feet and the ground. Such contact occurs when excitation or energy flows into the feet, creating a condition of vibrant tension similar to that described for the hands when one focuses his attention or directs his energy to them. One is, then, aware of the feet and able to balance himself properly on them.

It is common to speak of the modern individual as being alienated or isolated. Less frequently we hear him described as being uprooted or having no roots. James Michener characterized a segment of today's youth as *The Drifters.* As a cultural phenomenon it is a subject for sociological investigation. But it is also a bioenergetic phenomenon; the lack of a sense of being rooted must derive from some disturbance in bodily functioning. That disturbance is in the legs, which are our mobile roots. Just like the roots of a tree, our legs and feet interact energetically with the ground. One can sense the feet becoming charged and alive when one walks barefoot on the wet grass or the hot sand. One can also get the same feeling from a bioenergetic body-experience exercise. The one I generally use for this purpose is having a person bend forward and touch the ground lightly with his fingertips. The feet are about twelve inches apart, toes slightly turned in. Starting with bent knees, one straightens them until there is a strain on the hamstring muscles in the back of the legs. The knees should never be fully extended, however. The position is held for about a minute or more, while the person breathes easily and deeply. If the feeling flows into the legs, they will begin to vibrate. If it gets into the feet, they may start to tingle. Patients who do this exercise sometimes report they feel "rooted" when this happens; they may even feel their feet extending into the floor.

Being "rooted" or "grounded," having "standing" or "standing for" important human values are, I believe, rare qualities in people today. The motorcar has deprived us of the full use of our legs and feet. And air travel has taken us completely off the ground. However, their major effect on bodily functioning is more indirect than direct. The cultural impact that affects us most is the change in the mother-child relationship, notably in the decrease of close body contact between mother and child. I have discussed this change at some length in my last book.* A mother is an infant's first ground, or to put it differently, an infant is grounded through its mother's body. Earth and ground are symbolically identified with the mother, who is a representative of ground and home. It is interesting to note that the word "rooting" is also used to describe an infant's instinctive movements in search of a nipple. My patients failed to develop a sense of being grounded or rooted because of a lack of sufficient pleasurable contact with their mothers' bodies. No doubt their mothers were not fully grounded people themselves. A mother who is herself uprooted cannot provide the sense of security and grounding a baby needs. If we fail to recognize these

*Lowen, *Depression and the Body, op. cit.*

bioenergetic facts, we will be unable to prevent the disastrous effects on human life of a highly mechanized and technological culture.

Body Signs and Expressions

The language of the body is called nonverbal communication. There is a considerable interest in this today, for it is realized that a great amount of information is conveyed or can be gathered from body expression. The tone of a person's voice or his look often has greater impact than the words he utters. Children in my youth used to chant the refrain "Sticks and stones can break my bones, but names can never hurt me," a refrain suggesting that they were impervious to verbal taunts. But we also have a saying "Looks can kill." If a mother gives her child a murderous look, it cannot easily be dismissed. Children are more aware of the language of the body than adults who have been taught through long years of schooling to pay attention to words and ignore body expression.

Every intelligent student of human behavior knows that words can be used to tell a lie. Often there is no way of knowing from the words themselves whether the information they convey is true or false. This is especially true of personal statements. For example, when a patient says, "I feel fine," or "My sex life is great; there's nothing wrong with it," one does not know from the words if the statements are the truth or not. We frequently say what we want people to believe. By contrast, the language of the body cannot be used to deceive, if the observer knows how to read it. If my patient really feels fine, his body should reflect that state of being. I would expect his countenance to be bright, his eyes to have a shine, his voice to have resonance, and his movements to be animated. In the absence of these physical signs, I would question his statement. A similar consideration applies to remarks about sexual responsiveness. When the body of a person shows by its pattern of muscular tension that he holds his feeling in—a tight ass and a choked neck—it is impossible for him to have a "great" sex life since he's incapable of letting go to a strong sexual excitation.

The body doesn't lie. Even when a person tries to hide his true feelings by some artificial postural attitude, his body belies the pose in the state of tension that is created. No one is fully the master of his own body, which is why a lie detector can be used effectively to distinguish truth from falsehood. Telling a lie creates a state of body tension that is reflected in blood pressure, pulse rate and the electrical conductance of the skin. A newer technique is analysis of the voice itself to make the distinction. Its tone and resonance reflect every feeling a person has. It is logical, therefore, that it can be used in lie-detection procedures.

We are familiar with the use of handwriting to determine personality traits. And there are people who claim they can read character from the way a person walks. If each aspect of bodily expression is revealing of who we are, then, certainly, our whole body must tell our story more fully and more clearly.

Actually, we all respond to other people in terms of their bodily expression. We constantly size each other up as bodies, quickly evaluating a person's strength or weakness, his aliveness or deadness, his age, his sexual appeal, etc. From a person's bodily expression we often decide whether we can trust him, what his mood is and what his basic attitudes are to life. Young people today speak of a person's vibes, or vibrations, as being good or bad depending on how his body affects the observer. In psychiatry, especially, the subjective impressions one obtains from a patient's bodily expression are the most important data one has to work with, and almost all therapists use this information constantly. However, there is a reluctance in psychiatry, and in the public generally, to regard this information as valid and reliable since it cannot easily be verified objectively. I think it is essentially a question of how much one trusts his own sensing and senses. Children who have little reason to doubt their senses rely more heavily on this information than adults. It is the story of "The

Emperor's New Clothes." In a time like today, when there is such a strong tendency to manipulate people's thinking and behavior by words and images, this source of information is of paramount importance.

When presenting the bioenergetic concepts to professional people, I am often confronted with the demand for statistics, figures, hard-nosed facts. I can understand the desire for such information, but it should not cause us to dismiss as insignificant the evidence of our senses. We are biologically provided with distance receptors—eyes, ears and nose—which make it possible for us to assess a situation before we bump our noses into it. If we distrust our senses, we undermine our ability to sense and to make sense. By sensing another person, we can make sense out of the story he tells us about his life, his struggles and his misfortunes. We can then understand him as a human being, which is the basic condition for being able to help him.

Sensing another person is an empathic process. Empathy is a function of identification—that is, by identifying with a person's bodily expression, one can sense its meaning. One can also sense what it feels like to *be* that other person, though one cannot feel what another feels. Each person's feelings are private, subjective. He feels what is going on in his body; you feel what is going on in yours. However, since all human bodies are alike in their basic functions, bodies can resonate to each other when they are on the same wavelength. When this happens, the feelings in one body are similar to those in the other.

Practically, this means that if one assumes the bodily attitude of another person, one can sense the meaning or have the feeling of that body expression. Suppose you see another person whose chest is up, whose shoulders are raised and whose brows are elevated, and you want to know what this attitude signifies. Assume that attitude. Suck in the air, raise your shoulders, and lift your brows. If you are in touch with your body, you will immediately perceive that you have adopted an expression of fear. You may or may not feel afraid. That depends on whether it evokes a fear that is in you, but you will correctly identify the expression. You will then understand that, in the language of the body, the other person is saying, "I am afraid."

The other person may not feel afraid despite his expression of fear. If he doesn't, it means he is out of touch with the expression of his body. That generally happens when an attitude is of long standing and has become structured in the body. Chronic holding or tension patterns lose their effective or energetic charge and are removed from consciousness. They are not perceived or experienced. The body attitude becomes "second nature" to the person, at which point we say that it is part of his character. One will eventually recognize him by this pose, although at first impression it may strike one as strange. Our first impressions of people are body responses which we tend eventually to ignore as we focus on their words and deeds.

Word and actions are to a large extent subject to voluntary control. They can be used to convey impressions that contradict the expression of the body. Thus, an individual whose body expression is one of fear may speak and act with a show of bravery, an attitude with which he feels more closely identified on an ego level than the fear his body manifests. In this case we describe the conscious attitude as compensatory—that is, as an effort to overcome the underlying fear. When a person goes to an extreme length to deny a fear manifested in the body, his behavior is called counterphobic. The language of the body doesn't lie, but it speaks in a tongue that can be understood only by another body.

Duplicating another person's body expression is only necessary to make its meaning clear at first. After the meaning has been determined, one associates it with the expression whenever it is seen. Thus we know that tight, compressed lips express disapproval, a forward position of the jaw defiance and wide-open eyes fear. However, to convince ourselves of the validity of our interpretation, we can assume these expressions. Now I would ask the reader to assume the following position and see if he can follow the interpretations I give. In a standing position pull the buttocks forward and tighten the muscles of the ass. You may notice two effects: one, that the upper half of the body tends to collapse about the diaphragm, and, two, that the tension pattern in the pelvic area is one of containment or "holding in." The collapse is a loss of body stature and, therefore, of self-affirmation. If one could visualize a human being with a tail, one could picture that organ as being tucked between the legs. A whipped dog assumes the same pose. I believe we are justified, therefore, in interpreting this bodily posture as a sign of having been beaten, defeated or humiliated.

The holding in is sensed as a tightness and constriction of the pelvic outlets, anal, urinary and genital. Many psychological studies have shown that ego collapse with a concomitant sense of having been humiliated and defeated plus the tendency to hold in one's feelings are typical of individuals with masochistic tendencies. The next step involves the correlation of this constellation of psychological traits with a certain physical attitude. Once this correlation is established, it is checked repeatedly against observations of other patients. Finally, the character structure becomes identified with a definite bodily posture. When I see a person whose buttocks are pulled forward and whose ass is tightened, it denotes a masochistic element in his personality.

Reading the body's expression is often complicated by the presence of what is called compensatory body attitudes. Thus, some individuals with body postures revealing masochistic tendencies such as the pulled-in buttocks may conversely adopt an attitude of defiance in the upper part of the body—jaw thrust forward, chest thrust out—to try to overcome the masochistic submissiveness expressed in the lower part of the body.

Similarly an exaggerated aggressiveness could serve to cover an underlying passivity and compliance. Ruthlessness could hide the sense of having been beaten, and a thick-skinned insensitivity could deny the humiliation. In such cases we speak of sadomasochism, for compensating behavior calls attention to the weakness it is designed to hide.

Reading the language of the body requires that one be in touch with his own body and sensitive to its expression. Bioenergetic therapists themselves therefore undergo a course of treatment designed to get them in touch with their own bodies. Few people in our culture are free from muscular tensions that structure their responses and define the roles they will play in life. These tension patterns reflect the traumas they experienced in growing up—rejection, deprivation, seduction, suppression and frustration. Not everyone has experienced these traumas with an equal intensity. If, for example, rejection dominated the life experience of a child, he will develop a schizoid pattern of behavior that is both physically and psychologically structured in his personality. This becomes second nature to the individual and cannot be changed except by a recovery of one's first nature. The same is true for all other patterns of behavior.

The expression "second nature" is often used to describe psychological and physical attitudes that, though "unnatural," have become so much a part of the person they seem natural to him. The term implies that there is a "first nature," one free of these structured attitudes. We can define this first nature negatively or positively. We can say that it is the absence, on the body level, of chronic muscular tensions that restrict feeling and movement and, on the psychological level, of rationalizations, denials and projections. Positively it must be a nature that retains the beauty and grace that all animals are normally endowed with at birth. It is important to recognize the distinction between second and first nature, for too many people accept their bodily tensions and distortions as "natural," not realizing they belong to the order of "second nature," which feels natural only because of long habituation. It is my deep conviction that a healthy life and a healthy culture can be built only on man's first nature.

IV. Bioenergetic Therapy

A Voyage in Self-Discovery

Bioenergetics is not only concerned with therapy, just as psychoanalysis is not exclusively limited to the analytic treatment of emotional disorders. Both disciplines are interested in the development of the human personality and seek to understand that development in terms of the social situation in which it takes place. Nevertheless, therapy and analysis are the cornerstones on which this understanding rests, since it is through the careful working through of individual problems that insights into personality development are gained. Furthermore, therapy provides an effective testing ground for the validity of insights which otherwise might be no more than pure speculation. Bioenergetics cannot be dissociated, therefore, from bioenergetic therapy.

In my view therapy involves a voyage in self-discovery. It is not a short and simple journey, nor is it free from pain and hardship. There are dangers and risks, but then, life itself is not free from hazards, for it, too, is a journey into the unknown of the future. Therapy takes us backward into a forgotten past, but this was not a safe and secure time, else we would not have emerged from it scarred by battle wounds and armored in self-defense. It is not a journey I would recommend anyone to make alone, although I am sure some brave people have made the trip unaided. A therapist acts as guide or navigator. He has been trained to recognize the dangers and he knows how to cope with them; he is also a friend who will offer support and courage when the going is rough.

A bioenergetic therapist is required to have made this journey, or to be in the process of making it, and sufficiently advanced so that he has a solid sense of himself. He has to be, as we say, sufficiently grounded in the reality of his own being so he can serve as an anchorage for his client when the waters get choppy. There are basic requirements for any person who wishes to function as a therapist. He has to be grounded in personality theory and know how to deal with such problems as resistance and transference. A bioenergetic therapist, in addition, has to have a "feel" for the body so he can accurately read its language. However, he is not a perfect human being (is anyone?), and it would be unrealistic to expect that he is free of personal problems. This brings me to an important point.

The journey of self-discovery is never finished, and there is no promised land at which one finally arrives. Our first nature will continually elude us, though we get closer to it all the time. One reason for this paradox is that we are living in a highly technical, civilized society that is rapidly carrying us farther away from that state of living in which our first nature evolved. Even with a successful therapy we do not become free from all our muscular tensions since the conditions of modern living constantly impose a state of tension on us. It is questionable whether any therapy can fully eliminate the effects of all the traumas experienced in growth and development. Even if the wounds are completely healed, scars often remain as permanent effects.

One might ask, then, what is gained by going into therapy if there is no complete release from tension and no final end to the journey? Fortunately, most people who enter therapy do not seek a state of nirvana or a Garden of Eden. They are troubled, often desperate, and they need help on their forward journey through life. Taking them backward can provide such help if it can increase their self-awareness, promote their self-expression and further their self-possession. With a stronger sense of self they are better equipped to cope. Therapy can help a person in this way because it liberates him from the restrictions and distortions of a neurotic second nature and brings him closer to that first nature which is the source of his strength and his faith.

If therapy cannot return us to our first nature, which is the state of grace, it can bring us closer to it and so diminish the alienation most of us suffer. Alienation, more than any other word, describes the plight of modern man. He is like a "stranger in a strange land," never free from the questions "What am I living for? What is it all about?" He struggles with a lack of meaning in his life, a vague but persistent feeling of unreality, a pervading sense of loneliness that he tries hard to overcome or deny, and a deep fear that life will escape him before he has had a chance to live it. Although as a psychiatrist I focus my attention on a patient's presenting symptom or complaint, I do not see the goal of therapy as limited to that specific problem. If I cannot help him get more in touch with himself (for me, that means with his body and through his body with the world around him), then I feel that my efforts to overcome his alienation have failed and the therapy is unsuccessful.

Although we speak of alienation as the estrangement of man from nature and from his fellowman, its base is the estrangement of the person from his body. I have discussed this theme more fully elsewhere,* and if I reintroduce it here, it is because it is central to bioenergetics. Only through your body do you experience your life and your being in the world. But it is not enough to get in touch with the body. A person must also keep in touch, and that means a commitment to the life of the body. Such a commitment does not exclude the mind, but it does exclude a commitment to a dissociated intellect, a mind that is not mindful of the body. A

*Lowen, *Betrayal of the Body, op. cit.*

commitment to the life of the body is the only assurance that the journey will end successfully in the discovery of the self.

This view of therapy as an unending process raises a practical question: "How long," my patients ask, "do I have to come to see you?" A practical answer is: "You will stay in therapy as long as you feel it is worth the time, effort and money you invest." It is also practical to point out that many therapies end for reasons beyond the control of therapist or client, such as a change of residence to another city, for example. I may also end a therapy when I feel it is going nowhere in order to prevent a patient from using it as a continual crutch. The client will end the therapeutic relationship when he feels capable of assuming the responsibility for his further growth himself, in other words, when he feels he can continue the journey unaided.

Movement is the essence of life; growth and decline are its two aspects. There is, in reality, no standing still. If growth in terms of personality development stops, then a decline sets in that may be imperceptible at first but that sooner or later becomes evident. The true criterion of a successful therapy is that it starts and promotes a growth process in the client that will continue without the therapist's help.

In the first chapter I related some of my personal experiences in therapy with Wilhelm Reich and my subsequent therapy with John Pierrakos which laid the basis for the bioenergetic method. Although I gained an immeasurable increase in my sense of self (self-awareness, self-expression and self-possession), I did not feel I had reached the end of my journey. For the time being my boat was sailing smoothly, and I had no premonition of troubles or difficulties, but such conditions do not prevail indefinitely. In the course of the following years I went through some personal crises that I was able to handle well owing to my therapy. A personal crisis occurs only when some rigidity in the personality is under severe strain. It is, therefore, both a danger and an opportunity for further release and growth. Fortunately growth proved to be my direction as my life unfolded. Without going into the crises themselves, I shall describe one set of personal experiences pertinent to the subject of therapy.

About five years ago I became aware of a pain in my neck. At first I experienced it only occasionally, but in time it became more noticeable each time I turned my head sharply. I had not ignored my body in the years since I stopped active therapy. My fairly regular practice had been to do the bioenergetic exercises I use with my patients. Although they helped me greatly, they had no effect on the pain, which I suspect was a cervical arthritis. I never confirmed this suspicion by X-ray examination, so it remains only an hypothesis today.

Whether this pain was due to arthritis or not, I could palpate some fairly tense muscles in my neck that were related to the pain. There were other muscular tensions in my upper back and in my shoulders as well. I also noticed in films made of me while working with patients that I tended at times to carry my head bent forward. This posture created a slight rounding of my back between the shoulder blades.

For about a year and a half I did some exercises regularly in the attempt to relieve the pain and straighten my back. I also had a regular massage from one of the bioenergetic therapists. He could feel the tense muscles which he worked on strongly to induce some relaxation. The exercises and the massage helped temporarily. I felt freer and better after them, but the pain persisted, and the tension returned.

I had one other experience during this time which I believe played a role in the resolution of the problem. At the conclusion of a professional workshop two of the participants, themselves trained bioenergetic therapists, said I deserved a turn and offered to work with me. This is not a practice I normally follow, but on this occasion I let myself go. One worked with some tension in my throat. The other was working on my feet. Suddenly I felt a sharp pain as if someone had taken a knife and cut my throat. I had the immediate feeling that this was something my mother had done, psychologically, not literally. I realized the effect was to stop me from speaking out or crying out. I have always had some difficulty in voicing my feelings, although that problem had steadily diminished over the years. In some situations the failure to do so had resulted in my developing a sore throat, especially when I was tired. When I felt the pain, I threw the therapists off me and cried out in anger. Then I experienced a deep relief.

Shortly after this incident I had two dreams that brought the first problem to a climax. They occurred on two successive nights. In the first I was convinced I was going to die of a heart attack. Then I felt that it would be all right since I would die with dignity. Strangely I had no anxiety in the dream or when I awoke in the morning and recalled it.

The next night I dreamed I was the trusted adviser to an infantile king who believed I had betrayed him. He had ordered my head cut off. In the dream I knew I had not betrayed him and was confident that he would discover his error and that I would be reprieved and restored to my position. As the execution time approached, I was still confidently awaiting reprieve. When the day arrived and I was led to the block, I was still sure the reprieve would come, perhaps at the last minute. In the dream I sensed the executioner standing next to me with a big ax. He was not clear. However, I was still awaiting my reprieve. Then the executioner bent down to take off the chain that had bound my legs. He did this with his hands, for the chain around my ankle was made of flimsy wire. I suddenly realized, "Why, I could have done that myself" and I awoke. Again in this dream there was no anxiety about my approaching death.

This absence of anxiety made me feel the two dreams had a positive significance. I made no great effort to interpret them, therefore. The first hardly needed any interpretation. Prior to that dream I had been concerned about the possibility of a heart attack. I was approaching sixty, when such attacks are not uncommon, and I knew this was my main vulnerability. I had been aware of rigidity in my chest since my first session with Reich, and I had never fully released it. In addition, I was an inveterate pipe smoker, though I did not inhale. The dream did not reassure me about not getting a heart attack; rather it made that possibility an event of secondary importance. The important thing was to die with dignity, but that also meant, as I realized immediately, to live with dignity. This realization seemed to cancel the fear of death in me.

At first I did not communicate these dreams to anyone. Some months later, though, I related both to a group of bioenergetic therapists at a workshop in California. We were devoting an evening session to dreams. On that occasion we did not go deeply into the interpretation of the second dream. I had the feeling it was telling me I had played second fiddle too long to an infantile aspect of my personality, something that would only get me in trouble. I had to take my rightful place as ruler of my kingdom (my personality, my work) since I was carrying the responsibility for it. I felt good about that decision.

I met with another group of bioenergetic therapists on the East Coast about a month and a half later, and I recounted the dreams to them. In the interim I had some further thoughts about the second dream. I felt it was connected with the pain in my neck. In the dream I was to have my head cut off; the ax would come down on my neck. Accordingly I began by describing the chronic pain in my neck, which I now sensed had something to do with not holding my head up high. In fact, when I did adopt this posture, the pain disappeared. Yet I knew I could not do this consciously through the use of my will, for it would look artificial and I would not be able to sustain it. Holding my head high would have to be an expression of the dignity which would conform to the meaning of the first dream.

After recounting the dreams, I related some childhood impressions. I was the firstborn and only son in my family. My mother was devoted to me, the apple of her eye. In many ways she regarded me as a young prince. On the other hand she always insisted she knew best and was often cruel when I was obstreperous. She was ambitious and transferred this attitude to me. My father was also devoted to me. His personality was almost the opposite of my mother's. He was easygoing and pleasure-loving. Though he worked hard, he tended to be a failure in his small business. I used to help him with his records, for I was quick with figures. Throughout my childhood my mother and father fought with each other, generally over money, and I was regularly caught in the middle. On one hand, I felt I was superior to my father, but on the other, he was bigger and stronger, and I was afraid of him. I don't believe this fear of my father was of his creation. He was not cruel, and he spanked me only once. But my mother had set me up to compete with him, something no small boy can ever do successfully.

I realized I had never fully resolved this oedipal situation, for such it clearly was. My father was the infantile king I could not dethrone, and so I had to remain as the young prince, full of promise, but consigned to a secondary role.

When I related this situation and described myself in terms of it, I suddenly knew that it was over. It was the past. All I had to do to free myself was to take apart the flimsy chain that bound my ankles. My father had died several years before. Without thinking of that fact, I knew I was now the king, and as is natural for a king, I could hold my head up high naturally.

The interpretation ended on this note, and I gave the matter no further thought, for I now knew where I stood. Also without thinking about it, I discovered one day that the pain in my neck was gone. And I have remained free of it since.

Since then I have become aware that I have a different attitude in my dealings with people. Others have commented on a change. They say I have become softer, easier-going, less challenging, less insistent that others accept my views. Before I was fighting for recognition—for recognition as a man, not a boy, as a king, not a prince. But no one could give me a recognition I had denied myself. Now there was no longer any need to fight.

I was very pleased with this outcome, but it did not mean I had completed my journey. Following the release of tension in my neck, I was more aware of the tension in my shoulders and chest.

These tensions, however, did not reach the level of pain. Nevertheless, I continued the bioenergetic exercises working with breathing, with grounding and with hitting a sandbag to free my shoulders. Grounding refers to getting feeling into the feet. My dream had said that I was bound at the ankle.

One other experience is relevant to this story. About two years ago I became acquainted with a singing teacher who was familiar with bioenergetic concepts and understood the role of the voice in self-expression. Earlier I mentioned the feeling that my mother had cut my throat. This created some difficulty for me in speaking, in crying, but especially in singing. I have always wanted to sing but rarely did. I was afraid my voice would crack and I would start to cry. No one sang in my family when I was a child. So I decided to take some singing lessons from this teacher to see what it would do. She assured me that she understood my problem and that since it was a private lesson, I could just go ahead and cry if I felt like doing so.

I went for the lesson with considerable excitement. She started me making a sound, any free and spontaneous sound. Then I sang a word, "diabolo," which allowed me to open my throat and vocalize fully. I let myself go. I moved around and hammed it up. My voice became freer. At one point I made a sound that came out so effortlessly, so fully that it seemed I was the sound, the sound was me. It reverberated through my whole being. My body was in a constant state of vibration.

To my surprise I didn't feel like crying once. I just opened up and let it out. I knew then that I could sing, for some of the sounds had a beautiful, musical quality. As I left the session, I had a sense of joyfulness such as I have known on only a few occasions. Of course, I continued the lessons. I mention this experience because I am sure it played a part in the next step. In the course of the next year I did not pay much attention to my dreams, though they were not far from my consciousness. I thought about them occasionally and about my parents. Then, one day, it hit me. I knew who the infantile king was. It was my heart. The second dream took on an entirely different meaning: I had betrayed my heart. Not trusting it, I had kept it locked up in a rigid thoracic cage. The "I" in the dream was my ego, my conscious mind, my intellect. This "I," the intellect, was the trusted adviser who would run things for the benefit of the imprisoned, infantile king.

When I realized who the king was, I never doubted the correctness of this interpretation. Of course, the heart is king or should be. For years I had maintained that one should listen to his heart and follow it. The heart is the center or core of life, and its rule is love. It is also an infant, for the heart never grows old. The feelings in the heart of an infant and those in the heart of an older person are the same—it is the feeling of love or the pain of being unable to love. But while I proclaimed this principle, I didn't fully follow it myself. I had used the expression "infantile king" which had a derisive quality, as if maturity were a function of the intellect. Further, I had not forgiven my mother for the pain she caused me which my heart would have gladly sanctioned. Oh, yes: I had betrayed the king, and he had reasserted his authority. "Off with your head," he ordered, "I don't need that kind of false counsel."

But I was right, too, somehow. I hadn't really betrayed him, for I was really protecting him and acting in his best interest. How like my mother that sounds to me now. Yet there is a truth to it. I had known the heartbreak of betrayal when I was an infant. I had seen my mother turn on me in anger when all I asked was to be close to her. I was protecting my heart so it could not be so badly hurt again. Unfortunately the protection took the form of imprisonment, of closing the channel of communication between my heart and the world, and my poor heart was languishing to death. I was destined for a heart attack.

My head didn't roll and my heart didn't suffer an attack. I became free when I realized in the dream that the leg iron was not steel, that I was bound only by an illusion. I could have set myself free at any time. But until we know what is illusion and what is reality, the former acts with all the force of the latter.

Every king needs an adviser. Every heart needs a head which will provide it with eyes and ears so it can be in touch with reality. But do not let the head presume to rule; that is a betrayal of one's heart.

This new interpretation of my dreams can be called a bioenergetic interpretation, because it refers to the dynamic interaction between the parts of my body which are aspects of my personality. The previous interpretation was more a Freudian analysis. I regard both interpretations as correct; the latter simply goes deeper than the former. I have recognized that dreams are subject to different interpretations, and each one is valid to the degree that it casts light on the behavior and attitudes of the dreamer.

The insights the dreams provided still left me with the problem of the rigidity of my chest. The muscular tensions involved had to be released if I were to free my heart. The insights the dream provided didn't open my heart; they did, however, open the way for that change.

It is an important thesis of bioenergetics that changes in personality are conditioned on changes in bodily functions—namely, deeper breathing; increased motility; fuller and freer self-expression. In these respects the rigidity of my chest represented a limitation of being. I was aware of this rigidity in the past, and I had worked with it. In addition, my masseur, who was trained in bioenergetics, had attempted to relax the muscles of the thoracic cage. The results had been negligible. My chest stiffened against any pressure on it, and much as I wanted to give in, I was incapable of doing so. This situation began to change in the course of the past year.

The change was an awareness that the resistance had decreased. I sensed that if the pressure were applied now, I could give in. Accordingly, I asked one of the bioenergetic therapists to apply a gentle, rhythmic pressure to the chest wall as I lay over the breathing stool. As he did so, I began to cry; the cry gradually deepened into a full-throated agonizing sound. I felt this sound to be coming from the pain in my heart, from a longing for love and to love that I had kept firmly under control all these years. To my amazement the agonized sobbing didn't last very long. I suddenly began to laugh, and a feeling of joyfulness spread through my body. This experience made me realize how close laughter is to tears. The joy represented the fact that, for the moment, my chest was soft and my heart open.

Just as one swallow doesn't make a springtime, so one experience doesn't make a new person. The process had to be repeated, perhaps many times. Shortly after this experience I had a similar reaction to a different procedure. My wife and I were doing some bioenergetic exercises one Sunday afternoon. My shoulders felt tight, so I asked her to work on them for me. The most painful area was at the angle between neck and shoulders close to where the scalene muscles insert into the upper ribs. I was sitting on the floor, and she stood over me. She pressed into this area with her fists, and the pain was excruciating. I broke into sobs, which took on a very deep-throated quality. And again, after a minute or so, the laughter of release broke through, and the feeling of joy returned.

Summarizing my experiences over the past five years leads me to several conclusions. The first supports the idea expressed earlier that therapy seen as a process of growth and development is unending. The work with a therapist lays the foundation for this process. It also sets in action forces within the personality that operate to enlarge and expand all aspects of the self—self-awareness, self-expression and self-possession—forces that function on both the conscious and the unconscious levels. Dreams are a manifestation of the operation of these forces on the unconscious level. Consciously, the individual has to be committed to change—that is, to continued growth and development.

A second conclusion is that a commitment to growth involves a commitment to the body. Many people today are fascinated with the idea of growth, the human potential movement is based on this idea, and they pursue a number of activities that aim to promote personality growth. Such activities can have a positive benefit, but if the body is ignored, they can also become games which may be interesting, perhaps even fun, but not serious growth processes.

The self cannot be divorced from the body, and self-awareness cannot be separated from body awareness. For me, at least, the way of growth is by being in touch with my body and understanding its language.

The third conclusion introduces a note of humility to this discussion. We cannot change ourselves by any effort of will. That is like trying to pull one's self off the ground by one's bootstraps. The change will occur when one is ready, willing and able to change. It cannot be forced. It begins with self-acceptance* and self-awareness and, of course, with a desire to change. The fear of changing, however, is momentous. My own fear of death through a heart attack is an example. One must learn patience and gain tolerance. This is a body phenomenon. The body gradually develops a tolerance for a more energetic way of life, stronger feelings and a freer and fuller self-expression.

The Core of Therapy

My personal journey in self-discovery from the time I had my first therapy session with Reich to the present covered a period of thirty years. In view of the experiences I described in the preceding section I could say it took me thirty years to reach my heart. But that isn't strictly true. My heart was reached many times in that long period of time. I have been deeply in love, and in fact, I still am. I had experienced the joy of love previously. There was a difference, now, though. In the past my heart was reached by someone or something outside me—a person, a song, a story, Beethoven's Ninth Symphony and so on. My heart opened but, then it closed again, for I was frightened and thought I had a need to protect it. The fear is gone now, and my heart stays relatively open.

The thirty years during which I was a practicing bioenergetic

*Lowen, *Pleasure, op. cit.*, explains the importance of self-acceptance in the therapeutic process.

therapist have also taught me much about people. Working with people, I have learned *from* them. In some ways their struggles paralleled mine, and in helping them, I was also helping myself. We all were striving for the same goal, although few of us knew it. We talked of our fears, our problems and our sexual hang-ups, but we did not mention the fear of opening our hearts and keeping them open. My Reichian background had oriented me toward the goal of orgastic potency—which is certainly valid—but the connection between an open heart, the ability to love fully and orgastic potency was not stressed.

For many years now this connection was not unknown to me. The thesis of *Love and Orgasm,* published in 1965, is that love is the condition for the full orgastic response. Love and sex were equated, for sex was seen as an expression of love. However, the book dealt specifically with sexual problems, only incidentally touching on the person's fear of and inability to open his heart to love. I have no doubt it was my own fear that prevented me from pursuing that aspect of the subject more fully. Only after I had resolved my fear could I get to the core of the therapeutic problem.

The core is the heart. In Latin *cor* means heart. Our word "coronary" reflects this meaning.

We must realize that the heart is probably the most sensitive organ of the body. Our existence depends on its steady, rhythmical activity. When that rhythm is even momentarily affected, for example, when the heart stops a beat or races, we experience anxiety at the very core of our being. An individual who has experienced such anxiety early in life will develop many defenses to protect his heart against the danger of any disturbance of its functioning. He will not allow his heart to be easily touched, and he will not respond to the world from his heart. These defenses become elaborated in the course of life, until finally they form a powerful barrier against any attempt to reach it. In a successful therapy these defenses are studied, analyzed in relation to the individual's life experience and carefully worked through until the heart of the individual is reached.

To do this, however, the defenses must be understood as a

developmental process. This can best be explained diagrammatically by showing the defensive layering as concentric circles:

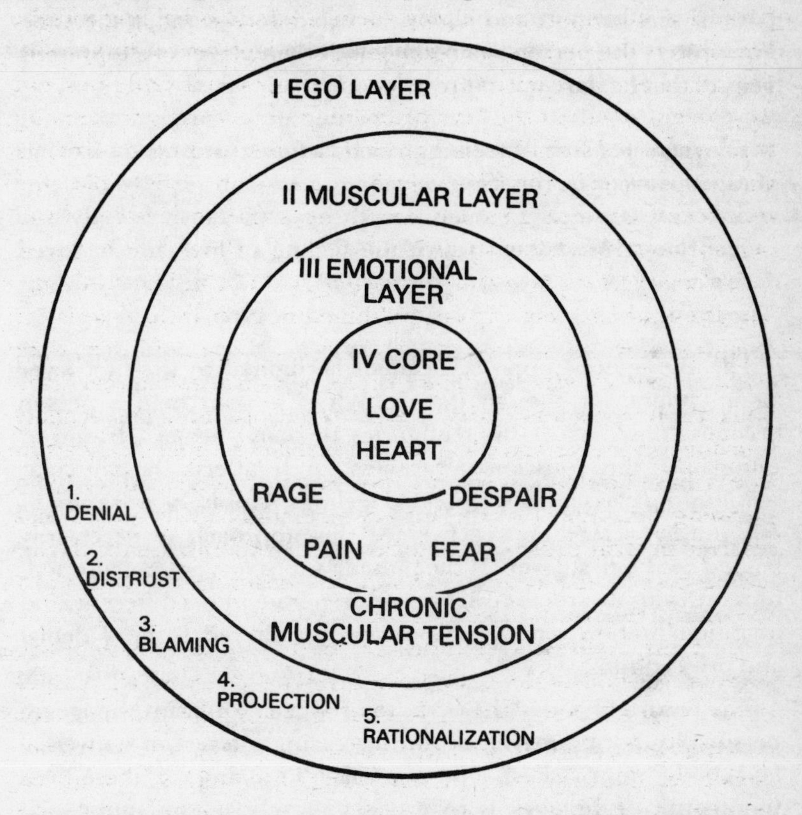

The layers can be summarized as follows, starting from the outermost: The *ego layer* which contains the psychic defenses and is the outermost layer of the personality. Typical ego defenses are

A. Denial
B. Distrust
C. Blaming
D. Projection
E. Rationalizations and intellectualizations.

The *muscular layer* in which are found the chronic muscular tensions that support and justify the ego defenses and at the same time protect the person against the underlying layer of suppressed feelings that he dare not express.

The *emotional layer* of feelings which includes suppressed feelings of rage, panic or terror, despair, sadness and pain.

The *core or heart* from which the feeling to love and be loved derives.

The therapeutic approach cannot be limited to the first layer alone, important though that is. While we can help a person become conscious of his tendencies to deny, project, blame or rationalize, this conscious awareness rarely affects the muscular tensions or releases the suppressed feelings. This is the weakness of the purely verbal approach since this approach is necessarily limited to the first layer. If the muscular tensions are not affected, the conscious awareness can easily degenerate into a different kind of rationalization with a concomitant but altered form of denial and projection.

The failure of verbal therapies to produce significant changes in personality is responsible for an increasing interest in nonverbal and body approaches. The tendency in many of these new therapeutic techniques is to evoke and release the suppressed feelings. The emphasis is often on getting out the screams. Not infrequently the patient will also experience his rage and his sadness and may express his longing.

Screaming does have a powerful cathartic effect on the personality. It has been one of the standard techniques of bioenergetics for a long time. The scream is like an explosion within the personality that momentarily shatters the rigidity created by chronic muscular tension and undermines the ego defenses in the first layer. Crying and deep sobs produce a similar effect by softening and melting body rigidities. The release of rage is also beneficial when the rage is expressed under control and in the therapeutic situation. Under these conditions it is not a destructive reaction and can be integrated into the ego of the person—that is, made ego syntonic. Fear is more difficult to evoke and more important to elicit. If the panic or terror is not brought to the surface and worked out, the cathartic effect of releasing the screams, the rage and the sadness is short-lived. As long as a patient fails to confront his fear and understand the reasons for it, he will continue to scream, cry and rage with little change in his overall personality. He will have substituted a cathartic process for an inhibiting one, but he will not significantly change in the direction of growth. He will remain caught between the inhibiting forces he has not understood and worked through and the desire to obtain a a momentary cathartic release.

It is, nevertheless, important for a therapy that these suppressed feelings be allowed expression. Readers who are familiar with my previous writings on bioenergetics know it is our consistent policy to open up and vent these feelings, for their release makes available the energy necessary to the process of change. One has to tap these feelings again and again to make available the energy necessary for growth.

In my opinion, working with the third layer alone will not produce the desired results. Bypassing layers one and two does not eliminate them. They are momentarily inoperative—that is, as long as the cathartic effect lasts. However, when the person has to go out into the world and function as a responsible adult, he will reinstate his defenses. He cannot do otherwise since the regressive or cathartic way is inappropriate outside the therapeutic situation. It would seem logical to work with both the first and third layers, since these complement each other, the first dealing with intellectual and the third with emotional defenses. But such an amalgam is difficult to achieve since the only direct connection between these layers is through the layer of muscular tensions.

If one works directly with layer two, one can move into the first or third layer whenever necessary. Thus, working with the muscular tensions, one can help a person understand how his psychological attitude is conditioned by the armoring or rigidity of his body. And when advisable, one can reach and open up the suppressed feelings by mobilizing the contracted muscles that restrain and block their expression. For example, screaming is blocked by muscular tensions in the throat. If a firm pressure is applied with the fingers to the anterior scalene muscles along the side of the neck while the person is making a loud sound, that sound will often turn into a scream. The scream will generally continue after the pressure has been removed, especially when there is a need to scream. Following the screaming, one moves into the first layer to determine what the screaming was about and why it was necessary to suppress it. In this way all three layers are involved in the analysis and working through of the defensive position. Keeping the focus on the body problem, in this case the tight and constricted throat, shifts the procedure from a purely cathartic maneuver to an opening-up, growth-oriented process.

It is unnecessary for me to stress that working with muscular tensions alone, without analyzing psychic defenses or evoking suppressed feeling, is not a therapeutic process. Body work as massage and yoga exercises has a positive value, but it is not specifically therapeutic in itself. However, we feel that it is so important for each person to keep in touch with his body and reduce its state of tension that we encourage all our patients to do their bioenergetic exercises alone or in classes, as well as to have regular massage.

Let us assume for the purpose of discussion that it is possible to eliminate every defensive position in the personality. How would a healthy person function? What would our diagram look like?

The four layers would still exist, but now they would be coordinating and expressive layers rather than defensive ones. All impulses would flow from the heart, which is to say that the person

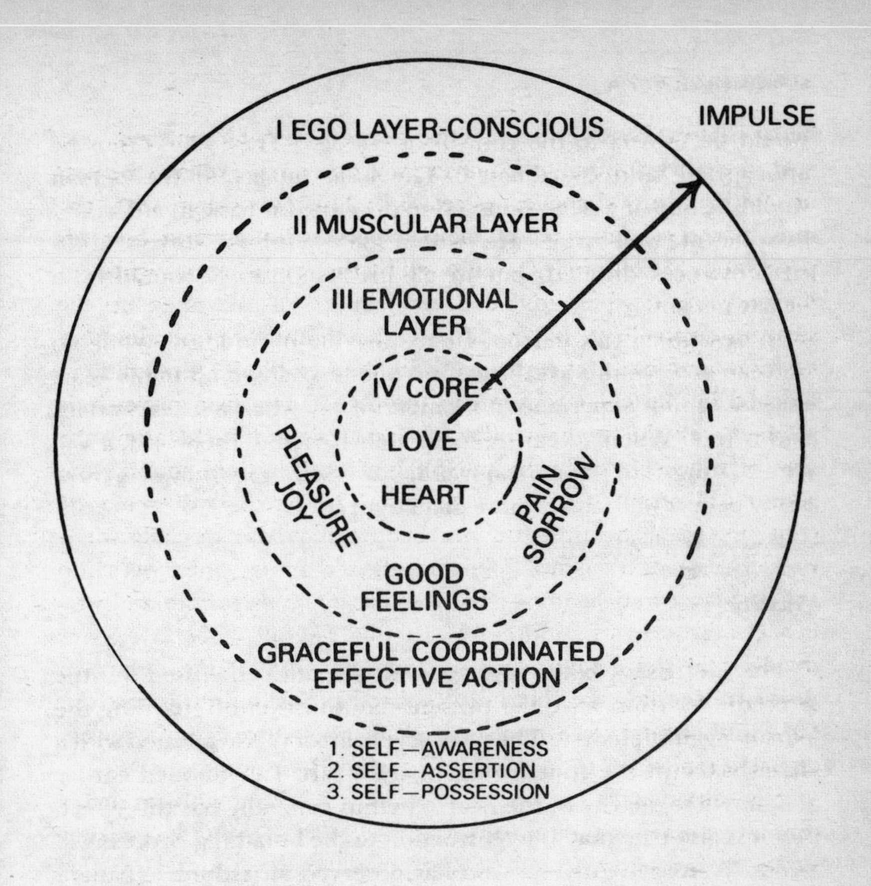

would put his heart into everything he does. This means he loves doing whatever he does, whether it is work, play or sex. He would also respond emotionally in all situations: his responses would always have a feeling base. He could be angry, sad, frightened or joyful depending on the situation. These feelings would represent genuine responses since they would be free from contamination by suppressed emotions stemming from childhood experiences. And since his muscular layer would be free from chronic tensions, his actions and movements would be graceful and effective. On the one hand, they would reflect his feelings, and on the other, they would be subject to the control of his ego. They would thus be appropriate and coordinated. The basic quality of the person would be one of ease as opposed to dis-ease; his basic mood would be one of well-being. He would be joyful or sorrowful as circumstances dictated, but in all his responses he would be a hearty person.

In describing this person, I am speaking of an ideal. While no one can achieve this ideal state, no one is so closed off in his heart that he cannot experience a moment of joy when his heart opens and is free. When a heart is completely closed to the world, it will stop beating, and the person will die. It is sad to see, however, how many people walk about more dead than alive.

Anxiety

The defenses, both psychic and somatic, discussed in the preceding section have the present-day function of guarding the person against anxiety. The most severe anxiety is associated with a disturbance in the functioning of the heart. I mentioned earlier that any irregularity in the heart rhythm generally has this effect. But it is also true that any obstruction to the breathing process will produce anxiety. Anyone who has observed an asthmatic patient struggling to get his breath can appreciate the intense anxiety that results from difficulty in breathing. In a broad way we can postulate the concept that any set of circumstances that inteferes with the operation of an organism's vital functions will produce anxiety. Respiration is hardly less important to the life of an organism than circulation.

The connection between respiratory difficulty and anxiety was known to Freud. In my last book, *Depression and the Body,* I quoted an observation by Ernest Jones, Freud's biographer, that shows Freud's awareness. "In a letter a year later, he [Freud] also remarked that anxiety being the response to obstructions in breathing—an activity that has no psychical elaboration—could become the expression of any accumulation of tension." Translating from the technical language of psychoanalysis, what this means is that the accumulation of tension would produce an obstruction to breathing and elicit anxiety. Unfortunately neither Freud nor traditional psychoanalysis followed up this lead, which would have opened the way to a biological understanding of personality disorders. This connection which Reich discovered on his own and explored became the basis of his therapeutic approach and led to bioenergetics.

Another lead to the nature of anxiety was supplied by Rollo May, who traced the word "anxiety" to its German root *Angst,* which means a "choking in the narrows." The narrows can refer, for example, to the birth canal through which everyone of us passes on his way to an independent existence. This passage can be fraught with anxiety since it represents the transition to independent breathing for the organism. Any difficulty the mammalian organism would have in establishing its independent respiration would threaten its life and produce a physiological state of anxiety. But the narrows can also refer to the neck, a narrow passageway between the head and the rest of the body through which air passes to the lungs and blood flows to the head. Choking in this area is also a direct threat to life and would result in anxiety.

I had an occasion to observe a dramatic incident of spontaneous choking and to see the intense anxiety it produced. It happened during the first session with a patient while she was lying over the breathing stool and allowing her respiration to become deeper and fuller. Suddenly she bolted upright in an absolute state of panic, saying in a choking voice, "I can't breathe. I can't breathe." I reassured her she would be all right, and in less than a minute she broke into deep, racking sobs. As soon as she began crying, her breathing became easy again. What had happened was obvious to me. Not anticipating an emotional release, she had relaxed her chest and opened her throat, with the result that a powerful impulse to cry welled up in it. This impulse came from a deep sadness locked in her chest. She reacted unconsciously by attempting to choke off the impulse and ended by choking off her breath instead.

In the first chapter I mentioned how, under similar circumstances in my personal therapy with Reich, I had released a scream. If I had attempted, then, to block the scream, I am sure I would have choked on it and developed a severe anxiety. Following the release of her crying, which persisted for some time, my patient's breathing became deeper and freer than before the incident. I have seen many patients choke up on feelings that well up when their throats open and their breathing becomes deeper. The choking is always accompanied by anxiety. These observations support May's definition of anxiety and also show the mechanism by which tensions in the neck and throat create obstructions to breathing that produce anxiety.

A similar set of muscular tensions located in the diaphragm and about the waist can effectively obstruct breathing by limiting the movement of the diaphragm. This has been fully documented by radiological studies.* The diaphragm is the main respiratory muscle, and its action is very much subject to emotional stress. It reacts to situations of fear by contracting. If the contraction becomes chronic, a predisposition to anxiety is created. I have identified this anxiety as falling anxiety and shall speak of it later.

The diaphragm lies just above another passageway or narrows—the waist. This passageway connects the thorax with the abdomen and pelvis. Impulses pass through this narrows to the lower part of the body. Any obstruction in this area would choke off the flow of blood and feeling to the genital apparatus and to the legs, producing anxiety, by creating a fear of falling with a consequent holding of the breath.

The question that arises is: What impulses are choked off in the waist? The answer, naturally, is sexual impulses. Children learn to control their sexual impulses by pulling in the belly and raising the diaphragm. Victorian women achieved the same aim by wearing

*Carl Strough, *Breath* (New York, William Morrow, 1970). Contains an extended discussion of the role of diaphragmatic tension in respiratory disturbance.

corsets that constricted the waist and impeded diaphragmatic movement. Thus sexual anxiety is intimately related to an obstruction of respiration or in Rollo May's words to a "choking in the narrows."

It was a basic Reichian proposition that sexual anxiety is present in all neurotic problems. We, in bioenergetics, have seen this proposition validated in case after case. In this age of sexual sophistication not many patients come to therapy complaining of sexual anxiety. Sexual disturbances, however, are common complaints. Underlying these problems is a deep anxiety which doesn't become conscious until the tension about the waist is reduced. Similarly, most patients are not conscious of their breathing anxiety. The patient I described earlier had not been aware she was anxious about breathing. She had been able to keep this anxiety from surfacing by not fully opening her throat and not fully breathing. It was only when she attempted to do this that her anxiety manifested itself. In the same way people can defend themselves against sexual anxiety by not allowing sexual feelings to inundate the pelvis. By constricting the waist, they can cut off the feeling of love in the heart from any direct connection with the excitation in the genital apparatus. Their sexual feelings become limited to the genitals. This dissociation is then rationalized by the ego in the proposition that sex should be divorced from love.

It sometimes happens that strong sexual feelings stemming from the heart develop spontaneously while the defenses are still seemingly intact. This may happen in therapy or out of it. In the first chapter I pointed out that in unusual circumstances an individual can step "out of his world" or "out of himself." This breakthrough of energy and feeling produces a transcendental experience. The defenses yield temporarily, allowing the sexual feelings to flow freely and resulting in a full orgastic release with intense pleasure and satisfaction. In most cases, however, the person attempts to choke these feelings off, since he is not able to surrender his defenses. If that happens, he or she will develop a severe anxiety which Reich labeled orgasm anxiety.

I began this section by saying that defenses serve to guard a person against anxiety. I then discussed the nature of anxiety and related anxiety to the sensing of some disturbance in the normal functioning of the body; to an obstruction in breathing, typically, a choking in the narrows; and to a fear of falling. However, we saw ultimately that in the absence of defenses or when they yield, there is no anxiety, only pleasure. We must therefore conclude that it is the presence of defenses that predispose an individual to anxiety or, to put it differently, create the conditions for anxiety.

How do defenses operate in these two apparently contradictory ways, defending against anxiety and yet at the same time setting the stage for it? To answer, we must realize that a defensive position or posture did not develop to guard a person from anxiety—that is, its present-day function—but rather to protect him from a hurt, either an attack or a rejection. If a person has been subject to repeated attacks, he will erect defenses to their danger in the future. Nations do the same thing with military establishments. In time, both on a personal level as well as on the national one, maintaining defenses becomes part of the way of life. However, the existence of defenses maintains the fear of attack, and so one feels justified in further strengthening the defensive position. But defenses also close one in, with the end result that an individual becomes imprisoned behind his own defensive structure. If he makes no effort to get out, he will remain relatively free from anxiety behind his walls.

Danger arises—and anxiety is a signal of danger—only when one attempts to open up, get out or drop his defenses. The danger may not be real, and the person may know this consciously, but it *feels* real. Every patient who opens up or drops a defense remarks, "I feel vulnerable." Of course, he is vulnerable, we all are, that is the nature of life, but we don't *feel* vulnerable if we are not afraid of being attacked. We are all mortal, but we don't *feel* we are going to die unless we sense something is seriously amiss in our bodies. At the moment of vulnerability, anxiety can arise. If a person panics, closes up and tries to reestablish the defenses, he will experience a severe anxiety.

Let us look at this process bioenergetically. The main channels of communication from the heart pass through the narrows of the neck and waist to reach the peripheral points of contact with the world. If these channels are open, the person is open, and his heart is open to the world. Our defenses are erected around these straits of passage. They do not completely cut off all communication and contact, for that would be death. They allow a limited correspondence or a limited access. So long as the individual keeps within these limits he remains free from anxiety. But this is a confining and constricting life-style. We all want to be more open to life.

We are dealing with levels or intensity of feeling. As long as the amount of feeling flowing outward is within the limits set by the muscular tensions, there will be no anxiety. Anxiety will develop when a stronger feeling attempts to get through and is choked off in panic. The panic causes the individual to close down almost completely, jeopardizing the life of the organism.

In this view every effective therapeutic maneuver generally results initially in the experience of anxiety. This explains why the development of anxiety in the therapy is often regarded as a positive sign. It forces a person to look at his defenses more objectively and facilitates the working through of his fears on both the psychic and the muscular levels. Progress in therapy is marked by more feeling, more anxiety and finally more pleasure.

These ideas about the nature of anxiety can be pictured in a figure that shows the flow of feeling from the heart through the narrows to the peripheral organs of the body. It can be seen from the figure on page 130 that the flow of feeling parallels the flow of blood which carries life-supporting oxygen and nutrients to all the body's cells.

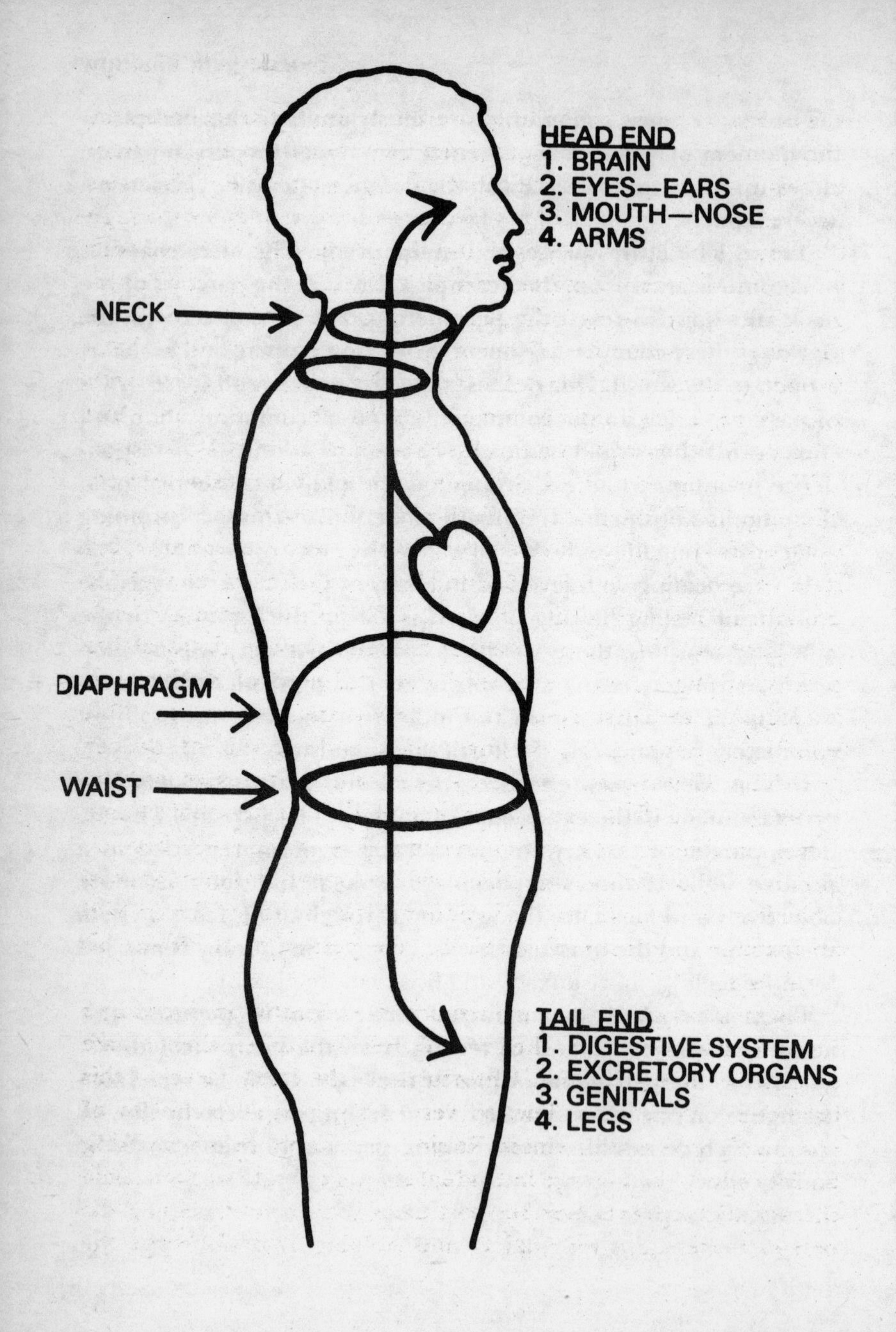
HEAD END
1. BRAIN
2. EYES—EARS
3. MOUTH—NOSE
4. ARMS
NECK
DIAPHRAGM
WAIST
TAIL END
1. DIGESTIVE SYSTEM
2. EXCRETORY ORGANS
3. GENITALS
4. LEGS

The main organs in the head are the brain, the sense receptors and the nose and mouth. Apart from the brain, the main functions of this part of the body are concerned with taking in. The arms further this. Oxygen, food and sensory stimulation enter through the head. The lower abdomen and the pelvis are concerned with giving out—namely, elimination and sexual discharge. In bioenergetics we regard the legs as organs of discharge since they move the organism or ground it. This polarity in body functions is the basis for the concept that the head end of the body is involved with processes that lead to increased energy charge or excitation, while the tail end is involved with processes that lead to energy discharge.

The maintenance of life depends not only on a constant supply of energy (food, oxygen and stimulation), but also on the discharge of an equivalent amount of energy. Health, let me emphasize, is a state of relative balance with due allowance of extra energy for growth and the reproductive functions. An insufficient intake leads to a depletion of energy reserves and the slowing down of life processes. When, on the other hand, the level of discharge is inadequate, the first result is the production of anxiety. This sometimes happens in therapy when, as a result of deeper breathing, the organism's energy or excitation increases and the person cannot discharge this excitation in an emotional release owing to inhibition in self-expression. The person will become nervous and uneasy, a state which will disappear, however, as soon as he has an effective release in either crying or anger. Faced with an inability to effect such a release, the person must restrict his breathing.

For most people anxiety is a temporary condition produced by a situation that overexcites the body. People tend to remain in a state of relative energy balance. Unfortunately the energy level of this balanced state is quite low, so very many people complain of chronic fatigue and tiredness. Raising the energy risks provoking anxiety which the average individual cannot tolerate without some therapeutic support. This support takes the form of helping the person understand his anxiety and helping him discharge the excitation through the expression of feeling. In people whose self-expression is unhampered, the energy level can be maintained at a high level, resulting in a body that is vibrantly alive and fully responsive to life.

One further point needs to be stressed. Life is not a passive operation. An organism has to *open up and reach out* to get and take in what it needs. This is as true of oxygen as it is of food. In an infant both the function of breathing and that of eating use the same physiological mechanism—sucking. An infant sucks air into its lungs just as it sucks milk into its mouth and digestive system. And because both functions use a common mechanism, a disturbance in one of the activities will affect the other.

Consider what happens to an infant who is weaned from the breast at a very early time. Most infants do not accept the loss of their first love object willingly. They cry and reach out for the breast with mouth and hands. This is their way of expressing love. Since they will be frustrated in this attempt, they will become restless and fitful and cry in anger. This behavior on the part of the infant often evokes a hostile reaction from the mother, and the infant or child soon realizes it must restrain the desire. It does so by choking off the impulse to reach out and the impulse to cry. The muscles of the neck and throat become contracted to constrict the opening and block the impulse. Now the breathing is affected, for the constricted throat also blocks the impulse to reach out and suck in air. The close connection between disturbances in nursing and in breathing was documented by Margaret Ribble in her book *The Rights of Infants.**

I have used nursing as an example of the active process of opening up and reaching out to take in. Opening up and reaching out are an expansive movement of the organism toward a source of energy or pleasure. The same action is involved whether a child reaches out for contact with the mother, for a toy or later as an adult, for a loved person. An affectionate kiss is a similar action.

*Margaret Ribble, *The Rights of Infants* (New York, Columbia University Press, 1948).

When a child has to block these actions, it sets up defenses on both psychic and muscular levels that would inhibit such impulses. Over time these defenses become structured in the body in the form of chronic muscular tensions and in the psyche as characterological attitudes. At the same time the memory of the experience is repressed and an ego ideal is created that sets the individual above the desire for contact, intimacy, to suck and to love.

In this example, we can see the connections between the different levels of the personality. On the surface—that is, the ego level—the defense takes the form of an ego ideal which says, "It's not manly to cry," and a denial, "I don't want it anyway." This defense is closely tied to the muscular tensions in the throat and arms which block the impulse to open up and reach out. On the body level the issue is not whether it is manly to cry. When the tensions are very severe, it becomes almost impossible for the person to cry. Similar tensions are found in the shoulders which make it equally difficult to reach out fully with the arms. On the deeper emotional level there are suppressed feelings of sadness, despair, rage and anger with impulses to bite, plus fear and longing. All this has to be worked through before a person's heart can be fully opened again.

Yet the person is not dead; his heart longs for love, his feelings demand expression, his body wants to be free. But if he makes any strong move in this direction, his defenses will choke off the impulse and throw him into anxiety. In most cases this anxiety is so severe that the person retreats and closes off, even if this means keeping his energy level low, his desires at a minimum and his life at a standstill. To live in fear of being fully alive is the state of most people.

V. Pleasure: A Primary Orientation

The Pleasure Principle

The primary orientation of life is toward pleasure and away from pain. This is a biological orientation, because on a body level, pleasure promotes the life and well-being of the organism. Pain, as we all know, is experienced as a threat to the organism's integrity. We open up and reach out spontaneously to pleasure, and we contract and withdraw from a situation that is painful. When, however, a situation contains a promise of pleasure, coupled with a threat of pain, we experience anxiety.

This concept of anxiety does not violate our previous view. The promise of pleasure evokes an outgoing impulse in the organism to reach toward the source, but the threat of pain forces the organism to choke off this impulse, creating a state of anxiety. Pavlov's work on conditioned reflexes in dogs clearly demonstrated how anxiety could be produced by combining in one situation a painful stimulus with a pleasurable one. Pavlov's experiment was very simple. He first conditioned a dog to respond to the ringing of a bell by offering it food soon after the bell rang. In a very short time the ringing of the bell alone would cause the dog to become excited and to salivate, anticipating the pleasure of food.

When this reflex was well established, Pavlov changed the situation by giving the dog an electric shock every time the bell rang. The ringing of the bell became coupled in the mind of the dog with the promise of food and the threat of pain. The dog was in a bind, wanting to move toward the food but afraid to do so, and so was thrown into a state of severe anxiety.

This pattern of being placed in a bind by mixed signals is the cause of the anxiety underlying all neurotic and psychotic personality disorders. The situations that lead to the bind occur in childhood between parents and children. Babies and children look to their parents as a source of pleasure and reach out to them with love. This is the normal biological pattern, since parents are the source of food, contact and sensory stimulation that infants and children need. Until it meets with frustration and suffers deprivation, an infant is all core—that is, all heart. But this doesn't last long in our culture where deprivation of emotional contact and frustration are common and where growing up is generally accompanied by punishment and threat. Parents, unfortunately, are not just a source of pleasure: they become quickly associated in the child's mind with the possibility of pain. The resultant anxiety is, in my opinion, responsible for the restlessness and hyperactivity so many children show. Sooner or later defenses are erected to diminish the anxiety, but these defenses also diminish the life and vitality of the organism.

This sequence—reaching out for pleasure⟶deprivation, frustration or punishment⟶anxiety and then⟶defense—is a general scheme to explain all personality problems. To understand an individual case, it has to be supplemented with knowledge of the specific situations that produced anxiety and the defenses erected to cope with it. Another important factor is time, for the earlier in life that anxiety arises, the more pervasive it is and the more deeply structured the defenses against it become. The nature and intensity of the threatened pain play an important role in determining the defensive position.

Almost all individuals in our society develop defenses against this striving for pleasure because it has been the cause of severe anxiety in the past. The defense does not totally block all impulses to reach out for pleasure. If it did, it would end in the person's death. In the final analysis, death is the total defense against anxiety. But since every defense is a limitation on life, it is also a partial death. The defenses allow certain impulses through, under certain limited conditions and to certain limited degrees. But as I have mentioned defenses vary among individuals, though they can be grouped in various types.

In bioenergetics the different types of defenses are subsumed under the heading "character structures." Character is defined as a fixed pattern of behavior, the typical way an individual handles his striving for pleasure. It is structured in the body in the form of chronic and generally unconscious muscular tensions that block or limit impulses to reach out. Character is also a psychic attitude which is buttressed by a system of denials, rationalizations and projections and geared to an ego ideal that affirms its value. The functional identity of psychic character and body structure or muscular attitude is the key to understanding personality, for it enables us to read the character from the body and to explain a body attitude by its psychic representations and vice versa.

We bioenergetic therapists do not approach a patient as a character type. We see him as a unique individual whose striving for pleasure is fraught with anxiety against which he has erected certain typical defenses. Determining his character structure enables us to see his deeper problems and so to help him free himself from the limitations imposed by his past life experience. Before I describe the various character types physically and psychologically, however, I would like to discuss the nature of pleasure and to prepare the theoretical framework for the descriptions.

Pleasure can be defined in a number of ways. The smooth and easy functioning of the organism gives rise to a feeling of pleasure, just as anxiety or pain is experienced when that function is disturbed or threatened. There is another situation that gives us a feeling of pleasure, and that is when we reach out. Naturally we reach out to what we think will be pleasurable, but I maintain that the act of reaching out is itself the basis for the experience of pleasure. It represents an expansion of the total organism, a flow of feeling and energy to the periphery of the organism and the world. In the final analysis, feelings are perceptions of movements in the organism. Thus, when we say that a person is in a state of pleasure, it denotes that the movements of his body, especially its internal movements, are rhythmical, unconstricted and outgoing.

We can define the feeling of pleasure, therefore, as the perception of an expansive movement in the body—opening up, reaching out, making contact. Closing off, withdrawing, holding in or holding back are not experienced as pleasure and may actually be experienced as pain or anxiety. Pain would result from the pressure created by the energy of an impulse meeting a block. The only way to avoid the pain or the anxiety is to set up a defense against the impulse. If the impulse is suppressed, the person will not feel anxiety or pain, but then, neither will he feel pleasure. What is going on can be determined from the expression of the body.

When a person is in a state of pleasure, his eyes are bright, his skin color pink and warm, his manner easy and lively, and there is a softness and ease in his bearing. These visible signs are the manifestation of the flow of feeling and of blood and energy to the periphery of the body which is the physiological counterpart of an outgoing, expansive movement or impulse in the body. The absence of these signs reveals a person is not in a state of pleasure but in a state of pain, whether the individual perceives it or not. In *Pleasure* I pointed out that pain is the absence of pleasure. There are body signs to support this view. A dulling of the eyes indicates the withdrawal of feeling from them. A cold, white skin is due to the constriction of capillaries and arterioles and indicates that the blood is being held back from the body surface. Rigidity and a lack of spontaneity suggest that the energetic charge is not flowing freely into the muscular system. This picture adds up to a state of contraction in the organism which is the somatic aspect of pain.

It should be pointed out that some bodies present mixed pictures, one part warm, soft and bright, while another is cold, tense and without color. The line of demarcation may not always be sharp, but one can see and feel the difference. A common picture of this disturbance shows good color and tone in the upper half of the body while the rest of the body from the waist down has an opposite appearance, poor color (brownish hue), poor muscle tone and a heaviness out of proportion to the well-shaped upper half. The meaning of this body picture is that there is a block to the flow of feeling in the lower half of the body, especially sexual feelings, and that this part of the body is in a state of holding or contraction. Another fairly common observation is a warm body with cold hands and feet. This condition indicates the tension or holding is in the peripheral structures, those that make contact with the environment. The saying "cold hands, warm heart" supports this interpretation.

Our primary orientation in looking at a body is to determine the degree to which the organism is capable of expanding or making a pleasurable response to the environment. Such a response as I have said, entails a flow of feeling, excitation or energy from the core or heart of the person to the peripheral structures and organs. The pleasurable response is also a warm and loving response, for the heart is then in direct communication with the outside world. A person handicapped by chronic muscular tensions blocking the heart's channels of communication and limiting the flow of energy to the body's periphery suffers in a number of ways. He may experience a sense of frustration and dissatisfaction with his life, he may experience anxiety and depression, he may feel withdrawn and alienated, or he may develop certain somatic disorders. Since these are the main complaints people present to psychiatrists, it should be realized that their elimination can occur only if the full capacity for pleasure is restored.

The human body has six major areas of contact with the external world: the face, including the sensory organs in that area; the two hands; the genital apparatus; and the two feet. There are minor areas of contact like the breasts in a woman, the skin in general and

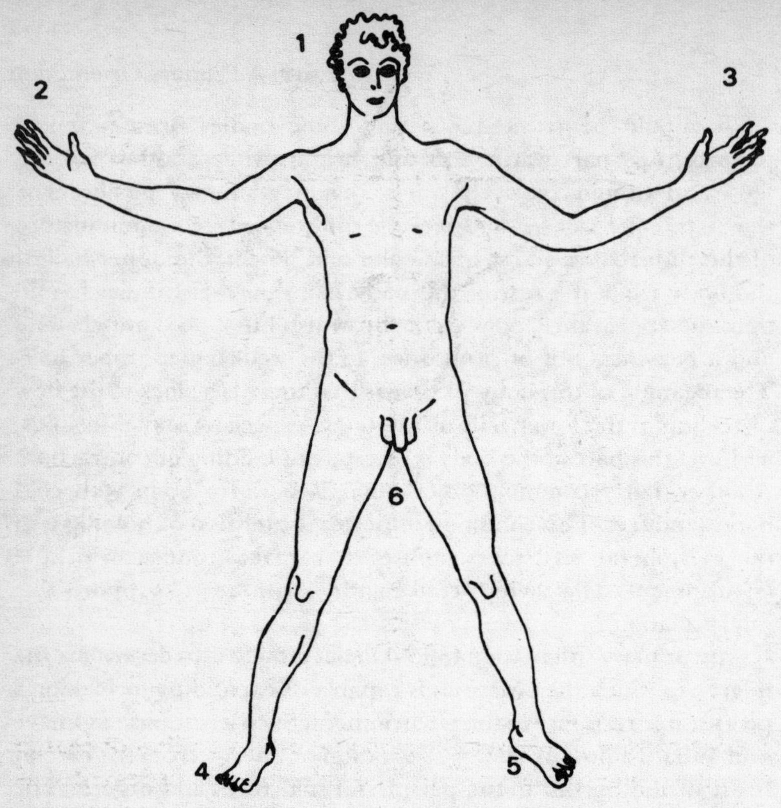

the buttocks when sitting. The six major areas form an interesting configuration best seen when a person is standing with legs and feet apart and arms and hands outstretched. The figure of the body would appear as in the above sketch which shows the six areas numbered.

If we convert this figure into a dynamic diagram, shown on the following page, the six areas represent the most extended parts of the body, energetically speaking.

In this diagram Point 1 represents the head, which is the locus of the ego functions and includes the sensory organs of audition, taste, vision and olfaction; Points 2 and 3 represent the hands which touch and manipulate (handle) the environment; Points 4 and 5 represent the feet which provide the essential contact with the ground; and Point 6, the genital apparatus, which is the main organ for contact and relationship with the opposite sex.

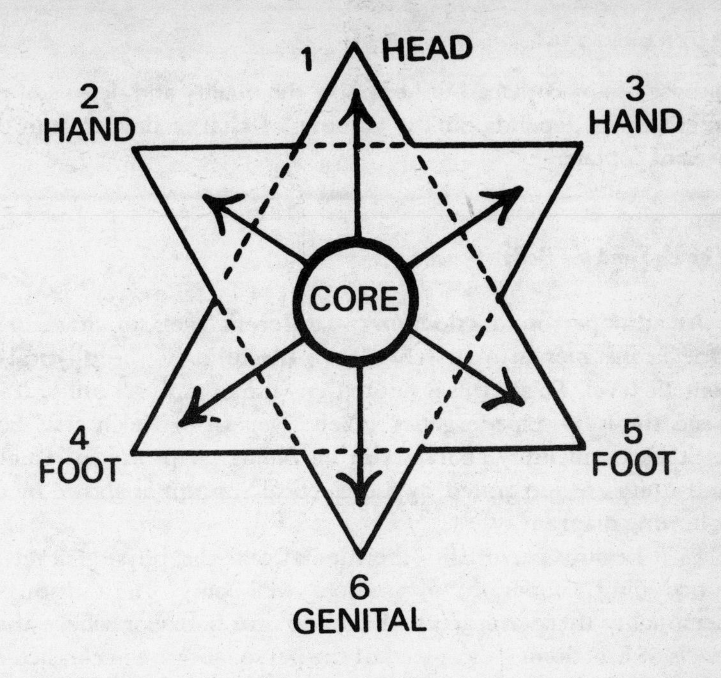

An expansive or pleasurable response involves a flow of charge from the center to all six points. The six points may be regarded as extensions of the organism like fixed pseudopodia of an amoeba. Despite the fact that they are fixed structures, a certain amount of extension is possible. The lips can be extended or withdrawn, the arms can lengthen or shorten depending on the extent of one's reach, and of course, the genitals in both men and women function like true pseudopodia when they become suffused with blood, charged with feeling and extended. The lower limbs are more fixed and show relatively little variation. Since the neck is a flexible organ, the head may be stuck out, held up or drawn in between the shoulders. When a strong contact is made with the environment, the energetic interchange at these points is intense. For example, when eye contact is made between two individuals who are excited, one can feel the charge that passes between the eyes. Similarly, when one is touched by hands that are charged, it is quite a different experience from being touched by cold, dry or tight hands. The energetic interaction in sex is, of course, the most intense of any contact, but here, too, the quality and degree of this interchange depends on the amount of charge flowing into this area of contact.

The Ego and the Body

An adult person functions on two different levels simultaneously. One is the mental or psychic level; the other is the physical or somatic level. To say this is not to deny the organism's unity. It is a basic thesis of bioenergetics taken over from Reich that both antithesis and unity characterize all biological processes. Duality and unity are integrated by a dialectical concept as shown by the following diagram.

In a healthy personality the mental and the physical levels of functioning cooperate to promote well-being. In a disturbed personality there are areas of feeling and behavior where these levels of functioning or aspects of the personality are in conflict. An area of conflict creates a block to the free expression of impulse

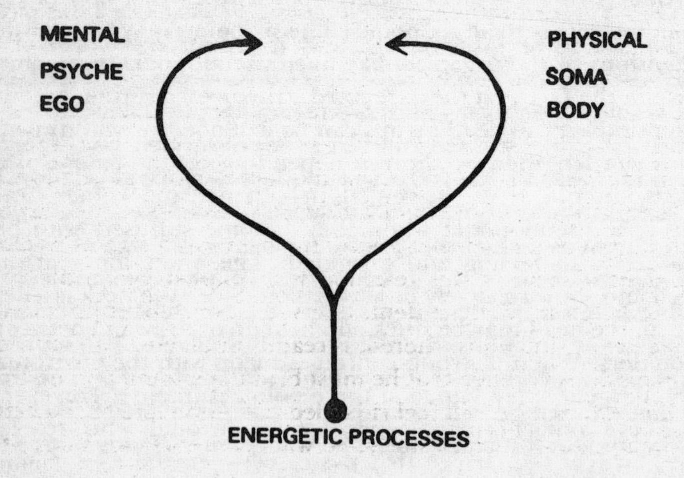

and feeling. I am not talking about a conscious inhibition of expression, which is subject to conscious control. The blocks I am referring to are unconscious restrictions of movement and expression. Such blocks limit a person's ability to reach out to the world for the satisfaction of his needs and represent, therefore, a reduction in his capacity for pleasure.

Putting the antithesis in terms of the ego and the body rather than mental and physical allows us to introduce the concepts of ego ideal and self-image as forces that can oppose the body's striving for pleasure. These concepts stem from the role of the ego as a synthesizing agent. The ego is the mediator between the inner and outer world, between the self and the other. This function derives from its position at the surface of the body and at the surface of the mind.* It forms a picture of the external world to which every organism must conform, and in doing so, it shapes the individual's self-image. In turn this self-image dictates what feelings and impulses are to be allowed expression. Within the personality the ego is the representative of reality.

But what is reality? The picture of it we have in our minds does not always accord with the real situation. We developed this picture in the course of growing up, and it reflects the world of our childhood and the family more than it does the world of adulthood and society. These two worlds are not totally different, for the world of the family reflects the larger one of society. The difference lies in the fact that the wider world offers a choice of relationships the limited world of the family didn't. For example, one may have been taught as a child that asking for help was a sign of weakness and dependency. If this teaching was coupled with ridicule for feeling helpless or dependent, one will have difficulty requesting help even in situations where it is readily available. The individual develops an ego image that he must be independent and do things for himself, and he will feel ridiculed and humiliated if he betrays this image. And unconsciously, he will choose relationships where

*Lowen, *The Physical Dynamics of Character Structure, op. cit.*

his pseudo independence is admired and encouraged, thus reinforcing a somewhat unrealistic self-image.

To understand character formation, we should know that there is a dialectical process at work in the interaction between the ego and the body. The ego image shapes the body through the control the ego exerts over the voluntary musculature. One inhibits the impulse to cry by setting the jaw, constricting the throat, holding the breath and tightening the belly. Anger as expressed in striking out can be inhibited by contracting the muscles of the shoulder girdle, thereby pulling the shoulders back. At first the inhibition is conscious and aims to spare the person further conflict and pain. However, the conscious and voluntary contraction of muscles requires an investment of energy and cannot therefore be maintained indefinitely. When an inhibition against some feeling must be maintained indefinitely because its expression is not accepted in the child's world, the ego surrenders its control over the forbidden action and withdraws its energy from the impulse. The holding against the impulse then becomes unconscious, and the muscle or muscles remain contracted because they lack the energy for expansion and relaxation. This energy can then be invested in other actions that are acceptable, a process which gives rise to the ego image.

Two consequences result from this surrender. One is that the musculature from which energy is withdrawn enters into a state of chronic contraction or spasticity which makes the expression of the inhibited feeling impossible. The impulse is, thus, effectively suppressed, and the person no longer feels the inhibited desire. A suppressed impulse is not lost. It lies dormant below the surface of the body where it does not affect consciousness. Under intense stress or with sufficient provocation the impulse can become so highly charged that it breaks through the inhibition or block. This happens in an hysterical outburst or a murderous rage. The second consequence is a diminution in the energy metabolism of the organism. Chronic muscular tensions prevent full natural respiration and so decrease the energy level. The person may get enough oxygen for ordinary activities, and so his basal metabolism may appear normal. However, his breathing difficulty will show up in situations of stress either as an inability to get sufficient air or more likely as an inability to cope with the stress.

Now the body condition forces the dialectic to work in reverse. The physical situation shapes the individual's thinking and self-image. A lower energy level forces him to make certain adjustments in his life-style. He will necessarily avoid situations that can evoke his suppressed feelings. And he will justify this avoidance by developing rationalizations about the nature of reality. These maneuvers are ego devices to prevent the emotional conflict from becoming conscious. For this reason they are called ego defenses. Other ego defenses are denial, projection, provoking and blame casting. These defenses are supported by the energy withdrawn from the conflict. The individual is now characterologically armored against the suppressed impulses. On the physical level, he is guarded by chronic muscular tensions. Immured as he is by this process, he can nevertheless function in a limited way or in restricted areas.

Having achieved some measure of stability and security, the ego takes pride in its accomplishment. The person derives an ego satisfaction from his adjustments and compensations. The man who can't cry regards this inability as a sign of strength and courage. He may even ridicule men or boys who cry easily, promoting his own neurotic trait as a virtue. The individual who cannot get angry or strike out makes a virtue of his handicap by claiming that seeing the other person's side is the mark of a reasonable man. The woman who cannot openly reach out for love will use sex and submission as a way to gain the needed contact and will see herself as particularly sexual and feminine.

Every muscular tension blocks the individual's reaching out directly to the world for pleasure. Faced with such restrictions, the ego will manipulate the environment in furtherance of the body's need for contact and pleasure. It will then justify such manipulation as necessary and normal, for it has lost touch with the

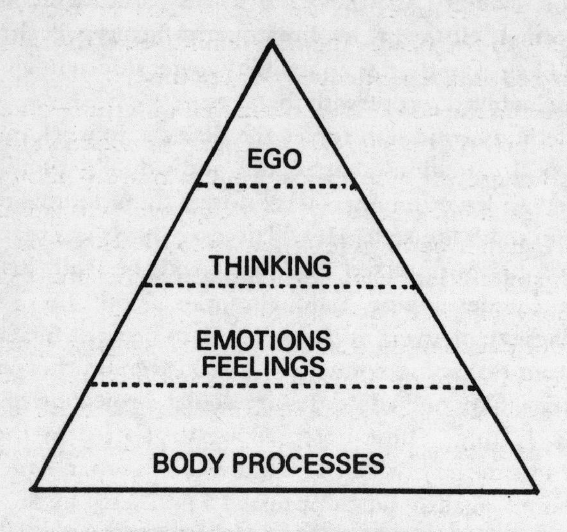

emotional conflict that forced it into this position. This conflict has become structured in the body and is beyond the reach of the ego. A person may give lip service to the idea of change, but until he confronts his problem on the body level, real changing is highly unlikely.

To comprehend the complex relationship between the ego and the body, we must integrate two opposite points of view of the human personality.* The first view is from the ground. In this view the hierarchy of personality functions appears as a pyramid as shown in the above diagram.

The base of the pyramid consists of the body processes that maintain life and support the personality. They rest on and are in contact with the earth or the natural environment. These processes give rise to feelings and emotions which in turn lead to thought

*A fuller discussion of this relationship is contained in my book *The Physical Dynamics of Character Structure, op. cit.*

processes. At the apex is the ego, which in bioenergetics is identified with the head. The dotted lines show that all functions are connected and dependent on one another.

The ego and the body can be compared with the relationship of a general to his troops. Without a general or commanding officer, troops do constitute not an army but a mob. Without troops a general is just a figurehead. When the general staff and the troops function together harmoniously and in touch with reality, we have a smooth and efficient army. When they conflict, there is disorder and trouble. This can happen when the general sees his troops as numbers or pawns in the game of war he is playing. He can forget that a war is fought not only by troops but for troops and not for his personal glory. So, too, the ego can lose sight of the fact that it is the body that counts, not the image it seeks to present.

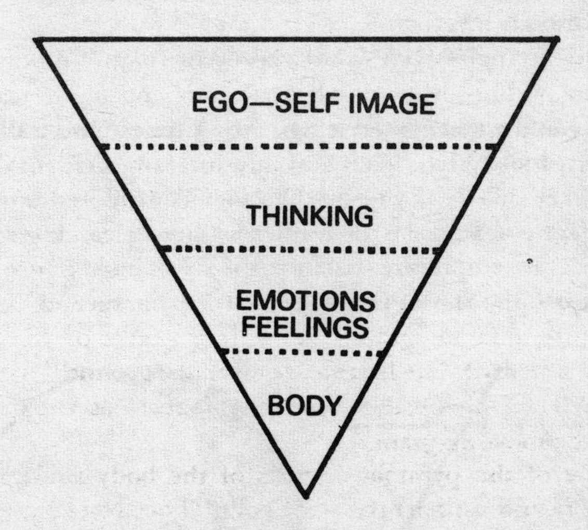

Seen from the point of view of the general, the normal hierarchy of authority within an army would be reversed. No general can function unless he sees himself as all-important. The same is true of the ego and the body. When viewed from above—that is, from the position of the ego—the pyramid of personality functions would be inverted. The view from above measures the degree of consciousness or control. More consciousness is invested in the ego than in any other function. Correspondingly, we are more conscious of our thoughts than of our feelings and least conscious of our bodily processes. This is the general's view of the army hierarchy in terms of power. It may be equated with a view of personality functions in terms of knowledge, which is an ego operation. On the other hand, the body has its wisdom which antedates and precedes the acquisition of knowledge.

These two views of the human personality can be integrated by superimposing one triangle upon the other. We then have the six-star figure that was used in the preceding section to represent the whole body. The dotted line shows where the conflict is most intense—the region of the diaphragm or waist where the two halves of the body meet.

The two triangles can also represent many other polar relationships in life—heaven and earth, day and night, male and female, fire and water. Interestingly, the Chinese use a different diagram to depict the duality of life-forces which in Chinese philosophy are called the yin and the yang. The difference between the two diagrams suggests two different life-styles. The circular Chinese diagram emphasizes balance; the six-pointed figure, which is also known as the Star of David, emphasizes interaction.

Not only do these forces interact within the organism to produce the drive that characterizes Western activity, but they compel the organism to interact aggressively with its environment. I am not using the word "aggressive" here in its destructive sense, but in opposition to "passive." Western aggressiveness has both its positive and its negative aspects. But whether positive or negative, it aims at change, in contrast with the Oriental attitude that aims at stability. For the sake of simplicity let me divide man's activities into four groups: intellectual, social, creative and physical, including sexual. The concept of interaction becomes clear if we place these groups at the four sides of our figure, as shown below.

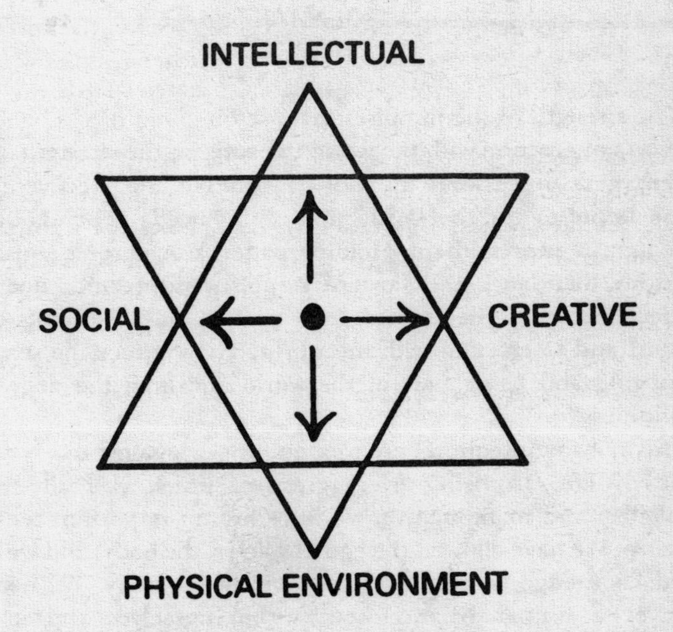

Now if we combine this diagram with the similar one in the preceding section, we will have a picture of the dynamic forces involved in the human personality (illustration, p. 150).

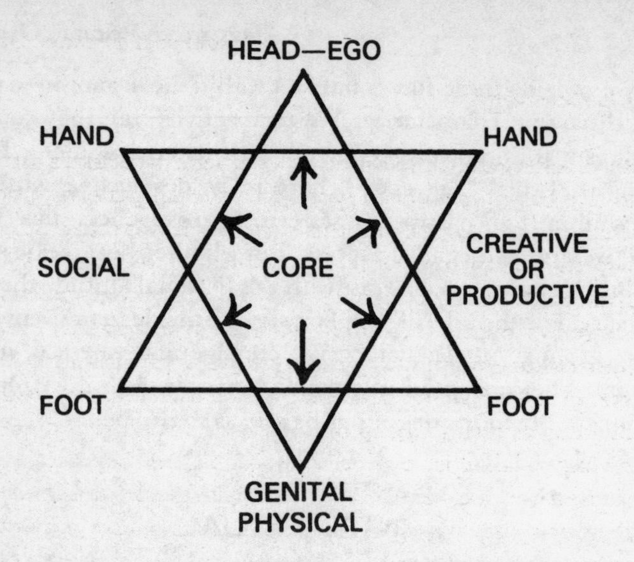

The strength of the impulses that are outgoing forces behind a person's interaction with the world depends on the strength of the bioenergetic processes in his body. In addition, the effectiveness of these impulses for the satisfaction of his needs depends on his freedom to express them. Holding patterns or chronic muscular tensions that block the flow of impulse and feeling not only undermine one's effectiveness as a person, but also limits one's contact and interaction with the world. They reduce the sense of belonging and being part of the world and limit the degree of soulfulness.

It is not my intention here to argue for or against the Western style of life. In being overaggressive, which is really being exploitive and manipulative, we have lost an important sense of balance. We have allowed the ego to subvert the body, and we have used knowledge to dismiss the wisdom of the body. We need to recover a proper balance both within ourselves and in our relationship to the world we live in. However, I doubt if that balance can be recovered by rejecting Western attitudes in favor of Oriental ones. We should be aware that the East is now strenuously trying to adopt Western ways.

A Characterology

In bioenergetics, the different character structures are classified into five basic types. Each type has a special pattern of defense on both the psychological and the muscular levels that distinguishes it from the other types. It is important to note that this is a classification not of people but of defensive positions. It is recognized that no individual is a pure type and that every person in our culture combines in different degrees within his personality some or all of these defensive patterns. The personality of an individual as distinct from his character structure is determined by his vitality—that is, by the strength of his impulses and by the defenses he has erected to control these impulses. No two individuals are alike in either their inherent vitality or in their patterns of defense arising from their life experience. Nevertheless, it is necessary to speak in terms of types for the sake of clarity in communication and understanding.

The five types are "schizoid," "oral," "psychopathic," "masochistic," and "rigid." We have used these terms because they are known and accepted definitions of personality disorders in the psychiatric profession. Our classification does not violate established criteria.

The following description of these types is presented in outline form since it is impossible, in this general view of bioenergetics, to enter into a detailed discussion of each disturbance. Since the character types are quite complex, only the broad aspects of each type can be mentioned.

The Schizoid Character Structure

Description

The term "schizoid" derives from "schizophrenia" and denotes an individual in whose personality there are tendencies to the schizophrenic state. These tendencies are: (1) to split the unitary functioning of the personality. For example, thinking tends to be dissociated from feeling. What the person thinks seems to have little apparent connection with how he feels or behaves; (2) to withdraw inwardly, breaking or losing contact with the world or external reality. The schizoid individual is not schizophrenic and may never become so, but these tendencies are present in his personality, usually well compensated.

The term "schizoid" describes a person whose sense of self is diminished, whose ego is weak and whose contact with the body and its feelings greatly reduced.

Bioenergetic condition

Energy is withheld from the peripheral structures of the body—namely, from those organs that make contact with the external world: the face, the hands, the genitals and the feet. These organs are not fully connected energetically to the core—that is, the core excitation does not flow freely out to them but is blocked by chronic muscular tensions at the base of the head, the shoulders, the pelvis and the hip joints. Functions performed by these organs become dissociated, therefore, from the feelings at the core of the person.

The inner charge tends to become frozen in the core area. As a consequence, impulse formation is weak. However, the charge is explosive (because of its compression), and it may erupt in violence or murder. This happens when the defense fails to hold and the organism becomes flooded with an amount of energy it cannot handle. The personality splits apart, and a schizophrenic state develops. Murder is not uncommon in this situation.

The defense consists of a pattern of muscular tensions that hold the personality together by preventing the peripheral structures from becoming flooded with feeling and energy. These muscular tensions are the same as those described above as responsible for the cutting off of the peripheral organs from contact with the core. Thus, the defense is the problem.

There is a splitting of the body energetically at the waist with the

The double lines indicate the contracted energy boundary of the schizoid character. The broken lines indicate the lack of charge in the peripheral organs and their lack of connection with the core. The broken line in the center of schizoid structure indicates the splitting of the two halves of the body.

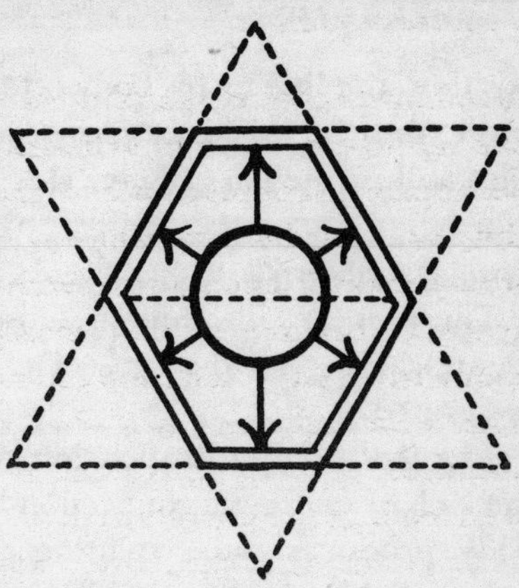

result that there is a lack of integration between its upper and lower halves.

This bioenergetic analysis is shown above diagrammatically.

Physical aspects

In the majority of cases, the body is narrow and contracted. Where there are paranoid elements in the personality, the body is fuller and more athletic in appearance.

The main tension areas are at the base of the skull, the shoulder joints, the leg joints, the pelvic joints and about the diaphragm. The latter is generally so severe that it tends to split the body in two. The dominant spasticities are in the small muscles that surround the articulations. One can see, therefore, in this character type either an extreme inflexibility or a hyperflexibility of the joints.

The face is masklike. The eyes, though not vacant as in schizophrenics, are not alive and do not make contact. The arms hang like appendages rather than extensions of the body. The feet are contracted and cold; they are often everted; the weight of the body is carried on the outside of the feet.

There is often a marked discrepancy between the two halves of the body. In many cases they do not look as if they belong to the same person.

Under stress, for example, when the person assumes a bow

position, the line of his body often appears broken. The head, the trunk and the legs are often seen to be at angles to one another. This is illustrated in Chapter II.

Psychological correlates

There is an inadequate sense of self because of a lack of identification with the body. The person doesn't feel connected or integrated.*

The tendency to dissociation represented on the body level by the lack of energetic connection between head and the rest of the body produces some splitting of the personality into opposite attitudes. Thus, one can find an attitude of arrogance coupled with one of debasement, of being a virgin coupled with the feeling of being a whore. The latter also reflects the split in the two parts of the body, lower and upper.

The schizoid character shows a hypersensitivity owing to a weak ego boundary which is the psychological counterpart of the lack of peripheral charge. This weakness reduces his resistance to outside pressures and forces him to withdraw in self-defense.

In the schizoid character there is a strong tendency to avoid intimate, feeling relationships. Actually such relationships are very difficult to establish because of the lack of charge in the peripheral structures.

Using the will to motivate actions gives schizoid behavior an ungenuine quality. It has been called "as if" behavior—that is, as if it were based on feeling, but the actions themselves are not expressive of feeling.

Etiological and historical factors

It is important here to present some historical data about the origin of this structure. The following remarks summarize the observations of students of this problem who have treated and analyzed many individuals with this disturbance:

*R.D. Laing, *The Divided Self* (New York, Pantheon, 1969).

In all cases there is clear evidence that there was an early rejection by the mother which the patient experienced as a threat to his existence. The rejection was accompanied by covert and often overt hostility on her part.

The rejection and hostility created a fear in the patient that any reaching out, demanding or self-assertion would lead to his annihilation.

The history reveals a lack of any strong positive feeling of security or joy. In childhood, night terrors were common.

Either withdrawal or nonemotional behavior was typical with occasional outbursts of rage, what is called autistic behavior.

If either parent made a secondary investment in the child during the oedipal period for sexual reasons, which is fairly common, a paranoid element is added to the personality. This would allow a certain amount of acting out during late childhood and in adulthood.

Given this history, the child had no choice but to dissociate himself from reality (intense fantasy life) and from his body (abstract intelligence) in order to survive. Since the dominant feelings were terror and a murderous fury, the child walled off all feeling in self defense.

The Oral Character Structure

Description

We describe a personality as being an oral character structure when it contains many traits typical of the oral period of life—namely, infancy. These traits are a weakness in the sense of independence, a tendency to cling to others, a decreased aggressiveness and an inner feeling of needing to be held, supported and taken care of. They denote a lack of fulfillment in infancy and represent a degree of fixation at that level of development. In some people these traits are masked by consciously adopted compensatory attitudes. Some personalities with this structure show an exaggerated independence which, however, fails to hold up under stress. The underlying experience of the oral character is deprivation, whereas the corresponding experience of the schizoid structure was rejection.

Bioenergetic condition

Energetically the oral structure is an undercharged state. The energy is not frozen in the core as in the schizoid condition; it flows out to the periphery of the body, but weakly.

For reasons that are not fully clear, linear growth is accentuated, resulting in a long, thin body. One possible explanation is that the delay in maturation allows the long bones to grow unduly. Another factor may be the inability of the underdeveloped muscles to hold the bony growth in check.

The lack of energy and strength is most noticeable in the lower part of the body, since development of the body in a child proceeds from the head downward.

All points of contact with the environment are undercharged. The eyes are weak with a tendency to myopia, and the level of genital excitation is reduced.

This bioenergetic condition is shown diagrammatically:

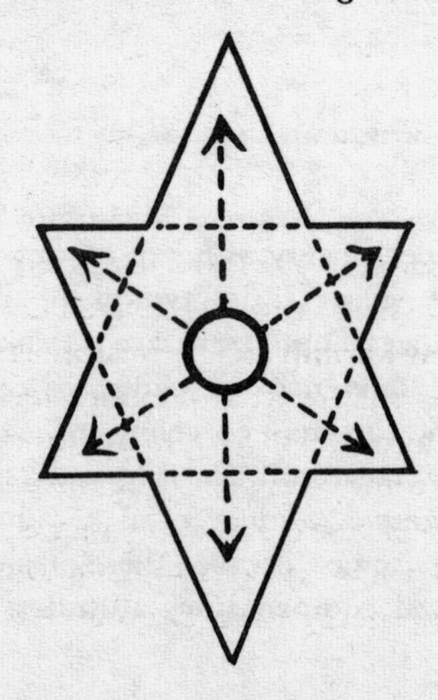

Physical characteristics

The body tends to be long and thin corresponding to Sheldon's ectomorphic type. It differs from the schizoid body in that it is not tightly contracted.

The musculature is underdeveloped, but it is not stringy as in the schizoid body. This lack of development is most noticeable in the arms and legs. Long, spindly legs are a common sign of this structure. The feet are also thin and narrow. The legs do not impress one as able to hold the body up. The knees are generally locked to provide the added support of rigidity.

The body shows a tendency to slump owing in part to the weakness of the muscular system.

There are often physical signs of immaturity. The pelvis may be smaller than normal in both men and women. Body hair is often reduced. In some women the whole process of growth is retarded, giving them childlike bodies.

The breathing of the oral character is shallow, accounting for the low-energy level of his personality. The deprivation on the oral level reduced the strength of the impulse to suck. Good breathing depends on the ability to suck in the air.

Psychological correlates

The oral character has difficulty standing on his own feet literally and figuratively. He tends to lean on or cling to others. But as I mentioned earlier, this tendency can be masked by an exaggerated attitude of independence. The clinging is also reflected in the inability to be alone. There is an exaggerated need for contact with other people, for their warmth and their support.

The oral character suffers from an inner feeling of emptiness. He looks constantly to others to fill him up, though he may act as if he were the one providing support. The inner emptiness reflects the suppression of intense feelings of longing, which, if expressed, would result in deep crying and a fuller respiration.

Because of his low-energy level, the oral character is subject to mood swings of depression and elation. A tendency to depression is pathognomonic of oral traits in a personality.

Another typical oral trait is the attitude that "it" is owing to him. This may be expressed in the idea that the world owes him a living. It stems directly from the early experience of deprivation.

Etiological and historical factors

The early deprivation may be due to the actual loss of a warm and supporting mother figure by death or illness or her absence caused by the need to work. A mother who herself suffers from depression is not available to a child.

The history often reveals a precocious development, learning to talk and to walk earlier than normal. I explain this development as an effort to overcome the feeling of loss by becoming independent.

There are often other experiences of disappointment in the early life as he or she tried to reach out to the father or to siblings for contact, warmth and support. Such disappointments may leave a feeling of bitterness in the personality.

Depressive episodes in late childhood and early youth are typical. The oral child does not, however, show the autistic behavior of the schizoid child. We must recognize that there can be schizoid elements in an oral personality just as there can be oral elements in the schizoid structure.

The Psychopathic Character Structure

Description

This character structure requires some words of introduction. It is the one character type that has not been described or analyzed in my previous studies. It can be a very complex structure, but for the sake of brevity and clarity I will describe a simple form of this disturbance.

The essence of the psychopathic attitude is the *denial* of feeling.

This attitude contrasts with the schizoid character who *dissociates* from his feelings. In the psychopathic personality the ego or mind turns against the body and its feelings, especially the sexual feelings. That is why the term "psychopathology" arose. The normal function of the ego is to support the body's striving for pleasure, not to subvert it in favor of an ego image. There is in all psychopathic characters a great investment of energy in one's image. The other aspect of this personality is the drive for power and the need to dominate and control.

The reason why this character type is complex is that there are two ways to gain power over others. One is by bullying or overpowering another in which case, if one does not challenge the bully, one becomes in a sense his victim. The second way is by undermining a person through a seductive approach which is very effective against naive people who fall into the psychopath's power.

Bioenergetic condition

There are two body types that correspond to the two psychopathic structures. The overpowering type is more easily explained bioenergetically, and I will use it for my illustration. Gaining power over another is achieved by rising above the other. In this type there is a marked displacement of energy toward the head end of the body, with a concomitant reduction of charge in the lower part of the body. The two halves of the body are noticeably disproportionate, the upper half being larger and more dominant in appearance.

There is generally a definite constriction about the diaphragm and waist which blocks the flow of energy and feeling downward.

The head is energetically overcharged, which means there is a hyperexcitation of the mental apparatus, resulting in continuous consideration of how to gain control and mastery over situations.

The eyes are watchful or distrustful. They are not open to see interrelationships. This closing of the eyes to seeing and understanding is characteristic of all psychopathic personalities.

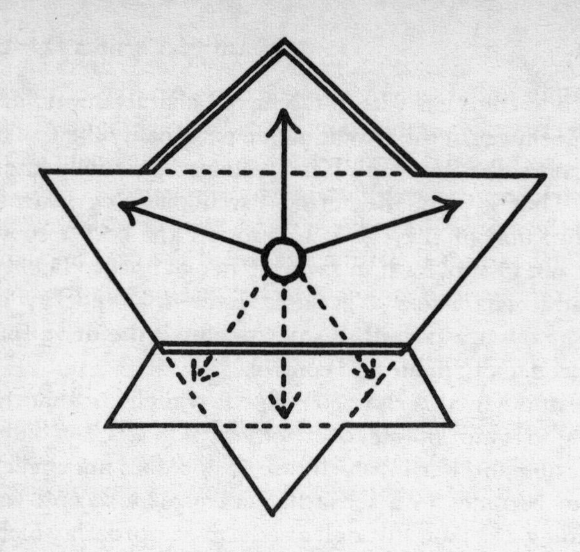

The need to control is also directed against the self. The head is held very tightly (one mustn't ever lose his head), but it in turn holds the body tightly in its grasp.

These energetic relationships are shown in the above diagram.

Physical characteristics

The body of the overpowering type shows a disproportionate development of its upper half. It gives the impression of being blown up and corresponds to the individual's blown-up ego image. One might say the structure is top-heavy. It is also rigid. The lower part of the body is narrower and may show the typical weakness of the oral character structure.

The body of the second type, which I have called seductive or undermining, is more regular and does not have a blown-up look. The back is generally hyperflexible.

In both cases there is a disturbance of the flow between the two halves of the body. In the first type the pelvis is undercharged and rigidly held; in the second it is overcharged but disconnected. Both types also have a marked spasticity of the diaphragm.

There are marked tensions in the ocular segment of the body, which includes the eyes and the occipital region.

Similarly severe muscular tensions can be palpated along the base of the skull in what may be called the oral segment. These tensions represent an inhibition of the sucking impulse.

Psychological correlates

A psychopathic personality needs someone to control, and though he may seemingly control that person, he is also dependent on him. Thus, there is a degree of orality in all psychopathic individuals. In the psychiatric literature they have been described as having an oral fixation.

The need to control is closely related to the fear of being controlled. To be controlled means to be used. We shall see that in the history of individuals with this character structure there was a struggle for dominance and control between parent and child.

The drive to be on top, to succeed is so strong that the person cannot admit or allow a defeat to occur. Defeat puts him in the position of victim; *ergo*, he must be the victor in every contest.

Sexuality is always used in this power play. He is seductive in his seeming power or in a soft, sly enticement. Pleasure in sex is secondary to performance or conquest.

The denial of feeling is basically a denial of need. The psychopathic maneuver is to make others need him so that he doesn't have to express his need. Thus he is always one up on the world.

Etiological and historical factors

As in all character types, the person's history explains his behavior. I would make the general statement that no person can understand his behavior if he doesn't know his history. Thus, one of the main tasks of every therapy is to elucidate the patient's life experience. That is often very difficult to do in the case of this personality because the psychopathic tendency to deny feeling includes the denial of experience. Notwithstanding this problem, much has been learned in bioenergetics about the background of this problem.

The most important factor in the etiology of this condition is a sexually seductive parent. The seduction is covert and is done to meet the parent's narcissistic needs. It aims to tie the child to the parent.

A seductive parent is always a rejecting parent on the level of the child's need for support and physical contact. The lack of the necessary contact and support accounts for the oral element in this character structure.

The seductive relationship creates a triangle which puts the child in the position of challenging the parent of the same sex. This creates a barrier to the necessary identification with the parent of the same sex and furthers an identification with the seductive parent.

In this situation any reaching out for contact would leave the child extremely vulnerable. The child will either rise above the need (upward displacement) or fulfill the need by manipulating the parents (seductive type).

There is also a masochistic element in the psychopathic personality, resulting from the submission to the seductive parent. The child could not rebel or walk away from the situation; its only defense was internal. The submission is only on the surface; nevertheless, to the degree that the child submits openly, he gains some measure of closeness with the parent.

The masochistic element is strongest in the enticing or seductive variety of this character structure. The initial gambit is to move into a relationship in a masochistically submissive role. Then, when the enticement has worked and the attachment of the other person is secure, the role is reversed, and a sadistic quality emerges.

The Masochistic Character Structure

Description

Masochism is equated in the public mind with the wish to suffer. I don't think that is true of an individual with this character structure. He does suffer, and since he is unable to change the situation, it is inferred that he wishes to remain in that condition. I am not speaking of a person with a masochistic perversion, the individual who seeks to be beaten so he can enjoy sex. The masochistic character structure describes an individual who suffers and whines or complains but remains submissive. Submissiveness is the dominant masochistic tendency.

If the masochistic character shows a submissive attitude in his outward behavior, he is just the opposite inside. On the deeper emotional level, he has strong feelings of spite, negativity, hostility and superiority. However, these feelings are strongly blocked out of fear that he would explode in violent behavior. He counters the fear of exploding by a muscular pattern of holding in. Thick, powerful muscles restrain any direct assertion and allow only the whine or complaint to come through.

Bioenergetic condition

In contrast with the oral structure, the masochistic structure is fully charged energetically. This charge is, however, tightly held in but not frozen.

Because of the severe holding in, the peripheral organs are weakly charged, which does not lead to discharge and release—that is, expressive action is limited.

The holding in is so severe that it results in a compression and collapse of the organism. The collapse occurs in the waist as the body bends under the burden of its tensions.*

*Another view of the operation of these energetic forces in the masochistic structure can be found in my book *The Physical Dynamics of Character Structure, op. cit.*, p. 191.

Impulses moving upward and downward are choked off in the neck and waist, accounting for the strong tendency in this personality to experience anxiety.

Body extension in the sense of extending oneself or reaching out is severely curtailed. The reduction of extension produces the shortening of the structure described above.

Here's the diagrammatic representation of the masochistic body:

Physical characteristics

A short, thick, muscular body is typical of the masochistic structure.

For reasons that are not known, there is generally an increased growth of body hair.

Particularly characteristic is a short, thick neck denoting a pulling in of the head. The waist is correspondingly shorter and thicker.

Another important characteristic is the pulling forward of the pelvis, which may be described more literally as a tucking in and flattening of the ass. This posture resembles the picture of a dog with his tail between his legs.

The tucking in of the ass is responsible, together with the weight of tension above, for producing a folding or collapse of the body in the waist.

In some women one sees a combination of rigidity in the upper half of the body and masochism in the lower half shown by heavy buttocks and thighs, a pulled-up pelvic floor and a dark hue to the skin caused by the stagnation of the charge.

The skin of all masochistic characters tends to have a brownish hue owing to stagnation of the energy.

Psychological correlates

Because of the severe holding in, aggression is greatly reduced. Self-assertion is similarly limited.

In place of self-assertion there is whining and complaining. The whine is the only vocal expression that comes easily through the choked throat. In place of aggression there is provocative behavior which aims at producing a forceful response from the other person strong enough to enable the masochist to react violently and explosively in sex and otherwise.

The stagnation of charge owing to the strong holding in leads to the feeling of "being stuck in a morass," unable to move freely.

An attitude of submission and pleasing is characteristic of masochistic behavior. On a conscious level the masochist is identified with trying to please; on the unconscious level, however, this attitude is denied by spite, negativity and hostility. These suppressed feelings must be released before the masochistic individual can respond freely to life situations.

Etiological and historical factors

The masochistic structure develops in a family where there is love and acceptance combined with severe pressure. The mother is dominant and sacrificing; the father is passive and submissive.

The dominant, self-sacrificing mother literally smothers the child, who is made to feel extremely guilty for any attempt to declare his freedom or assert a negative attitude.

A strong focus on eating and defecation is typical. This amounts to pressure from above and below. "Be a good boy. Please your mother. Eat all your food. . . . And move your bowels regularly. Let mother see," and so on.

All attempts at resistance, including temper tantrums, were crushed. All people with a masochistic structure had temper tantrums as children which they were forced to give up.

Feelings of being trapped which allowed only a reaction of spite, which ended in self-defeat, were common experiences. The child could see no way out.

The patient struggled as a child with deep feelings of humiliation whenever he did "let it out freely"—in the form of vomiting, soiling or defiance.

The masochist is afraid to go out on a limb or stick his neck out (same for the genitals) for fear he will be cut off or it will be cut off. There is a strong castration anxiety in this character. Most significant is the fear of being cut off from parental relationships that provide love—but on condition. We shall see this significance more clearly in the next section.

The Rigid Character Structure

Description

The concept of rigidity derives from the tendency of these individuals to hold themselves stiff—with pride. Thus, the head is held fairly high, the backbone straight. These would be positive traits were it not for the fact that the pride is defensive, the rigidity unyielding. The rigid character is afraid to give in, equating this with submission and collapse. Rigidity becomes a defense against an underlying masochistic tendency.

The rigid character is on guard against being taken advantage of, being used or trapped. His guardedness takes the form of holding back on impulses to open and reach out. Holding back also means "holding in the back," hence rigidity. The ability to hold back stems from a strong ego position with a high degree of control over behavior. It is also supported by an equally strong genital position, thus anchoring the personality at both ends of the body and ensuring good contact with reality. Unfortunately the emphasis on reality is used as a defense against the striving for pleasure—letting go—and this is the underlying conflict in the personality.

Bioenergetic condition

In this structure there is a fairly strong charge at all peripheral points of contact with the environment, which favors the ability to test reality before acting.

The holding back is peripheral, which allows feeling to flow but limits its expression.

The main areas of tension are the long muscles of the body. Spasticities in the extensor and flexor muscles combine to produce rigidity.

There are, naturally, different degrees of rigidity. When the holding back is mild, the personality is alive and vibrant.

This bioenergetic condition is shown diagrammatically:

Physical characteristics

The body of the rigid character is proportionate and harmonious in its parts. The body looks and feels integrated and connected. Despite this, one may see some elements of the disturbances and distortions described above for the other types.

An important characteristic is the aliveness of the body: bright eyes; good skin color; aliveness of gesture and movement.

If the rigidity is severe, there is a corresponding reduction of the positive elements noted above, coordination and grace in movement are diminished, the eyes lose some of their luster, and the skin tone may become pale or grayish.

Psychological correlates

Individuals with this character structure generally are worldly-oriented, ambitious, competitive and aggressive. Passivity is experienced as vulnerability.

The rigid character can be stubborn, but he is rarely spiteful. In part his stubbornness derives from his pride; he is afraid that if he lets go, he may look foolish, so he holds back. In part it derives from his fear that submission would entail a loss of freedom.

The term "rigid character" was adopted in bioenergetics to describe the common factor in several differently labeled personalities. Thus, it includes the phallic, narcissistic male whose focus is on erective potency and the Victorian type of hysterical female character Reich described in *Character Analysis* who uses sex as a defense against sexuality. The old-fashioned compulsive character also belongs in this broad category.

The rigidity of this character is like steel. Rigidity is also seen in the schizoid structure where, owing to the frozen state of his energy system, it is like ice and as brittle. Generally, the rigid character copes effectively with his world.

Etiological and historical factors

The history behind this structure is interesting in that the individual with this character did not experience the severe traumas that created the more serious defensive positions.

The significant trauma here is the experience of frustration in the striving for erotic gratification, especially at the genital level. This occurred through the prohibition of infantile masturbation and also in the relation to the parent of the opposite sex.

The rejection of the child's striving for erotic and sexual pleasure was viewed by him as a betrayal of his reaching out to love. Erotic pleasure, sexuality and love are synonymous in the mind of a child.

Because of his strong ego development, the rigid character did not abandon this awareness. As shown in the diagram, his heart is not cut off from the periphery. He or she is a person who acts with heart but with restraint and ego control. To surrender this control and let the heart take over would be the desired state.

Since the open expression of love as a desire for physical intimacy and erotic pleasure encountered a rejection from the parents, the rigid character moves indirectly and under guard to attain his end. He doesn't manipulate as the psychopathic character does; he maneuvers to gain closeness.

The importance of his pride lies in the fact that it is tied to this feeling of love. The rejection of his sexual love is a hurt to his pride. Similarly, an insult to his pride is a rejection of his love.

I have one final comment. I have not discussed the treatment of these problems because therapists do not treat character types but people. Therapy focuses on the individual in his immediate relationships: to his body; to the ground he stands on; to the people with whom he is involved; and to the therapist. This is in the foreground of the therapist's approach. In the background, however, is his knowledge of character, without which he could not understand the patient and his problems. A skilled therapist can move easily from one ground to the other without losing sight of either.

The Hierarchy of Character Types and a Bill of Rights

The character structure defines the way an individual handles his need to love, his reaching out for intimacy and closeness and his striving for pleasure. Seen in this light, the different character structures form a spectrum or hierarchy, at one end of which is the schizoid position—which is a withdrawal from intimacy and closeness because it is too threatening—and at the other, emotional health—where there is no holding against the impulse to reach out openly for closeness and contact. The various character types fit into this spectrum or hierarchy according to the degree that they allow for intimacy and contact. The order will parallel the one used in presenting the character types.

The *schizoid character* avoids an intimate closeness.

The *oral character* can establish closeness only on the basis of his need for warmth and support—that is, on an infantile basis.

The *psychopathic character* can relate only to those who need him. As long as he is needed and in a position to control the relationship, he can permit a limited degree of closeness to develop.

The *masochistic character* is, surprisingly, capable of establishing a close relationship on the basis of a submissive attitude. Of course, such a relationship can be described as only "half-assed," but it is more intimate than any relationship the previous three types can develop. The anxiety in the masochistic structure is that if he asserted any negative feeling or proclaimed his freedom, he would lose the relationship or be cut off from the closeness he has.

The *rigid character* forms fairly close relationships. I use the word "fairly" because he remains guarded, despite the seeming intimacy and commitment.

Each character structure contains an inherent conflict because within the personality there is at once the need for intimacy and closeness and for self-expression and a fear that these needs are mutually exclusive. The character structure is the best compromise the person was able to make in his early life situation. Unfortunately, he is stuck with that compromise, though the environmental situation changed as he became an adult. Let us look at these conflicts more closely. We will also see from this analysis how each character structure is a defense against the one lower down in the hierarchy.

Schizoid: If I express my need for closeness, my existence is threatened. Changing the order, it becomes: "I can exist if I do not need intimacy." He must stay, therefore, in a state of isolation.

Oral: The conflict could be expressed as: "If I am independent, I must give up needing any support and warmth." Such a statement, however, forces him to remain in a dependent position. It is modified, therefore, as "I can express my need so long as I am not independent." Giving up the need to love and be close would drop this person into a schizoid state, which is far more life-denying.

Psychopathic: In this structure there is a conflict between independence or autonomy and closeness. This could be expressed as: "I can be close if I let you control me or use me." This he cannot permit, for it involves a complete surrender of the feeling of self. On the other hand, he cannot give up his need for closeness as the schizoid did, nor can he risk becoming dependent, as an oral character. In this bind as a child, he was forced to reverse the roles. In his present relationships he becomes the controlling and seductive parent vis-à-vis another person who is reduced to an oral position. Thus, by keeping control over the other, he can allow some measure of closeness. It could be said as follows: "You can be close to me for so long as you look up to me." The psychopathic element is in the reversal, "You can be close to me" instead of "I need to be close to you."

Masochistic: Here the conflict is between love or closeness and freedom. Simply stated, it is: "If I am free, you will not love me." Faced with this conflict, the masochist says, "I'll be your good boy, and you will love me."

Rigid: The rigid character is relatively free, relatively because he constantly guards that freedom—guards it by not letting his heart's desire turn his head too much. His conflict could be stated as: "I can be free if I do not lose my head and surrender fully to love." In his mind surrender has the connotation of submission, which he believes would reduce him to the level of a masochistic character. As a result, his wanting and loving are always guarded.

We can further simplify the above. The conflict becomes sharper.

Schizoid = existence vs. need
Oral = need vs. independence
Psychopathic = independence vs. closeness
Masochistic = closeness vs. freedom
Rigid = freedom vs. surrender to love

A resolution of any one of these conflicts means that the antagonism between the two sets of values disappears. The schizoid person finds that existence and needing are not mutually exclusive and a person can have both. The oral character discovers that one can need and also be independent (stand on one's own feet) and so on.

Personality growth and development are a process in which the child becomes progressively conscious of its human rights. These are: *The right to exist*—that is, to be in the world as an individual organism. This right is generally established during the first months of existence. If it is not well established, the failure creates a predisposition to the schizoid structure. However, any time that this right is seriously threatened, to the point where the person feels uncertain of his right to be, a schizoid tendency will result.

The right to be secure in one's needing, which derives from the support and nourishing function of the mother during the first years. A basic insecurity on this level leads to an oral structure.

The right to be autonomous and independent—that is, not to be subject to the needs of others. This right is lost or fails to become established if the parent of the opposite sex is seductive. Yielding to the seduction would put the child in the parent's power. The child counters this threat by being seductive, in turn, to gain power over the parent. This situation generally results in a psychopathic structure.

The right to be independent, which the child established through its self-assertion and its opposition to the parent. If self-assertion and opposition are crushed, the individual develops a masochistic personality. Self-assertion begins generally at eighteen months of age, when the child learns to say no and continues to develop during the next year. This period coincides with toilet training, and the problems created by forced training become associated with the issue of self-assertion and opposition.

The right to want and to move toward the satisfaction of these wants directly and openly. This right has a big ego component and is the last of the natural rights to become established. I would relate its emergence and development approximately to the period between three and six years of age. It is strongly tied to the early sexual feelings of the child.

The failure of these basic and essential rights to be established results in a fixation at the age and in the situation which caused the arrest of full development.

Since every person has some degree of fixation at each of these stages, or levels, each of these conflicts will require some working through. At this point I do not know if there is any order to this therapeutic process. It would seem the best procedure is to follow the patient as he or she confronts each of these conflicts in his life. If this is done correctly, the patient would end his therapy feeling very strongly that he has the right to be in the world, needing but also independent, free but also loving and committed.

VI. Reality: A Secondary Orientation

Reality and Illusion

At the end of the section on character types I mentioned that these types are kept in the background of the therapist's mind in his approach to a patient. In the foreground is the patient's specific life situation. This would include the presenting complaint; how the person sees himself in his world—(how he sees the relationship between his personality and his difficulties); the degree of his relationship to his body (how aware he is of muscular tensions that may contribute to his problem); his expectations of therapy and, at all times, how he relates to the therapist as another human being. The initial focus is on the person's orientation in reality. I should add that this focus is never abandoned in the course of therapy but is constantly enlarged as more aspects of his life and history come into view.

Although the initial focus is on reality, I call it a secondary orientation. But it is secondary only in point of time—that is, a person's orientation in reality develops gradually as he grows to adulthood, whereas his orientation to pleasure is present from the inception of life. How well a person is oriented in reality will determine how effectively his actions fulfill his striving for pleasure. It is inconceivable to me that a person who is unrealistic about his life would be able to get the pleasure, satisfaction and fulfillment he so earnestly desires.

But what is reality? And how can we tell whether a person is realistic about his life or not? About the first question I am not sure that I really know. There are certain truths I believe are founded in reality, such as the importance of good breathing, the value of freedom from chronic muscular tensions, the need to be identified with one's body, the creative potential of pleasure and so on. I have been unrealistic about certain matters. Thinking I could make it the easy way, I lost money in the stock market. And there are issues about which I am confused. How realistic is it of me to see as many patients as I do? To carry a heavy burden of responsibility? I don't think anyone knows the full answers to the first question, so let us turn to the second.

Fortunately the person who comes to therapy admits that he is in trouble, that somehow his life hasn't worked out as he hoped and that he is uncertain of the reality of his expectations. Given this knowledge and the fact that it is easier to be objective about another person, a therapist can usually discern those aspects of the person's thinking and behavior that seem unrealistic. He could say that such thinking and behavior are based more on illusion than reality.

For instance, I was consulted by a young woman who was depressed because of the breakup of her marriage. She discovered her husband was involved with another woman, and this discovery shattered her image of herself as the "perfect little wife." The two adjectives she used were apt. She was a bright, small woman who believed she was devoted to her husband and indispensable to his success. It is easy to imagine her shock when she discovered he was interested in another woman. How could anyone offer him more?

It is pretty clear from this story that my patient was unrealistic about life. The idea that one could be a "perfect wife" is surely an illusion, human nature being what it is—far from perfect. The belief that a man would be grateful to his wife for making him successful is not founded in reality, for the effect of such an attitude is to deny the man and castrate him. The collapse of illusions always results in depression,* which offers the person an opportunity to uncover his illusions and reestablish his thinking and behavior on more solid ground.

I first became interested in the role of illusions through my study of the schizoid personality.† The desperate condition of the schizoid forces him to create illusions to sustain his spirit in its struggle for survival. In a situation where one feels helpless to change or evade a threatening reality, recourse to illusion prevents the person from giving way to hopeless despair. Every schizoid individual has his secret illusions he cherishes and hopes to fulfill. Sensing that his human nature was rejected, he will develop the illusion that he is superior to ordinary human beings by virtue of special qualities. He is nobler than other men; she is purer than other women. These illusions often run counter to the real-life experience of the person. For example, a young woman whose sexual behavior was loose and promiscuous believed she was pure and virtuous. The idea behind this illusion was the hope she would be discovered one day by a prince who would see through her outer wantonness and discover her heart of gold.

However, the danger of an illusion is that it perpetuates the desperation. This quote from *Betrayal of the Body* explains:

> As an illusion gains power it demands fulfillment, thereby forcing the individual into conflict with reality which leads to desperate behavior. To pursue the fulfillment of an illusion requires the sacrifice of good feelings in the present, and the person who lives in illusion is, by definition, unable to make demands for pleasure. In his desperation he is willing to forgo

*Lowen, *Depression and the Body, op cit.*
†See Lowen, *Betrayal of the Body, op. cit.*

> pleasure and to hold life in abeyance in the hope that his illusion-come-true will remove his despair.*

One of my patients expressed this idea beautifully when she said, "People establish unreal goals, then keep themselves in a constant state of desperation attempting to realize them."†

The subject of unreal goals came up again in my study of depression. A basic finding was that every depressed person has illusions that interject a note of unreality into his actions and behavior. From this it became clear that a depressive reaction invariably follows the collapse of an illusion. In my *Depression and the Body* there is a significant paragraph I would like to quote:

> Where a person has experienced a loss or trauma in childhood that undermines his feelings of security and self-acceptance, he would project into his image of the future the requirement that it reverse the experiences of his past Thus an individual who experiences a sense of rejection as a child would picture the future as promising acceptance and approval. If he struggled against a sense of helplessness and impotence as a child, his mind would naturally compensate this insult to his ego with an image of the future in which he is powerful and controlling. The mind in its fantasies and daydreams attempts to reverse an unfavorable and unacceptable reality by creating images and dreams. He will lose sight of their origin in childhood experience and will sacrifice the present to their fulfillment. These images are unreal goals and their realization is an unattainable objective.**

The significance of this paragraph is that it extends the role of illusion to all character types. Each character structure results from childhood experiences that have to some degree undermined the

**Ibid.*, p. 127.
†*Ibid.*, p. 121.
***Ibid.*, p. 25.

person's "feelings of security and self-acceptance." In each character structure, therefore, we will find images, illusions or ego ideals that compensate this injury to the self. The more severe the trauma, the greater is the investment of energy in the image or illusion, but in all cases the investment is considerable. Whatever energy is diverted to the illusion or unreal goal is unavailable for daily living in the present. The individual is handicapped, therefore, in his ability to come to grips with the reality of his situation.

Each person's illusion or ego ideal is as unique as his personality. We can, however, to further our understanding, broadly describe the kind of illusions or ego ideals typical of each character structure.

The schizoid character: I mentioned that the schizoid individual felt rejected as a human being. His response to this rejection was to see himself as superior. He is a prince in disguise and doesn't really belong to his parents. Some individuals even imagine they were adopted. One of my patients, for example, told me, "I suddenly became aware that I had an idealized image of myself as an exiled prince. I related this image to my dream that some day my father, the king, would come and claim me as his heir apparent. . . . I realize that I still have the illusion that someday I'll be discovered. Meantime I have to maintain my 'pretensions.' A prince can't demean himself by ordinary work. I have to show I'm special."

The extreme degree a person has to go to be special in the face of a rejection of his humanity is seen in schizophrenia, the decompensated state of the schizoid character. It is common to find schizophrenics who believe they are Jesus Christ, Napoleon, the goddess Isis and so on. In the schizophrenic state, the illusion takes on the quality of a delusion. The individual can no longer distinguish reality from illusion.

The oral character: The trauma to this personality was a loss of the right to need and the resulting unfulfilled state of his body. Consequently, the illusion that develops as a compensation is an image of being fully charged and filled with energy and feeling which he expends freely. When the mood of the oral character swings into elation, which is typical of this structure, the illusion is acted out. The person becomes excited and voluble, pouring out thoughts and ideas in a flood of feeling. This is his ego ideal—to be the center of attention as the one who gives fully. However, the elation is not more solid than the image, which cannot be sustained because the oral character doesn't have the necessary energy. Both collapse, and the oral character ends in one of his also typical depressive states.

I had a patient whom I had treated for some time many years ago whose story is relevant. One day he proposed that I should give freely of what I have, for he was fully prepared to do the same. "I am willing to share what I have," he said. "Why don't you?" "How much do you have?" I asked him. "Two dollars," was the reply. Since I had much more than that, it didn't seem to me a realistic proposition. He was nevertheless convinced of the generosity behind his offer.

The psychopathic character: This person has an illusion about power—that he secretly possesses it and that it is all-important. This illusion is his compensation for the experience of being helpless and powerless in the hands of a seductive and manipulative parent. But to fulfill the illusion in his own mind, he must also hold himself out as a person with wealth or power. When the psychopathic character gets power, as not infrequently happens, it becomes a dangerous situation, for he cannot separate his real power from his ego image of himself as a person of power. And so power will not be used constructively, but in the interest of furthering his ego image.

One patient told me that for years he had the image of himself carrying a money bag with $8,000,000—an image that made him feel powerful and important. When I saw him in therapy, he had amassed several million dollars, and the realization began to dawn that he was neither powerful nor important. The word "realization" denotes a facing of reality. The illusion of power—of what it can do for one—is very common in our culture. Its anithesis to pleasure is discussed in *Pleasure*.*

The masochistic character: Every masochistic character feels inferior. He or she was shamed and humilated as a child, but inwardly he thinks of himself as superior to others. Supporting this image are suppressed feelings of contempt for the therapist, for his boss and for everyone who, in reality, is in a superior position.

One of the reasons why working with this problem is so difficult is that a patient with this character structure cannot afford to let the therapy succeed. The success of the therapy would prove the therapist was a better (more competent) person than the patient. What a bind! This illusion explains in part why the masochistic character has such an investment in failure. Failure is always explained away on the basis of "I didn't try hard enough," which means he could really succeed if he wanted to. Failure, in an inverted way, supports his illusion of superiority.

The rigid character: This structure arises out of the rejection by a parent of the child's love. The child experienced a sense of betrayal and heartbreak. In self-defense he armored himself or set up his guard against expressing love too openly for fear of betrayal. His love is guarded. But though this is the reality of his way of being in the world, he doesn't see himself in this light. His illusion or self-image is that *he* is the loving person whose love is not appreciated.

The analysis of the rigid character raises an interesting thought. He *is* a loving person. His heart is open to love, but its communication is guarded, not free. If one holds back the expression of love, its value is reduced; so the rigid individual is a loving person in feeling, but not in action. The interesting point is that the illusion is not all false; there is an element of reality in it, leading one to wonder, "Is that true of all illusions?" Without having fully thought it out, my immediate answer is yes. There

*Lowen, *Pleasure, op. cit.*

must be some kernel of truth or reality in every illusion which may help us understand why a person holds onto them so tenaciously. Here are some examples:

There is some truth to the schizoid individual's image of being special. Some of them actually become special and outstanding in their lifetimes. Genius is not so far removed from insanity, as we all know. Can we say that their *rejection* by the mother was related to their being special in her eyes? I believe there is some validity to this view.

The oral character *is* a giver. Unfortunately, he has little to give. One can see his illusion, therefore, as based on feeling, not behavior. In the adult world, only the behavior passes for the real coin.

The psychopathic character *had* something his parent wanted; otherwise he would not have been an object of seduction and manipulation. As a child he must have been aware of this and got from it his first taste of power. True, he was really helpless, and so his power was only in his mind, but he learned a fact of life he used later: Whenever anybody needs something from you, you have power over them.

It is hard to find a basis for the masochistic character's illusion of superiority, yet I know one must exist. The only thought that occurs to me, which I must offer hesitantly, is that he is superior in his ability to put up with a painful situation. "No one else but a masochist could put up with it," is a common saying of people. He puts up with it and maintains a relationship others would long since have abandoned. Is there any virtue in this attitude? In some cases there may be. When another person is absolutely dependent on you, your submission to the situation may have a noble quality. I suspect this was the masochistic character's experience of his relationship to his mother, and it left him with some inner sense of worth.

The danger with an illusion or ego image is that it blinds a person to reality. The masochistic character cannot tell when it is noble to submit to a painful situation and when it is self-defeating and masochistic. Similarly, the rigid character cannot tell when his behavior is loving or not. We not only are blinded by illusions, but are hung up on the ego images they contain. Being hung up, we do not have our feet on the ground and cannot discover our true selves.

Hang-Ups

A person is said to be "hung up" when he is caught in an emotional conflict that immobilizes him and prevents any effective action to change the situation. In such conflicts there are two opposing feelings, each blocking the other from expression. The girl who is hung up on a boy is a good illustration. On one hand, she is attracted to the boy and feels she needs him; on the other, she fears his rejection and senses she will be hurt if she moves toward him. Unable to move forward for fear and away because of desire, she is thoroughly hung up. A person can get hung up on a job to which he is not committed but which he is afraid to leave because of the security it represents. One is hung up in any situation where conflicting feelings prevent any effective movement from occurring.

Hang-ups can be conscious or unconscious. If a person is aware of the conflict but cannot resolve it, he *feels* hung up by it. However, a person can be hung up by conflicts that occurred in childhood, whose memory has been long repressed. In this case, he is not conscious of being hung up.

Every hang-up, conscious or unconscious, limits an individual's freedom to move in all areas of life, not just in that of conflict. A girl hung up on a boy will find her work or study will suffer and her relationships with family and friends will also be affected. And this is true, though to a lesser degree, of unconscious hang-ups, which, like all unresolved emotional conflicts, become structured in the body in the form of chronic muscular tensions. These muscular tensions actually hang up the body in ways I shall describe shortly.

It is not generally appreciated that every illusion a person has hangs him up. He is caught in an unresolvable conflict between the demands of reality, on one hand, and the attempt to fulfill the illusion, on the other. The person is unwilling to surrender his illusions, for this would represent a defeat to his ego. At the same time he cannot fully ignore the demands of reality. And since he is to some degree out of touch with reality, it often has a frightening and threatening aspect. He still sees reality through the eyes of a desperate child.

The problem is further complicated by the fact that illusions have a secret life, or to put it differently, that illusions and daydreams are part of the secret life of most people. It may surprise my readers if I tell them this secret life is rarely spontaneously revealed to a psychiatrist. That, at least, has been my experience, and I don't think it is unique. I don't believe the withholding of this information is deliberate; most patients simply do not see its relevance. They focus on the immediate problem for which they seek help and do not think that their images, illusions and fantasies are important. Of course, they are important, and we must assume there is an unconscious denial operative in keeping this information hidden. But sooner or later it must and does come out.

I treated a young man for a depression of very long standing. The therapy involved intensive body work, breathing, movement and expressing feeling to which the patient responded favorably. At the same time he revealed quite a lot of information about his childhood which seemed to explain his problem. But the depression continued, although with each session there was some slight improvement in his attitude. And so it went for several years. He firmly believed bioenergetics would help him, and I was prepared to stay with him.

One of the significant events of his childhood was the death of his mother when he was nine. She died of cancer and had been bedridden for some time before that. At her death my patient said he felt very little emotion, though he recounted that his mother was devoted to him. He denied feeling any grief, which was very difficult to understand. One could see this denial as the cause of his later depression, but it was a barrier we could not penetrate.

The breakthrough occurred at a clinical seminar when I presented this young man to my colleagues. At the presentation we analyzed his body problem, using the language of the body, and reviewed his history. He admitted to still being depressed. Then one of my associates made a surprising remark. "You believed you could bring your mother back from the dead," she said. My patient looked at her with a sheepish grin on his face as if to say, "How did you know?" and then said, "Yes."

How she knew, I don't know. It was a beautiful intuition, and it uncovered an illusion on which this patient had been hung up for more than twenty years. I don't believe he would have revealed it voluntarily. He may have been trying to hide it from himself, perhaps out of shame. Its coming to light made a marked difference in the course of the therapy.

Every therapy needs some intuitive insights by the therapist. It also needs the therapist's understanding of where the patient is as a person. If we cannot easily uncover the illusions a patient has, although some are easily exposed, we can determine that the person is hung up and see some of its mechanics. We can do this because the hang-up is revealed in the physical expression of the body. Seeing the hang-up, we can infer the illusion, whether we know its exact nature or not.

There are two ways to determine from the body's expression whether a person is hung up or not. The first is to see how well grounded he is. Being grounded is the opposite of being hung up. Having one's feet on the ground is body language revealing that the person is in touch with reality; it means he is not operating under any illusions, conscious or unconscious. In a literal sense everyone has his feet on the ground; in an energetic sense, however, this is not always the case. If a person's energy does not flow strongly into his feet, his energetic or feeling contact with the ground is very limited. A light contact, as in electrical circuits, is not always sufficient to ensure the flow of the current.

To appreciate the validity of the energetic view, consider what happens when a person is on a high. There are all kinds of highs, but characteristic of all is the sense that one's feet are off the ground. In an alcoholic high, for example, the individual has great difficulty sensing the earth under his feet and his contact is insecure. This could be blamed on his alcohol-induced lack of coördination. However, the same sensation is felt when the high results from some very exciting news. One feels as if he were sailing along. A person in love dances along, his feet hardly touching the ground. A drug high gives the sensation of floating—one which is also occasionally experienced by schizoid individuals. When a person moves through his environment seemingly without contact with his surroundings, we call him a floater.

The bioenergetic explanation for the high is the withdrawal upward of energy from the feet and legs. The greater the withdrawal, the higher the person seems to rise, since in an energetic or feeling sense, he is further removed from the ground. In a high produced by an exciting event—the achievement of an important objective, for example—the withdrawal of energy from the legs and feet is part of an upward surge of excitation and energy to the head. It is accompanied by a corresponding flow of blood, flushing the face with color and animating the whole person. In a drug high, on the other hand, this upward flow occurs initially; then energy is withdrawn from the head, as it is also from the lower part of the body. The face loses color, the eyes become dull or glazed, and there is a loss of animation. Nevertheless, there is a sense of being high owing to upward withdrawal of energy from the ground. At the other end of the body the withdrawal of energy from the head produces a dissociated state of the mind, which seems to float free from its bodily confines.

The second way one can see the hang-up physically is in the carriage or posture of the upper half of the body. There are several common hang-ups; the one most frequently seen is what I have called the coat-hanger type. It is almost exclusive to men. The shoulders are raised and somewhat squared off, head and neck incline forward. The arms hang loosely from their joints, and the chest is also raised. I call this the coat hanger because it looks as if the body were held up by an invisible hanger:

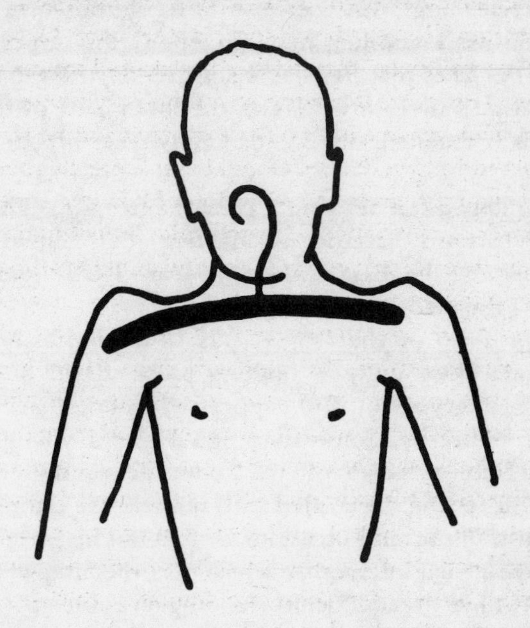

An analysis of the body expression reveals the dynamics of this hang-up. The raised shoulders are an expression of fear. One can prove this by assuming an expression of fright. Notice that the shoulders go up automatically and there is a gasp of air as the chest becomes inflated. When the reaction is love, the shoulders normally drop. Habitually raised shoulders reveal that the person is locked in an attitude of fear he cannot shrug off, since he is unaware of being frightened. Generally, the situation that caused the fear is forgotten, and the emotion itself has been suppressed. Such habitual postures do not develop from a single experience but represent a continued exposure to a frightening situation. This could, for example, be the experience of a boy who was long afraid of his father.

The compensation for this attitude of fear is to bring the head forward as if to confront the threat or at least to see if there is a threat. Since leading with the head is dangerous in a physical confrontation with another man, in effect, this aspect of the posture is a denial of fear. It says, "I don't see anything to be afraid of." This posture necessarily affects the lower part of the body. When one is frightened, one treads lightly. Fear lifts one off the ground.

Being frightened but denying it creates a hang-up. The person can't move forward because of his fear, but neither can he withdraw because he has denied his fear. He is immobilized emotionally—the nature of a hang-up.

The suppression of the fear results in a suppression of the related anger. Since there is nothing to be afraid of, there is nothing to be angry about. But suppressed feelings have a way of coming out indirectly. Some time ago I saw a young man in consultation who was a leader in the student activist movement. He complained of feeling dissatisfied with himself. He did not feel at ease with girls. On several occasions he had lost his erection while trying to have sexual intercourse which disturbed him very much. He also said he had great difficulty deciding on a career.

An examination of this young man's body revealed that his shoulders and chest were raised and pulled up, his belly pulled in, his pelvis tilted forward and tightly held, and his head tilted forward on a short neck. This posture made the upper half of his body appear to lean forward. He had watchful eyes and a hard, grimly held jaw.

Looking at his legs, I saw that they were tight and rigid and that he had some difficulty in bending his knees. His feet were cold to the touch and seemingly without feeling or charge. When he tried to assume the bow position, his pelvis was retracted, breaking the arch of the body. I sensed that very little feeling or charge flowed into the lower part of his body, which explained his sexual difficulty. He admitted he sensed a lack of feeling in his legs. I should add, too, that his breathing was very shallow with almost no abdominal involvement in the respiratory movements.

Given his personal problems, it might surprise the reader to learn that this young man decided not to go into therapy. As we discussed his problem, it became evident to me he was too hung up on the student movement to *let down* sufficiently to face the reality of his personal situation. What illusions he had about how this activity could help him resolve his personal difficulties I never learned. But it was apparent that he had transferred the fight for personal dignity and freedom to the social scene, where he could maintain the image of an aggressive male against the reality of personal failure.

A common hang-up in women is represented by the dowager's or widow's hump which is a mass of tissue that accumulates just below the seventh cervical vertebra at the junction of the neck, shoulders and trunk. This protuberance derives its name from the fact that it is rarely seen in young women but is not uncommon in older ones. From its appearance, I call this a meat-hook hang-up because it seems to me that a meat hook would produce such a configuration (below).

The location of the hump is the point where the feeling of anger would flow out into the arms and upward into the head. In animals,

a cat or a dog, the feeling of anger is manifested by the erection of hair along the spine and by the arching of the back. Darwin pointed this out in *The Expression of the Emotions in Man and Animals.** My reading of the body tells me the hump is produced by the pileup of blocked anger. Its occurrence in older women indicates that it represents the gradual piling up of unexpressed anger as a result of a lifetime's frustration. Many older women have a tendency to become shorter and heavier as they pull into themselves with advancing years.

I should make it clear that what is blocked is the physical expression of anger in hitting, not its verbal expression. Some dowagers or widows are noted for their sharp tongues.

My analysis of the problem represented by the hump is that it involves a conflict between an attitude of submission—that is, being a good girl to please father and family and strong feelings of anger at the sexual frustration such an attitude entails. The problem had its origin in the oedipal situation in which young girls are trapped by conflicting feelings toward their fathers—love and sexual feelings on one side and anger and frustration on the other. This results in a hang-up, since a girl cannot express her anger for fear of disapproval and the loss of his love, nor can she move toward her father with sexual feeling, since this would lead to rejection and disgrace. I am not speaking of sexual contact with a father but of pleasurable erotic contact which is part of the normal expression of affection. What is involved is a father's acceptance of his daughter's sexuality. Submission to the requirement that she be a good girl, which, of course, implies an acceptance of the double standard of sexual morality, immobilizes a woman in her striving for sexual pleasure. It forces her to assume a passive role. We can

*Charles Darwin, *The Expression of the Emotions in Man and Animals* (London, Watts & Co., 1934). Darwin says, "I saw the hair on the Anubis baboon, when angered, bristling along the back from the neck to the loin," p. 40. With carnivores, Darwin notes this action "seems to be almost universal, often accompanied by threatening movements, the uncovering of the teeth, and the utterance of savage growls," p. 41.

imagine the illusions a girl develops to compensate her loss of sexual aggressiveness.

There is another way a woman gets hung up by sexual morality and that is by being placed on a pedestal. I have described such a case in *Depression and the Body.* Elevation to a pedestal takes one off the ground just as surely as any other hang-up. In the case I treated the patient's body from the pelvis down *looked* like a pedestal. It was rigid and immobile and seemed to serve only as a base for the upper half.

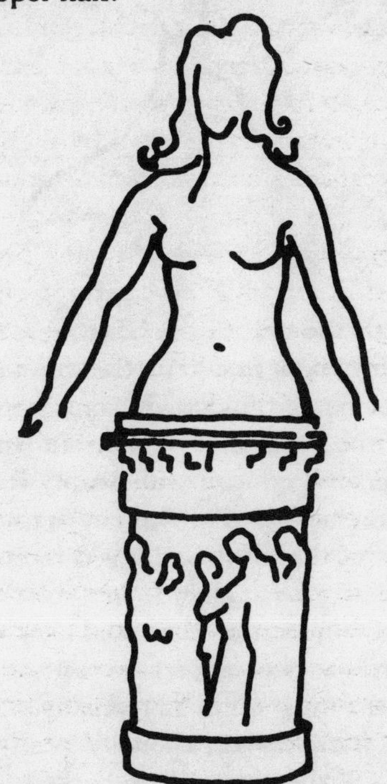

Two more hang-ups deserve mention. One is associated with the schizoid character structure and it is called the noose because the posture of the body resembles the figure of a man who has been hanged. The head hangs slightly to the side (illustration, p. 192),

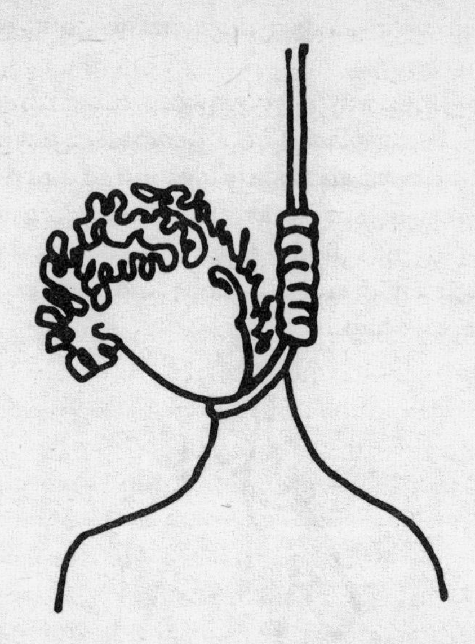

as if its connection with the rest of the body were broken. In the schizoid structure there is a break in the connection of head functions or ego functions and body functions. Being hung up by the neck pulls one off the ground. The schizoid personality is not grounded, and the person's contact with reality is tenuous. Most significant, however, is the fact that the key tension area in this structure is at the base of the skull, and it is this tension that splits the unity of the personality. Actually the muscular tensions in this area form a ring at the junction of head and neck which operates like a noose. In bioenergetics considerable work is done on these tensions to reestablish the unity of the personality.

Finally, there is a hang-up occasionally seen in borderline schizophrenics that I call the cross. If one asks such a person to hold his arms out to the sides, one is struck sometimes by the very strong impression that the body posture resembles pictures showing Christ crucified or just after he was taken down from the cross. Many schizophrenics have a strong identification with Jesus Christ, and some even develop the delusion that they *are* Christ. To see this identification acted out on the body level is astonishing.

These body attitudes revealing an individual's hang-ups are not intended as a complete list. I have seen several people whose bodies and facial expression bore a striking resemblance to the pictures of Moses as he is commonly portrayed. I am sure this indicates a hang-up in the personality, but I have not studied this problem in sufficient depth to make any definitive statement about it. Others on the body level may come to light in the future.

Knowing what a person's hang-up is by reading it from the body is a great help in understanding him. But if we can't describe his hang-up by looking at the body because its expression is not always clear, we can know with certainty that every person who does not have his feet firmly planted on the ground, energetically speaking, is hung up and has unresolved emotional problems. To the extent that he is not grounded, he is not fully in touch with reality. This knowledge governs my approach to every patient, for I begin by helping him become more firmly grounded and more in touch with all aspects of his reality. Sooner or later in every therapy the underlying conflicts come to the surface, and the nature of the person's hang-up, together with the illusions that are its psychic counterpart, becomes evident to both of us.

Grounding

In bioenergetics grounding means getting a person down to solid ground. Being grounded is the opposite of being hung up. But like so much of bioenergetics, it also has a literal meaning—namely, of establishing adequate contact with the ground, on which one stands.

Most people think they have their feet on the ground and in a mechanical sense they do. We can say they make mechanical contact but not a feeling or energetic contact. But one doesn't know the difference until one has experienced it. At Esalen some years ago, during one of my semiannual visits to teach bioenergetics, I was approached by a young woman who conducted *t'ai chi* classes for residents and guests. She told me that though she had tried the bioenergetic exercises, she had never been able to develop any vibrations in her legs. She had seen them occur in the legs of people participating in my workshop, and she wondered why they eluded her. I may add that this young woman had been a dancer before she became a teacher of *t'ai chi*. When I offered to work with her, she accepted eagerly. I used three exercises. The first was the bow position described in Chapter II which would help line up her body and deepen her breathing. Some people respond to the stress of this exercise by vibrating slightly, but not this person. Her legs were too tight and too rigid. She needed a stronger stress to break down the rigidity so that the vibratory movements could occur. It involved standing on one leg with bent knee and balancing herself by touching a chair at her side. All the weight of her body was on the bent leg. She was told to hold the position as long as she could and then, when the pain became too great, to collapse onto a blanket placed on the floor in front of her. She did this exercise twice on each leg alternately. The third exercise involved bending forward with knees slightly bent and touching the ground with the fingertips (illustration, opposite page).

As a result of the first two exercises, her breathing had become fuller and deeper. As she did the third, in which the only stress is on the hamstring muscles if they are tight, her legs began to vibrate. She remained in this position for a while, sensing the feeling. When she got up, she said, "I've been *on* my legs all my life. This is the first time I've been *in* them." I believe that statement is true of many people.

In very disturbed individuals, there may be almost no feeling in their feet. I recall another young woman who was close to a schizophrenic state. She had come to her appointment with me wearing only a pair of sneakers though it was a rainy, winter day in New York. When she took off her sneakers, I saw her feet were blue with cold. Yet when I asked her if they were cold, she said no. She didn't feel them as cold—she just didn't feel them.

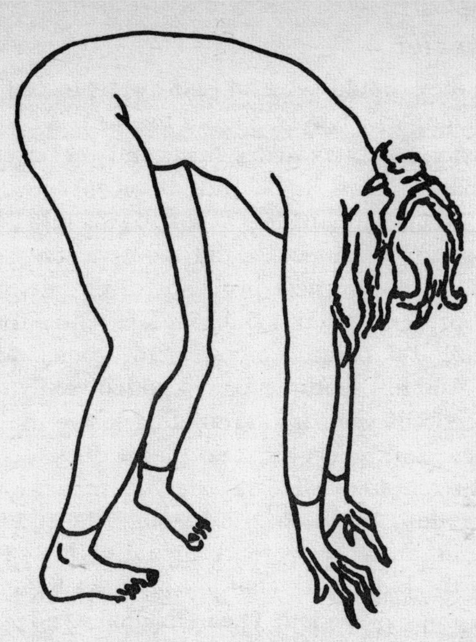

In demonstrating some of the bioenergetic techniques to professionals, after explaining the concept of grounding, I get them to do a few of the simple grounding exercises to develop vibrations in their own legs. The vibratory phenomenon increases sensation and feeling in the legs and feet. Very often when this happens, they report, "I really feel my legs and feet. I never felt them this way before." This experience gives some idea of what grounding is about and that it is possible to sense one's self more fully in contact with one's base of support.

A few exercises do not fully ground a person, though. One has to work with them regularly to achieve and maintain the feeling of security and sense of being rooted that a well-grounded position provides. In the dream recalled in Chapter III, I described how I was bound by a flimsy wire about my ankle which I could have easily removed. In the dream all I had to do was bend down and take it apart. But what did that mean in reality? Working with my legs more recently, I experienced how bound my ankles were. True, they are not as tight as most ankles I see, but neither are they as loose as they should be. And I am aware, too, of tensions in my feet. For example, it is very painful for me to sit on my heels with my feet extended. My ankles hurt, and the arches of my feet develop spasms. One day during a bioenergetic exercise class conducted by my wife, my legs shook so violently I felt they would not hold me up. Of course they did, but it was a new experience for me. I could attribute these problems to my age, past sixty-three now, but I prefer to think I still have a potential for growth that I could realize if I became more deeply rooted and more fully grounded. And so I continue to work with myself.

Bioenergetically speaking, grounding serves the same function for the organism's energy system that it does for a high-tension electrical circuit. It provides a safety valve for the discharge of excess excitation. In an electrical system the sudden buildup of charge could burn out a part or cause fire. In the human personality the buildup of charge could also be dangerous if the person were not grounded. The individual could split off, become hysterical, experience anxiety or go into a slump. The danger is especially great in people who are poorly grounded, such as borderline schizophrenics. My associates and I make it a practice with these people to balance exercises that build up the charge (breathing) with activities that discharge the excitation (the expression of feeling) and exercises that ground the person. When a person leaves a session or a workshop feeling very high, there is good probability he or she will crash. This is not serious if the person anticipates and can handle the down. However, when a person leaves feeling good and solid, the odds are he will hold this feeling.

In the present state of our knowledge we do not fully understand the energetic connection between the feet and the ground. That there is one, I feel certain. What I do know surely is that the more a person can feel his contact with the ground, the more he can hold his ground, the more charge he can tolerate and the more feeling he can handle. This makes grounding a prime objective in bioenergetic work. It implies that the major thrust of the work is downward—that is, to get the person *into* his legs and feet.

One may wonder why this should be so difficult. Clearly, the downward movement is always more frightening than going up. For example, the landing of a plane is more frightening than the takeoff. Coming down arouses in most people a fear of falling ordinarily suppressed. In the next chapter I will discuss the anxiety associated with the idea of falling, which, I have found, is one of the deepest in the human personality. At this point I would like to describe some of the problems encountered as one allows his energy and feelings to flow downward in his body.

Generally, the first feeling one experiences as one "lets down" is sadness. If the person can accept and give in to the feeling, he will begin to cry. We say that one "breaks down" into tears. There is a deep sadness in every person who is hung up, and many would prefer to stay hung up than face their sadness, for in most people it verges on despair. One can face the despair and go through the sadness if one has the help of an understanding therapist, but let me say that it is no easy undertaking. The sadness and crying are held in the belly, which is also the chamber where the charge accumulates for the breakthrough to sexual release and satisfaction. The way to joy invariably leads through despair.*

Deep pelvic sexual feelings are also very frightening to many people. They can tolerate the limited excitation of genital charge which is superficial and easily discharged and poses no demand for total surrender to the orgastic convulsions. The sweet, melting sensations of pelvic sexuality lead to this surrender and evoke the fear of loss of control that is one aspect of falling anxiety. The problem we encounter in therapy is not genitality but sexuality—the fear of melting or letting down into the fires of passion that burn in the belly and pelvis.

Finally, there is the anxiety of standing in one's own feet which connotes standing *alone.* As adults we all stand alone; that is the reality of our existence. But most people, I have found, are reluctant to accept this reality, for to them it means being alone. Behind a facade of independence, they cling to relationships and

*Lowen, *Pleasure, op.cit.*

become hung up. By hanging onto a relationship, they destroy its value, and yet they are afraid to let go and stand on their own feet. Once they do, they are surprised to find they are not alone, since the relationship improves so that it becomes a source of pleasure to both parties. The difficulty is in the transition, for in the interval between letting go and feeling one's feet solid on the ground, one experiences the sensation of falling and the anxiety it evokes.

VII. Falling Anxiety

The Fear of Height

Falling anxiety is commonly associated with a fear of heights; most people experience it when standing near the edge of a cliff. No matter that their feet are on solid ground and there is no real danger of falling; they become dizzy and sense a loss of balance. Falling anxiety must be a uniquely human experience, since all four-footed animals in a similar situation feel surefooted. In some people this anxiety is so severe that simply riding in a car over a bridge can produce a similar reaction; such a case is clearly pathological.

There are others who seem singularly devoid of this anxiety. I have watched in amazement and awe at steelworkers moving about easily on narrow girders high above the tumultuous city. I could not imagine myself being up there; my anxiety would be too great, for I have long been afraid of heights. I recall as a child of eight being lifted onto my father's shoulders to see a parade and feeling terrified. At this time, too, I was scared of the roller coaster when my father wanted to take me on it. Later I overcame that fear by riding one every day while working at an amusement park. Over the years my fear of height has greatly diminished which I attribute to the work I have done with my legs to become grounded and secure. Now I can work on a high ladder or look down from a height without feeling much anxiety.

There are two reasons for the seeming security of people who show no falling anxiety. Some, like American Indians, are definitely surefooted. They were among the first steelworkers to be employed in high construction jobs. Other people have unconsciously denied their fear. In *The Betrayal of the Body* I reported the case of a schizoid young man who had extremely tight, tense legs with little feeling in them. He suffered from a severe depression associated with a feeling that "nothing happens" to him in a meaningful, emotional way. This patient had no falling anxiety, however.

> Bill was a rock climber, one of the best, he said. He had made many ascents of steep cliffs without any fear or hesitation. He was not afraid of heights or of falling. He was not afraid because in one part of his personality he did not care if he fell. He related an incident about a time when he was climbing alone and lost his foothold on the cliff. For moments he dangled, holding on with his hands to a narrow ledge. while he groped for a toehold, his mind was detached. He wondered, "What would it be like if I fell?" He felt no panic.*

Bill felt no fear because he had cut off all feeling, and that was also why nothing ever happened emotionally in his life. But at the same time he was desperate for something that would break down or break open the icy cold, impersonal will enveloping him like a chrysalis. He wanted something to reach his heart, but first the chrysalis would have to be smashed. He was tempted; he had impulses to touch high-tension electric wires and to step in front of

*Lowen, *Betrayal of the Body, op.cit.*, p. 107.

speeding cars. He said he would like to jump off a cliff if he could do it safely. He wanted to fall so that, like Humpty Dumpty, his shell would crack, but he was afraid it would mean the end of him.

Bill was a cliff-hanger with all the implications this position implies. He seemed to have only two choices—hang on or let go. Letting go meant falling to his death, which Bill was not prepared to do, but as long as he hung on, he was hung up, and nothing happened.

Recently I saw a young woman who told me that as a girl she had absolutely no falling anxiety, but that lately it had emerged as a real terror. She had obsessive fantasies of falling. This development coincided with a change in her life. She had dissolved a bad marriage and was working hard to get her feet on the ground both in her life and in her therapy. She could not understand why she had become afraid of falling and asked me about it. I explained that she had begun to "let go," that she was not hanging on any longer, and so her suppressed fear of falling surfaced dramatically.

The fear of falling is a transitional stage between being hung up and having one's feet solidly on the ground. In the latter case there is no fear of falling; in the former it is denied by an illusion. If we accept this analysis, then every patient who starts to let go of his illusions and tries to get down to the ground will experience some falling anxiety. The same thing is true of choking anxiety that only arises when an impulse to reach out is choked off or back. As long as this impulse is allowed expression only within the limits imposed by the character structure, no anxiety is experienced. Transgressing these limits gives rise to anxiety.

In the general discussion of anxiety in Chapter IV, I observed that the overall degree of anxiety in a person was equivalent to the degree of choking anxiety. This means that a person who has choking anxiety will have an equal amount of falling anxiety and vice versa. This follows from the concept that the flow of excitation to all the peripheral points or organs of the body is roughly equal.

In our study of the different character structures we saw that each character type was related to a certain kind of falling anxiety, although that term was not used there. The schizoid character structure represented a *holding together* out of fear that letting go meant *falling apart.* If the term "falling apart" is taken literally, it implies that, for the schizoid character, the act of falling would lead to his coming apart or being smashed. We would expect, therefore, to find in this character structure an intense falling anxiety. Such is the case when this anxiety surfaces as it does occasionally in dreams.

One schizoid patient told me, "I used to dream about falling—one was especially bad. I dreamed that wherever I stood, the floor would give way. I changed my spot, and that began to give way. I climbed the stairs, but that, too, crumbled. So I decided to go to my father and have him hold me up, because I knew he couldn't fall. But it was uncertain. It was better than being alone but not fully safe. It was very terrifying."

We can easily understand why this dream would be terrifying. People experience the same terror in an earthquake when the ground under their feet loses its stability. The sense that there is no solid ground undermines our orientation as human beings. A person feels "spaced out," and unless he has undergone some rigorous training for such an experience, it is terrifying. The senses reel, and the very integrity of the personality is temporarily threatened.

In the other character types their fear of falling is also related to their structures. For the *oral character,* the fear of falling carries with it the anxiety that he would be alone because he would fall behind or fall back. If his legs let go, he would be like a little child who suddenly sits down when his legs no longer support him, only to discover his parents have moved on and there is no one there to pick him up.

In the *psychopathic character* the fear of falling is a fear of failing. As long as he is up, he is one up on the world. Down means defeat, which leaves him open to being used.

For the *masochistic character* falling means the bottom's falling out. This could signify the end of his world, or of his relationship.

There is also an anal element in this attitude. If he lets the bottom fall out (defecation), he would mess up, which would be the end of his role as a good little boy.

For the *rigid character* falling is a loss of pride. He would fall forward on his face, and his ego might be smashed. When one's personality is strongly linked with feelings of independence and freedom, this is no slight anxiety.

For every patient, then, falling represents a surrender or giving up of his holding pattern—that is, of his defensive position. But since this position was developed as a survival mechanism and to ensure some measure of contact, some degree of independence and freedom, its surrender will evoke all the anxiety that originally necessitated its development. One can ask a patient to risk doing this because his situation as an adult is different from that of his childhood. Realistically speaking, the schizoid individual will not fall apart if he lets go, nor will he be annihilated if he asserts himself. If we as therapists can help him get through the anxiety of the transition stage, he will find that the ground under his feet is solid and that he has the ability to stand on it. One of the procedures I use to achieve this end is an exercise in falling.

An Exercise in Falling

At the outset let me say that this exercise, which I find very effective, is only one of the many body mobilization procedures used in bioenergetics.

I place a heavy folded blanket or a mat on the floor and ask my patient to stand in front of it, so that when he falls, he will land on the blanket. There is no way a person can get hurt in this exercise, and no one has ever been hurt. As the person stands before me, I try to get an impression of his attitude, the way he holds himself or the way he stands in the world. Making this evaluation requires skill in reading the language of the body, experience with many different people and a good imagination. At this point I generally have some knowledge of the person—of his problems and his history. But if I cannot obtain a clear impression of the person's attitude, I count on the exercise itself to reveal his hang-up.

He is then asked to put all his weight on one leg, bending that knee fully. The other foot touches the floor lightly and is used only for balance. The directions are very simple. The person is to stand in that position until he falls, but he is not to let himself fall. Letting one's self down consciously is not falling since the person controls the descent. To be effective, the fall should have an involuntary quality. If the mind is set on holding the position, then the fall will represent the release of the body from conscious control. Since most people are afraid to lose control of their bodies, this in itself is anxiety-provoking.

In one respect this exercise resembles a Zen koan in that the ego or will is challenged, yet rendered powerless. One cannot stay in this position indefinitely yet one is obliged to use his will not to let himself fall. In the end, the will must yield, not by a voluntary act but by the superior force of nature, in this case gravity. One learns that giving in to the superior forces of nature does not have a destructive effect and that one does not have to use his will constantly to fight these forces. Whatever its origin, every holding pattern represents in the present the unconscious use of the will against the natural forces of life.

The purpose of this exercise is to uncover hang-ups that keep a person suspended and create an anxiety about falling. It probes a person's contact with reality. For example, a young woman standing in front of the blanket and looking at it said she felt she was a mile up in the air looking down on a plain. Falling from this height would be a frightening experience, and she was afraid of it. Then, when she finally fell with a scream and lay on the blanket, she experienced a great sense of relief and release. The ground was only a short distance away. I had her repeat the exercise using her other leg, and this time she did not feel so far above the ground.

People have different visions when they look at the blanket.

Some see a rocky terrain against which they will smash if they fall. Others see a body of water into which they will plunge. Both falling and water have a significance as sexual symbols that I will explore later. Still others see faces, of either their mother or father. For these people falling represents a surrender or giving in to the parents.

The exercise is made more effective if the person lets his body collapse while resting on one leg. He is encouraged to drop his chest and breathe easily to let feeling develop. And I also ask him to keep saying, "I am going to fall," for that is what is going to happen. At first when he says these words, the voice is without any emotional tone. But as the pain increases and the prospect of falling becomes clearer, the voice may rise in pitch and carry a note of fear.

Not infrequently the person will spontaneously exclaim, "I am *not* going to fall." This will be said with determination, sometimes with fists clenched. Now the struggle is on in earnest. I will then ask the person, "What does falling mean to you?" Often the answer is "failing." And, "I am *not* going to fail." One young woman struggled dramatically, going through this exercise four times, twice on each leg. These are her words:

First time: "I am not going to fall."

"I am not going to fail."

"I've always failed," and with that remark she fell and began to cry deeply.

Second time: "I am not going to fall."

"I am not going to fail."

"I always fail. I always will fail." Again she falls and cries.

Third time: "But I don't want to fail. I didn't have to fall. I could have stayed up forever."

"I'm not going to fall." But as the pain increased, so did the realization she would fall.

"I can't stay up forever. But I can't." And with that remark, she fell and began to cry.

Fourth time: "I'm not going to fail."

"Every time I try I fail."

"I'm not going to try."

"But I have to try." Then the falling and the realization it must end in failure.

Why must it end in failure? I asked her what she was trying to accomplish. Her answer was: "Be what people expect me to be." That's an impossible task, like staying up forever. If one undertakes such a task, one is bound to fail, for no one can be other than what he or she is. No body would continue such a senseless endeavor—that consumes so much vital energy—unless the ego (in Freudian terms, the superego) was driving it on. To throw off this tyranny, and to free oneself from the unreality of the goal and the illusion that it could be achieved one has to become painfully aware of its impossibility. This is what the exercise aims to accomplish and that is what eventually happened.

Every patient is engaged in a neurotic struggle to be different from who he is, since who he is proved unacceptable to his parents. When a person enters therapy, his hope is that the therapist will help him achieve this goal. It is true he needs to make some changes in his personality, but the direction of change is toward self-awareness and self-acceptance, not toward the fulfillment of an image. This direction is downward, toward the ground and reality. But as long as the person is engaged in this neurotic struggle to fulfill the demands of others he remains hung up on the conflicts of his childhood. There is no way out of this struggle except by surrender.

This problem of the neurotic struggle is vividly illustrated in the following case. Jim came to his session and reported this dream: "Last night I dreamed I was trying to pull myself along the ground on shriveled, dead legs. I had to use the upper half of my body to move." Then he added, "In the past I've had dreams of floating." The lower half of his body was very rigid and tight. He had undergone a spinal fusion in the lumbosacral region because of severe lower-back trouble. His dream was an accurate portrayal of his energetic condition.

Right after recalling the dream, Jim remarked, "I had a fantasy this morning of my mother being a snake. I could see her face as a snake. She was a boa constrictor wrapped around my waist constricting me. Her head was on my penis, sucking it. My mother told me that when I was little, I was so cute that she kissed me everywhere and on my penis. When I tell you this, I become hazy, spaced out, and begin to sweat."

He then went into the falling exercise which revealed the intensity of his struggle. He said, "It feels like I give up, but I don't fall. I'm going to hold on forever. I'm not going to fall."

To himself, he said, "Jim, you're going to hold on forever."

And addressing me, he remarked, "If I fall, I'll drop into a bottomless pit. You know the feeling of falling where your stomach tightens up and you can't breathe. I had fantasies of flying as a child. I even tried to fly, but I fell. My parents came and spanked me for frightening them.

"I should be able to hold. I have this idea very strong. I get angry at myself for letting go. I give up too soon. I'm a coward, cop-out, a cry baby. My mother made me feel a failure if I couldn't hold on and take it. Her motto was 'The difficult we do right away; the impossible takes a little longer.'"

At this time Jim was not prepared to abandon the struggle. His fear of falling was too great. Both Jim and I had to accept where he was at and continue to work with the problem. I gave him a turkish towel, which he twisted with both hands. As he was doing this, he remarked, "It's a snake. I've got to hold onto it or it"—(and he knew this referred to his mother)— "will get me."

Jim was a psychotherapist himself, so there was little need for me to offer any interpretations of his fantasies. He knew that his mother was seductive and that giving up meant giving in to his sexual feeling for her. If he had done that as a child, she would have swallowed him, not literally but in the sense that he would have been consumed by his passion for her and have lost any feeling of being independent. His defense was to constrict his waist and cut off his sexual feelings. This is a psychopathic defense, but

Jim had no alternative. Even now, he could not risk the surrender of that position. One has to bear with a patient as he works through these very deeply structured conflicts.

At a later session Jim returned to his fear of falling. When he came in, he told me "Driving my car, I found myself tapping the wheel. I put words to the action, and it was 'I'm going to kill you.' "

We started again with the falling exercise, and Jim said, "When you told me to say, 'I'm going to fall,' the feeling I had was that I'm going to die. I feel like it's a life-and-death struggle. If I let go, I'm going to be killed. If I kill them, then I'm going to be killed.

"The way I operate is very tricky. I can't stay in an intense situation for long periods, but I can hang in forever. When everybody else has quit, I continue to hang in until I win or accomplish the task." Saying this, he clenched his fists. "It's a long trip, and I just put one foot after the other, plodding on.

"My mother's needling was a kind of grinding away at me. I do the same thing to myself and others. I push, I push, and I struggle. Yet I believe I am a quitter. I say to myself, Jim, if you weren't a quitter, you'd work harder.' "

This struggle is now transposed to the falling exercise which Jim is doing. He says, "I'm going to fall, I'm going to fail. But I've got to win, I've got to succeed." And then reality asserts itself. He remarks, "Of course, I've already failed."

But Jim can't accept this reality yet. He pounds both thighs with his fists and says, "I'm going to kill myself if I don't hang in. But if I do hang in, I'm going to die. I'm afraid I will get cancer of the lungs. But the more I try not to smoke, the more I smoke."

In the course of this monologue, Jim fell and cried. This was a minor release. He then repeated the exercise on the other leg and continued to express his fears. Venting anxiety like this with strong feeling is a very therapeutic procedure. After the falling exercise was over, Jim recalled an episode out of his childhood that was very revealing.

"I'm afraid that as soon as everything is OK, then I'm going to die. I survive only by struggling. If I stop struggling, I'm going to die. I had septicemia as a child with a high fever, and I was in and out of the hospital for about a year. I was comatose at times. I had to be drained and transfused. I almost died. But I hung in, using all my willpower to live. I know how to exist when it's tough. I don't know how to exist when it's nice."

In view of this experience it is not difficult to see why Jim would associate falling with dying. For Jim both seem to involve a surrender of his will. But it would be foolish to think Jim could make a conscious choice to surrender and trust his body. Such a choice is using the will to deny the will which leads nowhere. Jim's fear of death, the death of his spirit if he gave in to his mother and the death of his body if he ceased to drive it, has to be thoroughly experienced and analyzed. At the same time he has to learn to trust his body and his sexual feelings. Jim is consciously prepared to accept the reality of his body and its sexual feelings, but trusting them will depend on a whole new set of body experiences that therapy should provide.

This specific exercise also helps provide these experiences. Standing with the weight on one leg puts sufficient pressure on the muscles of that leg to tire them. In a state of exhausion the muscles cannot maintain their tension or contraction. They have to let go, and gradually, a strong vibration sets in. This increases the feeling in the leg so that it no longer feels like a "shriveled, dead leg." At the same time the breathing becomes deeper. Tremors may pass through the body, yet the person doesn't fall, and he is surprised to find his leg continues to support him, even though his conscious control of his body has diminished. Then, when the leg does finally let go and the person falls, there is a considerable relief at knowing that one isn't made of iron and that the body will fall when it can no longer maintain its standing. Finally, there is the strong realization that falling is not the end—one is not destroyed, the body can rise again.

The symbolism behind the falling exercise deserves mention. The earth is a symbol for the mother, who in turn is a representative of the earth. Mother and mother earth are the sources of our strength. In one of his many battles Hercules fought with Antaeus. In the fight Hercules knocked Antaeus down repeatedly, but instead of winning the fight, Hercules was losing it. He was becoming tired while Antaeus rebounded from each contact with the earth stronger than before. Then Hercules realized the Antaeus was the son of mother earth and that each time he returned to the earth, he was renewed and strengthened. Hercules then lifted Antaeus and held him in the air until he died.

We are all children of mother earth and of mothers who should be a source of strength to us. Unfortunately, as in the case of Jim, a mother can, instead, be a threat to the child and has to be resisted rather than yielded to. One cannot, then, let *down* without a severe feeling of anxiety. To remain hung up creates a real threat to one's existence because of the energetic processes of the body, whereas to fall may evoke a fear of dying but presents no real danger. Doing the falling exercise brings up the conflict with the mother, which can then be analyzed and worked through, allowing the person to let down or fall with a sense of security. For the earth is there for us.

I recently received a letter from a man I had recommended to a colleague, Dr. Fred Sypher of Toronto for treatment of severe lower-back pain that irradiated down his right leg. "One of the very interesting aspects of treatment with Dr. Sypher," he wrote, "is the contact with the floor. The floor becomes a friend, a solid comforter which is always there, which can keep you from being badly hurt, even though you are hurting. You cannot fall if you are already there, and when you are there, you could deal with a lot of stuff that maybe would be difficult to deal with if you felt you could fall. It made it possible for me to release a lot of the terror that is in me."

In many cases following the exercise in falling, we will do an exercise in rising. I have heard many patients express the fear that if they fell, they would not be able to get up again. They know, of course, that they can pull themselves up by an effort of will. What they are not sure of is that they can *rise* up.

Rising is like growing. A plant, for example, rises from the earth; it doesn't pull itself up. In rising, the force comes from below; in being pulled up, the force comes from above. The classic example of rising is a rocket that rises in proportion to the amount of energy it discharges below. Ordinary walking belongs to this category of movement, for as we make each step forward, we press down on the ground which presses back, sending us forward. The physical principle involved is action-reaction.

In the rising exercise, the person is on both knees on a folded blanket on the floor. His feet are extended behind him. He then puts one foot forward and also leans forward so that part of his weight is shifted to that foot. I ask him to feel his foot on the floor and to rock back and forth on it to increase that feeling. Next, he lifts himself slightly and puts all his weight on the bent forward leg. Now, if he pushes down hard enough on that leg, he will find himself rising. If this is done correctly, one actually feels a force moving upward through the body from the ground, straightening one up from below. However, this is not an easy exercise to do, and most people have to lift themselves up a little to help the process. With practice it becomes easier, and one learns how to direct the energy downward into the leg in order to rise. Generally it is done twice on each leg to develop the feeling of pressing on the ground and rising.

Fat, heavy people have particular difficulty with this exercise. I have seen them try to rise but fall over like a baby. It is as if they had lost the capacity to rise and had therefore resigned themselves psychologically to an infantile level where eating, rather than running and playing, provided life's major interest and satisfaction. I see such people as functioning on two levels simultaneously, an adult level, in which the will is the force that enables them to lift themselves up and move, and an infantile level, in which eating and feeling helpless (especially about eating) are characteristic.

Rising and falling constitute a pair of antithetical functions that cannot exist without each other. If one can't fall, one can't rise. This is clear in the phenomenon of sleep, where we speak of falling asleep and rising in the morning. In place of the natural functions of falling and rising, people who use their will let themselves down and lift themselves up or lie down and get up. If the will is not mobilized, as when one first wakes in the morning, such individuals will have great difficulty getting themselves out of bed. Underlying this problem is falling anxiety, the inability to go to bed early and let oneself *fall* asleep easily. As a result such people are tired in the morning and lack the energy to rise easily.

After a patient has gone through the falling exercise, his body is much looser. Generally my procedure is to let him work with breathing over the stool. Often the breathing takes on a more involuntary character following these exercises with the production of body tremors that may develop into sobs and crying. The person is always encouraged to go with these involuntary body movements because they represent a spontaneous effort by the body to free itself from tension.

Before I move on to the question of how falling anxiety arises, I would like to present one further case: Mark was a homosexual in his middle forties whose basic problem was isolation and loneliness owing to his inability to express feelings openly. His body had a wooden, heavy quality, inside of which one could sense a frightened child unable to come out. Mark came to a session with the following dream and comment: "I dreamed last night I was having a dinner party, and my guests were Mr. Head and Mr. Body. This was probably in preparation for my coming here today. The two were short, muscle-bound, hardhearted, barrel-chested and fiercely independent. It was as if they wouldn't meld (flow together). The dinner wasn't too important. I wanted to bring them together, but we never did get together for the evening. The party never came off."

Mark then went into position for the falling exercise. As he stood in front of the blanket, he said, "I see a hole. I seem to be drawn into the hole. It's very deep like a well. One of my fantasies is trying endlessly to scramble out of it. I seem to be able to see out, but the next time I find myself still trying to get out.

"I've had falling dreams all my life. I used to dream of falling down flights of stairs, now in my dreams I fall from much higher. In Europe this summer I was in a hotel room on a high floor, and while wide awake I fantasized that I was going to be pulled off the bed, across the balcony and into space.

"I could climb trees as a child as long as I could hold onto a branch. I seemed to have no fear of height if there was something to hold onto. When I was eight, someone dared me to walk a two-by-eight-foot rail which was on top of a tower a hundred feet high. It was a distance of about two hundred feet around. I did it. But later when I was in college, I didn't dare go near that tower.

"Also at around the age of six, seven or eight I used to dream I could fly. It was so real I believed it could happen. I actually tried it with people watching. I would try to take off, but I would land on my face."

After Mark fell and was lying on the blanket, he said, "I feel a sense of relief at falling. I feel like I'm built up of blocks that are very unstable. I feel on top of something very shaky and that I am better off (lying) on the ground."

The Causes of Falling Anxiety

I suggested earlier that human beings might be the only animals that experience falling anxiety. Of course, all animals are subject to anxiety when they do fall. I have seen my parrot become anxious when he lost his balance on his perch while asleep. He would wake with a start, act flustered for a moment, then recover his hold. Human beings, however, are susceptible to anxiety about falling even when standing on a solid base. It can probably be traced back through our evolutionary history to the time when our forebears lived in trees like some of the apes.

It seems pretty well established anthropologically that the human ancestor was a forest dweller before he ventured onto the plains in search of food. In *The Emergence of Man* John E. Pfeiffer describes what it meant to live in the trees: "Even more significant, life in the trees introduced a unique feature, a new and chronic psychological insecurity or uncertainty."* The insecurity related to the danger of falling. And falls were common. Pfeiffer points out that studies of the gibbon, a tree-dwelling primate, show that about one out of every four adults had suffered at least one broken bone. But there were advantages to living in the trees. There was ample food, it was relatively safe from predators, and it encouraged the development of the hand for holding and handling.

The danger of falling is greatly minimized by the ability to hold onto a limb or branch of a tree. Baby monkeys wrap themselves around the mother's body with arms and legs and cling to her while she moves through the trees. She will also provide support with one arm when that is free. For an infant monkey, therefore, loss of contact with the mother's body raises the immediate prospect of falling and injury or death. Rodents, like squirrels, who also live in trees raise their young in nests in a hole in the tree where the young are secure even while the mother is away. But tree-dwelling apes and monkeys carry their young with them, and the infant's only security is its hold on the mother's body.

In a newborn human infant the instinct to grasp and hold on with its hand is present at birth, a carryover from its phylogenetic history. When suspended, some infants can support their weight through the grip of their hands. But this is only a vestigial ability, and human infants need to *be* held to feel secure. If this support is suddenly withdrawn and it is allowed to fall momentarily, it becomes frightened and anxious. Only two other conditions seem to threaten a newborn infant: An inability to breathe produces choking anxiety, and a sudden loud voice produces what is known as the startle reaction.

The phylogenetic history of the human animal reflected in the human infant's need to be held to feel secure is the predisposing

*John E. Pfeiffer, *The Emergence of Man* (New York, Harper & Son, 1969, p. 21).

cause of falling anxiety. The effective cause is the lack of sufficient holding and physical contact with the mother.

In 1945 Reich published an observation on falling anxiety in a three-week-old infant. It was included in his study of falling anxiety in cancer patients in whom this anxiety is very severe and deeply structured. This article made a very strong impression on me, though it took twenty-five years before I could come to grips with it in my own work.

Regarding the infant, Reich writes:

> At the end of the third week there was an acute *falling anxiety.* It occurred when he was taken out of his bath and put on his back on the table. It was not immediately clear whether the motion of laying him down had been too fast, or whether the cooling of the skin had precipitated the falling anxiety. At any rate the child *began to cry violently, pulled back his arms as if to gain support, tried to bring his head forward, showed intense anxiety in his eyes and could not be calmed down.* It was necessary to take him up again. At the next attempt to put him down, the falling anxiety appeared again in the same intensity. Only when taken up did he again calm down.*

Following this incident Reich noted that the child's right shoulder was pulled back. *"During the anxiety attack he had pulled back both shoulders, as if to gain a hold." This attitude seemed to persist in the absence of anxiety.*†

It was evident to Reich that the child had no conscious fear of falling. The anxiety attack could be explained only by the withdrawal of charge from the periphery of the body and, with it a loss of the sense of equilibrium. It was as if the child had gone into

*Reich, Wilhelm, *The Cancer Biopathy* (New York, The Orgone Institute Press, 1949), p. 329.

†*Ibid.*, p. 330.

a slight state of shock which Reich called anorgonia. In shock, the blood and charge are withdrawn from the periphery of the body, the person loses his sense of equilibrium, and he feels he is going to fall or does fall. The same reactions would occur in any animal organism in shock. As long as the state of shock persisted, it would have difficulty getting up on its legs and countering the force of gravity. Reich was interested to know why the child experienced what appeared to be a shock.

Reich was aware there had been some lack of contact between the baby and its mother. The infant was being nursed on self-demand, and this contact with the mother was pleasurable and satisfying. But when not nursing, the baby lay in a crib or carriage near the mother while she worked at her typewriter. Reich believed the baby's need for physical contact was not fulfilled. It was not held enough. Before the attack the baby had had a particularly strong reaction to nursing, what Reich called an orgasm of the mouth, manifested in trembling and contractions in the mouth and face. In Reich's words, "This increased the need for contact even further." When this was not forthcoming and the baby was put down, it went into a state of contraction.

To overcome the tendency to falling anxiety in this child, Reich used three approaches: "*The child had to be taken up when he cried. This helped.*" I think it would have been better to hold the child more often as primitive women do, using a halter. "*The shoulders had to be brought forward gently out of their backward fixation*" to prevent any characterological armoring from developing. Reich did this in a playful manner for about two months. "*It was necessary actually to 'let the child fall' in order to accustom him to sensations of falling. This was also successful.*" This, too, was done in a very gentle and playful manner which the baby learned to appreciate as a game.

Why does this anxiety persist in some people throughout life? The answer is that parents do not recognize the problem and so make no moves to alter the situation. The need of the baby to be held is unheeded out of ignorance. The impulse to reach out for contact persists but it becomes associated with an increasing fear that there is no basis to expect a response, no certainty of one's standing as a needing organism and, finally, no ground to stand on.

Reich studied the case of another infant whose progress was being followed at the Orgone Infant Research Center.* This child, after doing well for two weeks, developed bronchitis in the third week. Its chest became sensitive, its breathing uneasy, and the baby seemed restless, fretful and unhappy. Investigation revealed there was some disturbance in the emotional contact between mother and child. *"The mother seemed to feel guilty over not being a 'healthy' mother"* and not fulfilling all the expectations she had. She admitted resenting the amount of time and energy she had to give to the baby and she was surprised and overburdened by its demands. The baby responded to the mother's unease and anxiety by becoming anxious in turn.

The report of this case is interesting for several reasons. First, Reich observed that the diaphragmatic region "seemed to respond first and most severely to emotional bioenergetic discomfort." According to Reich, other blockings would extend in both directions from this area. Diaphragmatic tension is closely related to falling anxiety since it reduces the flow of excitation to the lower part of the body. Secondly, it is apparent that good contact involves more than just holding or touching. The *quality* of the holding or touching is important. For the baby to profit from the contact, the mother's body has to be warm, easy and alive. Any tension in her body communicates itself to the child. Thirdly, Reich described what I believe is the essential element in a mother-child relationship, "Let the mothers just enjoy their babies and the contact will develop spontaneously."

Falling anxiety and disturbances of breathing are two aspects of a single process. In the preceding section Jim had described the feeling of falling "where your stomach tightens up and you can't

*Reich, Wilhelm, *Armoring in a Newborn Infant,* Orgone Energy Bulletin (New York, Orgone Institute Press, 1951), Vol. 8, No. 3, pp. 120–38.

breathe." The falling anxiety, according to Reich "is connected with rapid contractions of the life apparatus, is, in fact, produced by them. Just as actual falling causes biological contraction, so does contraction, conversely, cause the sensation of falling."* The withdrawal of energy from the legs and feet produces a loss of contact with the ground which is the same sensation as if the ground dropped away from the person.

Falling in Love

The existence of falling anxiety leads not only to fear of height but also to a fear of any situation that can evoke the sensation of falling in the body. Our language identifies two such situations —namely, falling asleep and falling in love. But, we may ask, aren't these merely literary expressions? In what way does the transition from wakefulness to sleep resemble the act of falling? If there is a parallel between them on a body level, then we can understand why so many people have difficulty falling asleep and need a sedative to dull their anxiety and facilitate the passage from consciousness to unconsciousness.

This passage has long been regarded as a downward movement. Actually, if a person should fall asleep while standing, he would fall just as a person does who faints and loses consciousness. But very few of us ever fall asleep standing up. We do it while lying down, in which case there is no displacement of the body in space. The sensation of falling must stem, therefore, from an internal movement, a happening within the body as sleep overcomes the person.

A clue is provided by the expression "sink into sleep," and actually, one senses a "sinking" in the process of going to sleep. It starts with a feeling of drowsiness. The body suddenly becomes heavy. One experiences this in the eyes, the head and the limbs. It

*Reich *Anorgonia in the Carcinomatous Shrinking Biopathy of Sex and Orgone Research,* New York Orgone Institute Press, 1955. Vol IV p. 32.

requires an effort for the drowsy person to keep his eyes open or to hold his head up. If he dozes off, the head drops. The limbs feel as if they won't support the body. Sinking into sleep is like sinking into the ground. One has a strong desire to lie down and give up the struggle against the forces of gravity.

Sometimes sleep comes quickly. At one moment the person is still awake, but at the next he is unconscious. Sometimes sleep develops gradually, and one can sense the progressive loss of feeling in parts of the body. I have noticed, as I lay next to my wife with my hand on her body, that first I lost consciousness of her body then of my own hand. If, however, I pay too much attention to my sensations, I come awake again. Attention is a function of consciousness and increases it. Generally, for me this is a very short interlude, and before I fully know it, I am fast asleep. Of course, one can't know it, for the function of knowing is extinguished by sleep.

In falling asleep there is a withdrawal of excitation and energy from the body surface and from the surface of the mind. The same withdrawal of energy occurs in the process of falling, and thus the two situations are energetically equivalent. Of course, they are practically different in that one risks getting hurt when falling to the ground, while falling asleep in a bed is a safe procedure. Nevertheless, the anxiety associated with the falling can attach to going to sleep because of their common dynamic mechanism. At issue is the individual's ability to surrender ego control, for this is entailed in the withdrawal of energy from the surface of mind and body alike. Where ego control is identified with survival, as it is in people who function largely through the exercise of will, the surrender of such control is unconsciously fought and situations that require it produce severe anxiety.

Neurotic anxiety stems from an internal conflict between an energetic movement in the body and an unconscious control or block set up to limit or stop that movement. These blocks are the chronic muscular tensions mostly in the striated or voluntary musculature which is normally under ego control. Conscious ego control is lost when the tension in a set of muscles becomes chronic. This does not mean that control is surrendered but that the control itself has become unconscious. Unconscious ego control is like a watchman or a guard over whom the ego or personality has lost authority. It functions as an independent entity in the personality and gains power in direct proportion to the amount of chronic body tension. Charge, discharge, flow and movement are the life of the body which this guard must restrain and limit in the interest of survival. One wants to let go and flow, but the guard says, "No, it's too dangerous." We were similarly restrained as little children when we were threatened or punished for being too noisy, too active, too alive.

We all know that falling is less dangerous if one "lets go" or abandons any attempt at ego control. In fact, if a person anxiously attempts to control his fall, he may find he can break a bone before he even hits the ground. The break is caused by sudden muscular contraction. Children whose ego control is weak and drunks in whom it has been undermined generally fall without much injury. The secret of falling is to go with the fall, allowing the currents to flow freely in the body and not being afraid of the sensation. For this reason some athletes such as football players practice falling to avoid the serious injuries that otherwise might occur.

Not all neurotic people suffer from falling anxiety. I mentioned earlier that if feeling can be blocked out, one will not experience anxiety. This was true of Bill, the rock climber. It is the sensation that is frightening. If one can stop the flow of excitation or prevent its perception, the fear is gone. This helps explain why not all neurotics have difficulty falling asleep. Falling asleep is anxiety-producing or frightening only when one senses the withdrawal of energy from the surface. If there is no sensation connected with the transition from consciousness to the state of sleep, anxiety will not be aroused.

This sensation is not in itself frightening; it may be experienced as pleasure. But if it is frightening, it is because the withdrawal of energy from the surface of the body and the resulting fading of consciousness parallels dying. The same withdrawal happens in dying, except that it is not later reversed. Should one become aware on some level of the connection between falling asleep and dying, it would become impossible to surrender ego control to the natural process.

In *The Betrayal of the Body* I reported the case of a young woman who experienced this anxiety. She described a dream in which she said, "I vividly experienced the reality of death—what it means to be lowered into the ground and to be there until one disintegrates."

Then she added, "I realized that it will happen to me as it does to everyone. As a girl I couldn't fall asleep because of my anxiety that I would die during my sleep and wake up in a coffin. I would be trapped, no way out."*

This statement contains a strange contradiction. If one dies during one's sleep, one doesn't wake up in a coffin. She is afraid of dying but she is equally afraid of being trapped, which is equated with dying since life is movement. To die is to be trapped unable to move, but to be trapped is also to die. For this patient, consciousness is more than awareness; it is a heightened alertness against the possibility of being trapped. Falling asleep involves a surrender of this alertness and, therefore, poses the danger of being trapped or dying.

In interpreting her remark further, I would equate the coffin with her body. Normally, as one wakes up, the first awareness is of the body. Consciousness returns in the order in which it left—first of the body, then of the outer world. Much depends, therefore, on how one experiences his body. If it is unalive, it would feel like a coffin imprisoning the spirit. It would also be subject to decay and disintegration, which happen only to dead bodies. Waking up to an alive body in which one feels the stirrings of life is as much pleasure as surrendering to a tired body that needs to sleep.

Something very nice happens to the body when one surrenders to it in sleep. It sheds the cares of the day and retreats from the world into a state of quiet repose and peace. The change from wakefulness to sleep is most noticeable in a person's breathing. We can often tell when someone lying close to us falls asleep by the

*Lowen, *Betrayal of the Body. op. cit.*, p. 185

change in the quality and rhythm of his breathing. Its quality becomes deeper and more audible, its rhythm slower, more even. This change is the result of the release of the diaphragm from the state of tension in which it is held during daytime activities. One lets down in sleep to lower energy centers in the body. The same diaphragmatic release occurs when we fall in love or have an orgasm.

In ancient philosophy the body was divided into two zones by the diaphragm—the dome-shaped muscle that resembles the contour of the earth. The region above the diaphragm was related to consciousness and the day—that is to the region of light. The area of the body below belonged to the unconscious and the night; it was considered the region of darkness. Consciousness was equated with the sun. The rising of the sun above the horizon of the earth, which brings the light of day, corresponded to a rising of excitation within the body from the abdominal centers to those in the chest and head. This upward flow of feeling resulted in the awakening of consciousness. The reverse occurred in sleep. The setting of the sun or its fall into the ocean, as primitive people viewed its descent, corresponded to the downward flow of excitation in the body to the regions below the diaphragm.

The belly is symbolically equivalent to the earth and the sea, which are regions of darkness. But it is from these areas, as from the belly, that life comes forth. They are the abode of the mysterious forces involved in life-and-death processes. They are also the abode of the spirits of darkness that dwell in the nether regions. When these primitive ideas became associated with Christian morality, the nether regions were assigned to the devil: the prince of darkness. He lured men to their fall through sexual temptation. The devil dwells in the pit of the earth but also in the pit of the belly where the sexual fires burn. A surrender to these passions could lead to an orgasm in which consciousness becomes dimmed and the ego dissolved, a phenomenon called "the death of the ego." Water is also associated with sex, probably from the fact that life began in the sea. The fear of drowning that many patients connect with the fear of falling can be related to the fear of surrender to sexual feelings.

We have idealized love so much that we overlook its close and intimate relation with sex, especially with the erotic and sensual aspects of sex. I have defined love as the anticipation of pleasure,* but it is particularly sexual pleasure that lures one to falling in love. Psychologically, it involves a surrender of the ego to the loved object, who becomes more important to the self than the ego. But the surrender of the ego involves a descent of feeling in the body, a downward flow of excitation into the deep abdomen and pelvis. This downward flow produces delicious streaming and melting sensations. One literally melts with love. The same lovely sensations occur when one's sexual excitement is very strong and not limited to the genital area. They precede every full orgastic release.

Strangely, the act of falling gives rise to similar sensations which is why children take such pleasure in swinging. Going with the fall of the swing sends delightful currents of sensation coursing through the body. Some of us may remember those lovely feelings. They can also be experienced in the fall of the roller coaster, which, I am sure, is the reason why that ride is so popular. Many activities that involve falling yield a similar pleasure such as diving, trampolining, and so on.

The key to this phenomenon is the release of the diaphragm, allowing a strong excitation to flow into the lower part of the body. This becomes clear to us when we realize that holding one's breath in these activities introduces anxiety and destroys the pleasure. The same thing happens in sex. If one is afraid to go with the fall and so holds his breath, the melting sensation does not occur, and the climax is only partially satisfactory.

The term "falling in love" may seem to contain a contradiction, in that the feeling of being in love is a high. How can one fall into a high? But falling is the only way to reach a high state of biological excitement. The trampoline jumper falls before he rises; he

*Lowen, *Pleasure, op.cit.*

presses down into the trampoline to get the push for the rise. The rising up in turn allows another fall to occur, which then results in another rise. If orgasm is the great fall, then the high one feels following a highly satisfactory sexual act is the natural rebound from the discharge. In love we walk on a cloud, but this is only because we have previously allowed ourselves to fall.

To understand why falling has such a powerful effect, we should think of life as movement. The absence of movement is death. But this movement is not basically the horizontal displacement in space that we spend so much time doing. It is the pulsatory rise and fall of excitement within the body, manifested in leaping and jumping, standing and lying down, ever striving for greater heights but always needing to return to solid ground, to the earth and to the reality of our earthly existence. So much of our energy is devoted to the effort to rise higher and achieve more that we often find it difficult to come down or let down. We become hung up and are afraid to fall. If we are afraid to fall, we constantly strive to rise higher, as if we could gain more security that way. Children who develop falling anxiety as infants must necessarily become adults whose goal in life is to rise higher and higher. If one goes so far in imagination that one reaches the moon, there is danger of lunacy—bleakness, emptiness, isolation. Transcending the atmosphere of the earth spaces one out. The salutary effect of gravity, the earth's pull on our bodies, is lost, and one can easily become disoriented.

Sleep and sex are closely connected since the best sleep follows good sex. In the same way, as everyone knows, sex is the best antidote to anxiety. But for sex to have this effect, one must be able to give in to sexual feelings. Unfortunately, falling anxiety attaches to sex and limits its natural function as the main avenue for the discharge of tension and excitation. We can still perform the sexual act, but it is done on a horizontal level, energetically speaking, and there is neither the fall that releases nor the rise that exhilarates. We are obliged to help our patients overcome their falling anxiety if they are to fully enjoy their sex and their sleep and to rise from both renewed and refreshed from their surrender.

VIII. Stress and Sex

Gravity: A General View of Stress

Discussing stress and sex in one chapter should not surprise us in view of the fact that the sexual release, as everyone knows, serves the function of discharging tension. Any discussion of stress, therefore, should include an analysis of the sexual orgasm. My first task, however, is to present a general view of the nature of stress.

Stress results from the imposition of a force or pressure on an organism which it counters by mobilizing its energy. Obviously, if the organism can escape the force, it will not be subject to stress. There are, of course, natural stresses associated with living that no organism can escape, but which it is, normally, well-equipped to meet. Then there are the pressures resulting from the conditions of social living which vary with the individual's cultural situation. An example is driving on a crowded highway where one has to be in a state of constant alertness to avoid a dangerous accident. In a highly competitive society like ours such pressures are almost too numerous to detail. Interpersonal relationships are often stressful because of the demands to which one is subject. Whenever there is a threat of violence, one is under stress. Finally, there are the stresses of self-imposed constraints that act on the body the same as external forces.

Of the natural forces creating stress, the most universal is gravity. We can temporarily escape its stress by lying down, but whenever we stand up or move about we are subject to it. Standing and moving require the mobilization of energy to counter the force of gravity. Standing is no mechanical process. Though we are aided by the structural alignment of our bones, our muscles have to do considerable work to maintain this posture. When we become tired or lack energy, it becomes difficult, if not impossible, to stand up. Soldiers who are forced to stand immobile for long periods have collapsed when their energy became exhausted. Collapse also occurs when a person receives a shock, either psychological or physical, that results in the withdrawal of energy from the periphery of his body.

Falling or collapsing is nature's safeguard against the danger of unremitting stress. There is just so much stress a body can take before it breaks down. Soldiers who have exceeded this limit while standing have been known to die. We also know about death from heat exhaustion when the body's ability to counter the stress of high temperature fails. But even in this situation, falling or lying down greatly reduces the danger by eliminating the stress of gravity.

In general, stress can be viewed as a force pressing down on a person from above or pulling him down from below. Burdens weigh on us, pressing us down; gravity acts to pull us down. We counter these pressures with our energy by exerting a counterpressure on the ground. On the physical principle that action equals reaction, if we press on the ground, it presses back, holding us up. So we say a person "stands up" to a stressful or difficult situation.

Standing erect is a typically human position. Man is the only animal for whom this is a natural posture. However, it requires the expenditure of considerable energy. Despite the fact that man's body is anatomically adapted for it, I don't think we can explain his two-legged stance purely by mechanics. We must recognize that the human organism is a more highly charged energy system than that of other animals and that it is his greater energy or higher level of excitation that has enabled him to attain and to maintain his erect posture.

That the human organism is a more highly charged energy system hardly needs documentation. The record of man's activities and achievements is sufficient proof. Whether this energy has an antigravity quality, as Reich believed, or whether it is used by the organism to counter the force of gravity need not be decided at this time. The important thing is that it flows along the axis of the body, upward and downward in the human being. The effect of this strong pulsation is that both poles of the body are highly excited and become intense centers of activity.

We are accustomed to thinking that man's dominance of the earth stemmed ultimately from the superior development of his brain. That is certainly true. But it is equally true, as many anthropologists have pointed out, that important to his growth as the dominant species was the development of cooperative hunting, a shared society and a strong pair bonding between male and female. In the final analysis man's sociality is a reflection of his sexuality.* The escape of human female sexuality from its bondage to the estrous cycle played an important part in the stability of human society by providing an opportunity for continuous pleasure and sexual satisfaction within the family situation. This allowed the male to make the necessary commitment to the female and to her offspring that is essential to the security of human children.

My point is that the development of the large brain, the increased sexual interest and activity of the human animal and the erect posture are a result of the increased energy charge in the human organism. This increased charge is also responsible for

*Weston LaBarre, *The Human Animal* (Chicago, The University of Chicago Press, 1954). This book contains an excellent discussion of the importance of the human body, and human sexuality to human social relationships.

man's erect posture. Anatomical and physiological changes necessarily accompanied increased energy charge. I don't believe they preceded it, for all these special human activities require a degree of excitation or amount of energy not available to other animals.

Many human qualities that are worth mentioning have been directly attributed to the erect posture of our species. Most important is that it frees the forelimbs from their subservience to the functions of support and locomotion and allows their evolution into the human arm and hand. We can handle and manipulate objects, both tools and weapons, we have an extremely high degree of sensitivity in our fingertips, which allows our touching to be discriminating, and we are endowed with a range of movement in our arms and hands that has enriched our self-expression through gesture. A second result, however, is that man faces the world with the most vulnerable aspect of his body exposed, his ventral side. Thus, his chest and heart, his belly and loins are more accessible to touch and less protected from attack. It is conceivable that the quality of tenderness is related to this way of being in the world. Thirdly, the fact that man's head is held above the rest of his body is partly responsible, I believe, for the introduction and establishment of a hierarchy of values in his thinking.

Freud attributed the origin of disgust to the raising of the head from the ground. In most other mammals the nose is on the same level as the excretory and sexual outlets, and these animals are free from the feeling of revulsion at these functions typical of man. I am not prepared to argue this point, which Freud believed contributed in some way to the human predisposition to neurosis. Certainly, we have assigned higher values to the functions of the head end of the body than to those of the ass end. We cannot logically say "rear end" since the ass is actually the lower end of the body. Being human and civilized, I have accepted this value system, which I believe has merit, provided it does not cause one to turn against his basic animal nature so closely identified with the functions of the lower end of his body.

However, if we are to understand the problems that can ensue from the erect posture when it is under stress, one must look at its mechanics. In this connection the lowly ass plays an important role. Anatomically I would agree with Robert Ardrey that the change that stabilized the erect posture was the development of the buttocks. These two large muscular masses, acting together with the backward tilt of the pelvis, provide the structural support for the erect body.

The reason for my agreement with Ardrey is my observation that when the buttocks are contracted and the pelvis is tilted forward, the body goes into a state of partial collapse. This is seen in the masochistic character structure described earlier. Interestingly, in the masochistic character the body takes on an apelike appearance, owing partly to the collapsed posture and partly to a hirsute condition which can develop. The masochistic structure is caused by unremitting stress—pressure from above and from below—which the child could not escape or stand up to. His only alternative was submission. To tolerate the continuing stress, his musculature became overdeveloped, which is one of the physical signs of this structure.

Masochism is a third way people deal with stress. Unable either to escape it by moving out of the stressful situation or to stand up to the pressure and handle the stressful situation, the masochist submits and bows under to the stress. This personality pattern develops in a situation where one can neither escape nor stand up to the stressing force.

Unfortunately, the pattern one adopts is established early in childhood as one attempts to cope with pressures from parents and from school authorities. It will determine how one handles stress as an adult. In the masochistic structure, we saw that the pattern is one of submission, with the creation of an overdeveloped musculature to tolerate the stress. However, if the pressure is applied early, in the first year of life, submission is impossible because the infant cannot build the necessary musculature to develop tolerance. Physical withdrawal from the situation is also impossible. And of course, standing up to stress is out of the question at this age. Psychological withdrawal becomes the *modus vivendi.* The infant or child dissociates from the situation and from reality. He inhabits a fantasy world, he dreams of flying—a denial of the stress of gravity—or he escapes into autism. This pattern will be followed later in life when the individual confronts any overwhelming stress. When pressure is applied later in childhood, as in the case of the rigid character, he will stand up to the stress. However, if the stress is a continuing one, the standing up becomes a characterological attitude and leads to a rigidity of body and mind. A person with a rigid structure stands up to all stresses, even when it is unnecessary and may be damaging. And since he has become so structured, he will even seek stresses to prove how well he can withstand them.

It should be clear to the reader now that these patterns of reaction to stress are structured in the body and are part of an individual's character attitude. In effect, then, the person is reacting to stress even when no outside pressure is imposed on him. In this case we can speak of self-imposed pressures. The ego (or what Freud called the superego) incorporates the pressure as a necessary condition of living.

Let us take the case of a person whose shoulders are raised and squared off as an expression of his feeling that it is manly to shoulder one's burdens. He may not be conscious of the feeling or the attitude, but that is what his body is saying. If we assume, hypothetically, that the amount of muscular tension in his shoulders is equivalent to that required to carry 100 pounds of weight on one's shoulders, it would be logical to deduce that he is subject to that much pressure. He is acting on a body level as if that much weight were pressing down on him. It would be better for him if he really were carrying a weight, for then he would be conscious of the burden and sooner or later he would let it go. As it is, he is under a constant stress without being aware of it and unable, therefore, to drop it.

Every chronic muscular tension is a continuing stress on the body. This is a frightening thought. Continued stress, as Hans Selye has pointed out,* has a deleterious effect on the body. It matters little what the stress is; the body reacts to all with a general adaptation syndrome. This syndrome consists of three phases. Phase 1 is called the alarm reaction. The body reacts to an acute stress by an outpouring of adrenal medullary hormones which mobilize the body's energy to meet it. When the stress is a physical insult to the body, the alarm reaction takes the form of an inflammatory process. If this reaction is successful in overcoming the injury and removing the stress, the body quiets down and returns to its natural homeostatic condition. Should the stress continue, however, Phase 2 begins. In this phase the body attempts to adapt to the stress. This involves the adrenal corticosteroid hormones, which are anti-inflammatory in their action. But the process of adaptation also takes energy which must be mobilized from the body's reserves. Phase 2 is like a cold war, in that the body tries to contain the stressful agent since it cannot eliminate it. Phase 2 can go on for a long time, but eventually the body weakens. Phase 3 is called the stage of exhaustion. The body no longer has the energy to contain the stress and begins to break down.

This brief presentation of Selye's concept of the reactions to stress does little justice to his important contribution to our understanding of the body. The broad scope of our subject, however, makes it impossible to give his work the attention it deserves. On the other hand, one can't ignore it in any discussion of stress. Of particular significance to us here is Phase 3—the stage of exhaustion. If this is translated as fatigue or chronic tiredness, it is probably the most universal complaint in our culture. I interpret it as a sign that many people are on the verge of exhaustion as a result of the continuous stresses to which they are subjected by their chronic muscular tensions.

The existence of these bodily stresses limits the energy otherwise available to meet the stresses of daily living. When a person's

*Hans Selye, *The Stress of Life* (New York, McGraw-Hill, 1956).

muscular tensions are reduced in the course of bioenergetic therapy, he finds he can cope far more effectively with the stresses of his personal situation. The secret of coping with stress is simply to have sufficient energy to meet it, but this is only possible if one's body is relatively tension-free.

In summary I would describe the situation of many people as follows: They are laboring under great stress, yet they feel that if they fail to carry on, this would admit to weakness, to defeat, to their failure as human beings. In this desperate strait, they set their jaws more firmly, stiffen their legs, lock their knees and struggle on with what at times appears an unbelievable will. As my patient Jim said, "You can't be a quitter." In many respects this will to carry on is an admirable quality, but it can and does have some disastrous effects on the body.

Lower-Back Pain

An acute lower-back pain that immobilizes a person, sometimes sending him to bed for a time, is often the direct and immediate result of stress. The person lifts a heavy object when suddenly he feels a sharp pain in his lumbosacral region and finds he cannot straighten up. We say his back has gone into spasm. One or more muscles, generally on one side, do go into a severe spastic condition which makes any movement of the back almost excruciatingly painful. Sometimes as a result of the spasm, there is a herniation of an intervertebral disc which presses on one of the nerve roots, causing pain to radiate down one leg. Herniation of the disc is not common—the pressure on the nerve can come from the spastic muscle itself.

Although I am a psychiatrist, I have treated a number of people who suffered from this condition. Some were patients in bioenergetic therapy who had a tendency to lower-back troubles and in whom a spastic condition occurred. Others consulted me because bioenergetic therapy deals with muscular tension. Let me say at the outset that I have no quick or easy cure for this condition. If a person is immobilized by the pain, then bed rest is necessary until it subsides. Bed rest serves to remove the stress of gravity, and gradually the muscle begins to relax. At this point I institute a program of bioenergetic exercises designed to further the relaxation of the tense muscles and to prevent a recurrence of the spasm.

To understand these exercises, one has to know why such spasms occur. What postural attitude or holding pattern makes an individual vulnerable to a lower-back problem? It is erroneous to believe that people are susceptible to lower-back problems because of their erect posture. It is erroneous to assume that it is normal to suffer from this condition. The condition is widespread and common in our culture, but so are heart disease and myopia. Should we say that people are susceptible to heart disease because they have hearts or to myopia because they have eyes? There are cultures in which lower-back problems are unknown, where heart disease is rare and myopia doesn't exist. The difference is not in the people. They, too, walk erect and have hearts and eyes. But they are not subject to the kind and degree of stress that is the lot of what we call Western man.

Is it true that stress is responsible for lower-back problems? I have so far indicated the connection only where a person lifts a heavy object. But many people have developed lower-back spasm in apparently innocuous activities. One bends over to pick up a small object, and his back goes into spasm. That is not uncommon. I know of one case where the spasm occurred while the person was sleeping. She turned over, and that movement was enough to set off the spasm. Obviously the stress is not always in the action that provokes the spasm. Yet stress there is in each case.

One young man whose back went into severe spasm was in the process of moving into an apartment with his girlfriend. For two days he had been busy packing, and he was almost finished when he bent over to pick up a book and landed in a hospital. The story, as it emerged when I saw him, was that he was in conflict about the move. His relationship to his girl was an intense one, but it was rarely free from arguments, jealousies and uncertainties. He had grave misgivings about the move and felt under pressure to make it in order to preserve the relationship. Nature intervened, and he never did move. He had felt that he couldn't back out, and his back went out instead. I believe it was as simple as that. The stress became unbearable, and his back collapsed.

Another case involved an actress who was in a show she had wanted to leave for some time. She was not getting along too well with the director and some members of the cast. In addition, she was pretty close to exhaustion from added rehearsals and late hours. She wanted to quit but couldn't. Then she made what may be called a "wrong move," and she was out flat. She left the show but via a bed in the hospital. Her body simply quit on her. In her case, too, I would say the stress was unbearable.

The person whose back went into spasm while sleeping was under considerable pressure at the time. During the preceding day her back had begun to trouble her. She had been rushing around doing chores, but she noticed she was hobbling, wasn't standing straight. She had had a previous attack that had laid her up in bed for a week, and she knew the signs. Still she thought, "As soon as I finish, I'll go home and rest, get off my feet." She finished, went home and rested awhile, but obviously it wasn't enough. When the spasm struck, she was off her feet for a week.

Why is it the lower back that gives out? Why is this the area particularly vulnerable to stress? The answer is that the lower back is the place where two opposing forces meet to create stress. One is gravity—together with all the pressures that act on a person from above, demands of authority, duty, guilt and burdens both physical and psychological. The other is an upward force through the legs supporting the individual in his erect posture and in his standing up to the demands and burdens placed on him. These two forces meet in the lumbosacral region.

This concept becomes clear if we study the stress of gravity. It can become overwhelming if one is forced to stand for a long time in one position. The question then is: "How long can a person's legs hold him up?" Sooner or later they must collapse but when the legs collapse, the back is spared. The danger to the back arises when the legs won't give out. Then the back will.

I must mention that there is a condition in which a person can stand motionless for an unbelievable length of time—for one day, two days or more. Curiously, in this condition neither the legs nor the back give out. That condition is catatonia, which is a schizophrenic modality. When one thinks about catatonia, one realizes that the *person* has given out—that is, he has gone away. I mentioned earlier that dissociation is one of the ways people deal with overwhelming stress. The catatonic is a dissociated being. The spirit or the mind and the body are no longer unified. The body has become transformed into a statue. Catatonics stand in statuesque poses.

Our legs are naturally structured to deal with stress, not to cope with it but to respond to it. This capacity is a function of the knee. Knee action gives the body its flexibility. The knee is the organism's shock absorber. If the pressure from above is too great, the knee will bend, and when the pressure is unbearable, it will fold and the person will fall.

When falling anxiety is present in the personality, the knees lose this function. The person will stand with locked knees to brace himself against the pressure, and he will tense the muscles of his legs to make them function like rigid supports. He is afraid of flexibility because that implies the ability to give way.

If the legs are soft and flexible, the pressure from above is transmitted to the legs and discharged into the ground. But when a person locks his knees and stiffens his legs to meet pressure, the rigidity extends upward to include the sacrum and pelvis. All the pressure becomes localized at the lumbosacral junction, which becomes vulnerable to injury.

I will use three simplified figures of the human body to illustrate:

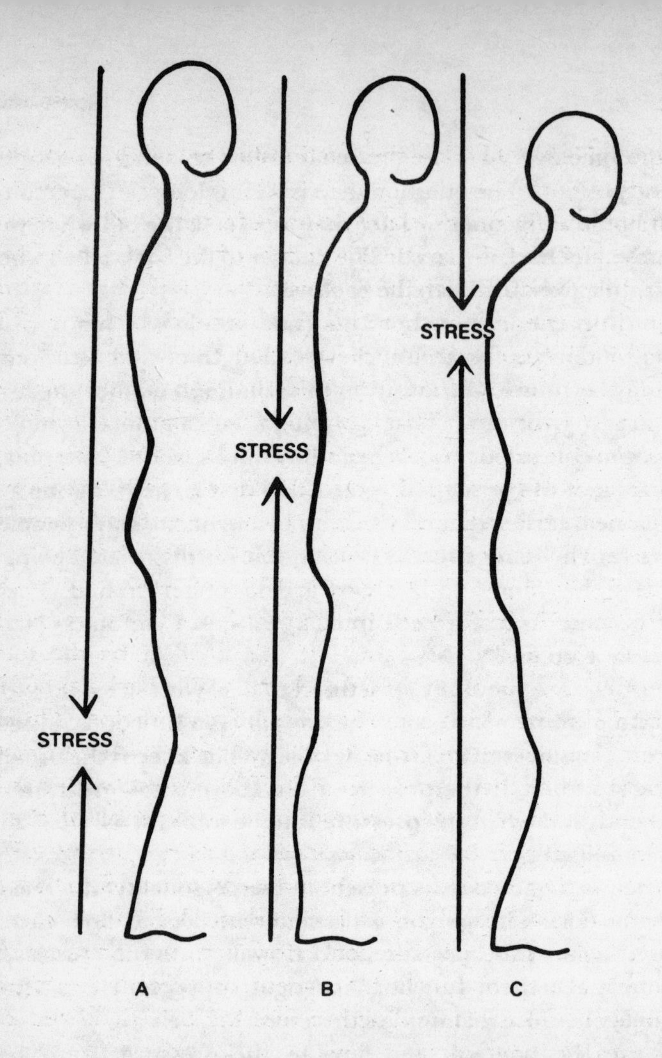

The figure at the left shows a fairly normal posture. The knees are bent and the pelvis is free—that is, not locked in a fixed position. This bodily posture allows the pressure to be transmitted to the knees, which act as shock absorbers. If the pressure is too great, the knees will give way. However, this rarely happens. Since a person with this posture is not afraid to fall, he is not afraid to quit. When the pressure becomes unbearable, he gets out of the situation. He would allow the relationship to collapse sooner than his body.

The central figure shows the posture of a person who stands with knees locked. In this case the lower part of the body, including the pelvis, functions as a rigid base. This position tells us the individual is very insecure, requiring a rigid base for support. The effect of this position is to focus all the stress on the lumbosacral region, forcing the muscles of this area to become extremely tense. Since the person is under continuous stress, any significant additional stress could result in a collapse of the back in this area. Another consequence of the state of contraction in the lumbosacral muscles is to cause undue wear and strain on the ligaments and bones of the invertebral joints, eventually causing an arthritic condition.

The figure at the right shows a different posture. The upper back is bowed, as if from the continual need to carry a heavy burden. The knees are bent, but this is offset by the forward position of the pelvis. In this posture the whole back has collapsed under the stress which spares the lumbosacral region. This is the typical posture of the masochistic character, who submits to pressure rather than stands up to it. The protection this attitude affords the lower back is bought at the expense of the total personality. It will fail if the individual makes a strong effort to stand up and fight back. When this happens, as it does in the course of therapy, lower-back tension is experienced. I always warn such patients that this will happen. However, the problem never becomes acute, because the patient is already engaged in bioenergetic exercises designed to free the pelvis and reduce the tension in the lumbosacral region.

It is significant that the adrenal glands which secrete the hormones that mobilize the body's energy to meet stressful situations are located in the lumbar region lying atop the kidneys against the body's posterior wall. They are in a position, therefore, to assess the degree of stress to which the body is subject. But how they do this is a question I cannot answer. I don't believe, however, that we can regard their location as purely adventitious.

The significance for me is that it shows the body is organized on bioenergetic principles. This is confirmed by the location of another important endocrine gland, the thyroid.

The thyroid gland regulates the organism's metabolism, the process by which food is oxidized to produce energy. One could say that the thyroid gland regulates energy production. It does this by producing a hormone, thyroxine, which circulates in the bloodstream, stimulating the oxidation of metabolites in the body cells. Too little thyroxine makes us feel sluggish because of a lack of energy; too much leads to a nervous hyperactivity. The hormone itself does not produce energy. That is directly determined by the amount and kind of food we eat, the amount of air we breathe and the body's energy needs. The hormone coordinates energy production with need.

The thyroid gland surrounds the trachea on three sides just below the thyroid cartilage. It is located in the narrows of the neck, just as the adrenal glands are located in the narrows of the waist. And just as the adrenal glands are positioned to be sensitive to stress, so the thyroid gland is positioned to be sensitive to respiration. It develops embryologically as an outpocketing of the pharynx, as do the lungs. What this suggests is that the secretion of thyroxine is directly related to the amount of air breathed. Medicine has known of this relationship for a long time and used it for testing a person's basal metabolic rate. Measuring an individual's breathing per unit of time while in a state of repose provides an indication of thyroxine secretion. It was not assumed, however, that the position of the gland had anything to do with this relationship. I believe it is not fortuitous, but that because of its position and embryological origin, the gland partakes of or responds to the slight expansion and contraction of the trachea occurring with respiration and thus is able to coordinate the body's metabolic activities with the oxygen intake.

Let us return again to stress, the lumbosacral region and the adrenal gland. It is public knowledge that the late John F. Kennedy suffered from severe lower-back trouble. Recall that he carried his shoulders very high and squared away, suggesting that he shouldered heavy responsibilities. This body attitude developed, however, long before he entered public life. Its origin must be sought in the experiences of his childhood. Once the attitude became structured in the body, it would predispose him to accept such responsibilities, regardless of personal cost, and he was that kind of a man. Kennedy was also a victim of Addison's disease, which is the almost complete loss of adrenal functioning owing to exhaustion of the gland. This could occur, in my opinion, if a person were subject to continual stress, producing first a hyperactivity of this gland, then its eventual exhaustion.

A person's physical health as well as his emotional health is adversely affected by stress. Since we live in times that are extremely stressful, we must learn how to guard our bodies and our minds against the harmful effects of stress. To reduce an individual's vulnerability to stress, the physical and psychic defenses against "letting down" must be worked through and released. This is no easy task in a culture that places an overriding value on success and achievement, on getting to the top and being able to take it. Our egos are not strong enough to accept failure, and so we force our bodies to stand up to situations harmful to our health. In the end our success is temporary and empty, for our bodies break down under the continuous stress. But the fear of failure is so great that until a final collapse occurs, the ego resists surrendering to the body. On a deep level failure is identified with this surrender. These ego defenses must be carefully analyzed in each case as part of the therapy.

In addition, the physical or structural elements in the body that block the letting down must be worked on consistently. We use two sets of exercises in bioenergetic therapy to help a person get in touch with and decrease the muscular tensions preventing the discharge of excitation or stress. The first includes all the exercises that aim to *ground* an individual through his legs and to overcome his falling or failing anxiety. I have described some of these exercises above and will refer to them again. The second has the special aim of freeing the pelvis and opening up sexual feeling. Some of these will be described in the next section dealing with the sexual release. It should be clear from what I have said earlier that if the pelvis is immobile and rigidly held in a fixed position, it will prevent any pressure from above passing down and into the legs where it can be discharged. The stress will then be focused in the lumbosacral region with the consequences we have seen.

Basic to any effective work with the lower part of the body is the flexible knee. Locked, knees prevent any excitation or feeling from flowing through the legs and into the feet. One of the first injunctions in bioenergetic therapy, therefore, is "keep your knees bent at all times." There are only a few other such injunctions as dropping shoulders and not pulling in or tightening the belly muscles. These simple injunctions can do much to promote better respiration and a greater flow of feeling and can be recommended for all people interested in a more alive, responsive body. They are necessary to counter the cultural dictate, "Shoulders back, chest out, belly in." The purpose of the dictate is ostensibly to help one stand straight, but it really forces one to stand stiffly.

The injunction to keep your knees bent is known to be important when lifting a heavy object. The failure to do so can lead to lower-back spasm. I have heard this injunction given by an announcer at a professional football game, pointing out that the running back who doesn't have his knees bent loses power and is liable to serious injury. Well, why not for everyone all the time when standing, since this position is a stressful one?

Patients who do not normally stand this way report it feels unnatural at first and may even give them a sense of insecurity. However, locked knees only create an illusion of security, and it is the illusion that vanishes with the bent knee position. To develop the habit of standing with bent knees will require conscious attention in the beginning. It can be practiced while shaving, washing dishes or waiting at a corner for the light to change. After a while one feels relaxed in this new position, and then it feels unnatural and awkward to stand with knees locked. One also becomes conscious of his legs and manner of standing. One may also feel more tired, but instead of fighting it, one gives in and rests.

The next step is to get some vibration into the legs. This is intended to reduce their rigidity. Vibration is nature's way of releasing muscular tension. When a person lets go, his body will vibrate like a spring released from tension. Our legs are like springs, and when we keep them tense too long, they stiffen and harden, losing their resiliency.

There are several ways the legs can be made to vibrate. The exercise most commonly used in bioenergetics is the bent-forward position with the hands touching the ground and the knees slightly bent. I described this exercise earlier in connection with grounding. It is always used after a person has been over the breathing stool and after he has used the bow position.

In my treatment of lower-back problems I alternate a patient between the bow position and the bent-forward position, allowing him to bend backward or forward as much as he can without too much pain. Alternating the bending loosens up the lower-back musculature, but it should be done gradually if a person is recovering from an acute back episode. Then, when his back is relatively pain-free, it is advisable for him to lie on the floor over a rolled-up blanket placed in the small of the back. This can be painful. The person is told to give in to the pain and not tense against it. If he can do this, the muscles in his back will let go. But one must not force or push this or any other exercise. Pushing creates the very tension we are trying to reduce. After a patient can do this exercise easily, he lies on a breathing stool with the pressure applied to his lower back. The stool is placed next to a bed so his head can rest on the bed. Here, too, the person is told to give in to the pain and let himself relax. One finds that as soon as one does let go, the pain disappears.

The biggest hurdle to overcoming a lower-back problem is fear, fear of pain. We have to help patients get over this fear if they are to become completely pain-free. Fear creates tension, and tension produces pain. They get caught in a vicious circle from which there seems no way out but surgery. I never advise surgery, since it does nothing for the muscular tension that is the root of the trouble. Splinting the back may remove the pain by reducing the back's motility, but I have known people who had more than one such operation with no significant benefit. These people made remarkable improvement with bioenergetic therapy.

By restoring the motility of the lower back, one can eliminate the pain. To do this, however, the fear has to be worked through. These patients are not just afraid of the pain; they are also afraid of what the pain implies—for pain is a danger signal. They are afraid their backs will actually *break.* This fear comes through when they lie over the stool on the lower back. If I ask what they are afraid of when it begins to hurt, the reply will invariably be: "I am afraid my back will break."

In my long experience no one has injured his back doing the bioenergetic exercises if he does them correctly. Doing them correctly means not using them to break through a problem but to get in touch with it on a body level. No exercise should be pushed beyond the danger point which is reached when a person becomes frightened. When this happens, an analysis of the fear is required. Questions should be asked, such as, "Where did you get the idea your back could break?" and "What could cause a back to break?" Sooner or later it becomes possible for a patient to associate his fear of breaking to a childhood situation. For example, he may recall the threat by a parent, "If I catch you, I'll break your back." This could be said to a rebellious child where the threat means the parent would break the child's spirit or the backbone of his resistance. Against this threat a child may react by stiffening his back as if to say, "You're not going to break me." But once the back has become chronically stiff, the fear of breaking is structured into the body as part of the defense.

A clearly expressed verbal threat is not always necessary to produce a stiff back. More commonly there is an open conflict of wills, in which situation the child may stiffen his back unconsciously to maintain his integrity. In all cases a stiffening of the back denotes unconscious resistance, a holding against yielding or giving in. While the holding has its positive aspect, the maintenance of integrity, it also has the negative effect of holding against needing, wanting and loving. The stiffness blocks the yielding to crying and the giving in to sexual longing. When people cry, we say they break down into tears and sobbing. The fear of breaking is fundamentally a fear of breaking down, of yielding and surrendering. It is important for a patient to make the associations that will enable him to understand where his fear came from.

A person can't get broken unless he is trapped as children are in their relationship with parents. Patients are not in this position. Every patient is told he is free to do or not do an exercise and to feel free to quit whenever he wants to. But patients and people in general are trapped by their stiffness and chronic muscular tensions, and they project this feeling into their relationships. Exercises should never be done compulsively, therefore, for this increases the feeling of being trapped. A person should do them as a means of sensing what goes on in his body and why. We cannot afford to go through life feeling that it will break us if we are not cautious, for then it surely will.

I mentioned that there were several ways to get the legs to vibrate. Perhaps the simplest exercise we use is having a patient lie on his back on the bed and extend both legs upward. If the ankles are flexed and the heels thrust upward, the stretch placed on the muscles of the back of the legs will generally cause them to vibrate.

Vibration of the body has another important function beyond that of releasing tension. It allows a person to experience and enjoy the body's involuntary movements. These are an expression of its life, of its vibrant force. If a person is afraid of them, feeling he must be in full control of himself at all times, he will lose his spontaneity and end up as a rigidly bound, automatized person.

Let me put it even more strongly. The body's involuntary movements are the essence of its life. The beat of the heart, the cycle of respiration, the peristaltic movements of the intestines—all are involuntary actions. But even on the total body level, these involuntary movements are the most meaningful! We convulse with laughter, cry for pain or sorrow, tremble with anger, jump for joy, leap with excitement and smile with pleasure. Because these are spontaneous, unwilled or involuntary actions, they *move* us in a deep, meaningful way. And most fulfilling, most satisfying and most meaningful of these involuntary responses is the orgasm in which the pelvis moves spontaneously and the whole body convulses with the ecstasy of release.

The Sexual Release

A satisfactory sexual release will discharge the excess excitation in the body, greatly reducing its overall level of tension. In sex the excess excitation becomes focused on the genital apparatus and discharged in the climax. The experience of a satisfactory sexual release leaves a person feeling quiet, relaxed, often sleepy. The experience itself is extremely pleasurable and fulfilling. It may give rise to the thought "Ah! So this is what life is about. It feels so good, so right."

This implies that there are sexual experiences or encounters that are not satisfying and that do not lead to such a conclusion. One can have an unsatisfying sexual contact where the excitation builds but does not reach a climax and is not discharged. If this happens, the person is often left in a state of frustration, restlessness and irritability. But the lack of a climax does not necessarily lead to frustration. When the level of sexual excitation is low, the failure to reach a climax does not disturb the body. It may create psychic distress if one regards the failure as a sign of impotence. But one can avoid this psychic distress by recognizing that the lack of a climax was due to the low level of sexual excitation, in which case the sexual contact, if it is between individuals who care for each other, can be pleasurable in itself.

Furthermore, not every climax is fully satisfying. There are partial releases, where only a fraction of the excitation is discharged. One may speak of a partial satisfaction, but this is a contradiction in terms. Satisfaction denotes completeness or fullness, yet such contradictions can and do exist in people's feelings. One can be satisfied with an 80 percent discharge if this is the best one has been able to achieve, because psychic factors enter into feelings and modify them. A woman who has not previously experienced a climax in the act of sex and then has one will experience it as rewarding and satisfying regardless of the degree of discharge. We can describe a feeling only by comparing it with previous experience; in this case the comparison is very favorable.

So far I have avoided the word "orgasm" because this is a much misused and misunderstood term. To say, as Albert Ellis does, that an "orgasm is an orgasm" is a play on words. He equates orgasm with climax, which is erroneous and makes no distinction between degrees of discharge and satisfaction. As everyone should know, no two acts of sexual intercourse are identical in feeling or experience. No orgasm is like any other. Things and events are alike only when there is an absence of feeling. Where feelings are involved, every experience is unique.

Reich used the term "orgasm" in a very special sense to refer to the complete surrender to sexual excitation with the total involvement of the body in the convulsive movements of discharge. The orgasm, as Reich described it, does occasionally happen to people, and it is an ecstatic experience. But it is also quite rare, as Reich himself recognized. A totality of response to any situation is unusual in our culture. We are all in too much conflict to surrender fully to any feeling.

I think we should use the word "orgasm" to describe a sexual release in which there are pleasurable spontaneous convulsive and involuntary movements of the body and the pelvis and which is experienced as satisfying. When only the genital apparatus is involved in the sensation of discharge and release, I would say this is too limited a response to be called an orgasm. That should be described as an ejaculation in a man or a climax in a woman. To qualify as an orgasm, the release should extend to other parts of the body—the pelvis and the legs, at least—and there should be some pleasurable involuntary movement in the body. An orgasm should be a *moving* experience. We are moved by it. If our whole body or being is moved spontaneously, especially if our heart responds, then one would have a full orgasm. This is what we all hope for in our sexual activity.

An orgasm, whether full or partial in terms of body involvement, releases tension in those parts that actively respond. The release, however, is not a permanent one. Since we are daily subject to stress in our lives, tensions can build again. One needs a satisfactory sexual life, not just one experience, to help keep down the level of tension in our bodies.

I don't want to create a mystique about orgasm, though I believe this funtion is critically important. It is not the only way to release tension, nor should it be used consciously for that purpose. One doesn't cry to release tension; one cries because one is sad, yet crying is a basic way of discharging tension. Even if the full orgasm is the most satisfying and effective discharge mechanism, it doesn't follow that sex without such an orgasm or the sexual union without climaxing is meaningless and devoid of pleasure. We engage in sex for pleasure, and that has to be the major criterion for our sexual behavior. All I am arguing is that the full orgasm is more pleasurable, so much so that it can reach the height of ecstasy. But since the degree of pleasure is dependent on the amount of preliminary excitation which is beyond our will or control, we must be grateful for whatever pleasure we experience.

The problem most people face is that the tensions in their body are so deeply structured that orgastic release rarely occurs. The pleasurable convulsive movements are too frightening, surrender too threatening. Regardless of what they say, most people are afraid and unable to give in to strong sexual feelings. And yet many patients say at the start of their therapy that their sex is good, that they are satisfied, that they have no sexual problem. In some cases they don't know any better, and the little pleasure they have is what they assume sex is about. In other cases self-deceit is operative. The male ego in particular will set up a defense of denial against any feeling of sexual inadequacy. As therapy progresses, both types become aware of how inadequate their sex was. They gain this realization by experiencing a more fulfilling and satisfying sexual discharge.

In all cases the person's body shows the true state of his sexual functioning. A person whose body is relatively free from major tensions will manifest the orgasm reflex while lying on the bed and breathing. I described this body response in the first chapter while discussing my personal therapy with Reich. It is important to repeat that description here.

The person lies on the bed, his knees bent so that his feet make contact with the bed. His head is back to get it out of the way, so to speak. The arms lie at one's sides. When the breathing is easy and deep and no muscular tensions block the respiratory waves as they pass through the body, the pelvis will move spontaneously with each breath. It will rise upward with the exhalation and fall backward on inspiration. The head moves in a reverse direction, upward with inspiration and backward with expiration. However, the throat moves forward with the expiration. This is shown in the figures on page 248.

Reich pictured the reflex as a movement in which the two ends of the body come together. The head, however, does not take part in this forward movement but falls back. (See the figure on p. 249.) If one looks at the figure and can picture the arms also reaching up, the movement could be described as an encircling or enclosing action. It resembles the action of an amoeba that flows around a particle of food to enclose and engulf it. The movement is far more primitive than sucking, in which the head plays the dominant role. Sucking is related to breathing in, to inspiration. When inhalation occurs, the head comes forward, and the throat and pelvis move backward.

This movement is called an orgasm reflex because it occurs in every case of a full orgasm. In a partial orgasm there is also some involuntary pelvic movement, but the whole body doesn't fully give

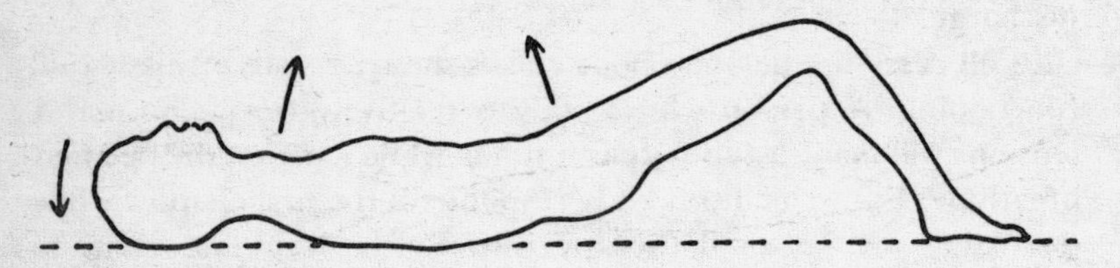
EXPIRATION—FORWARD MOVEMENT OF PELVIS

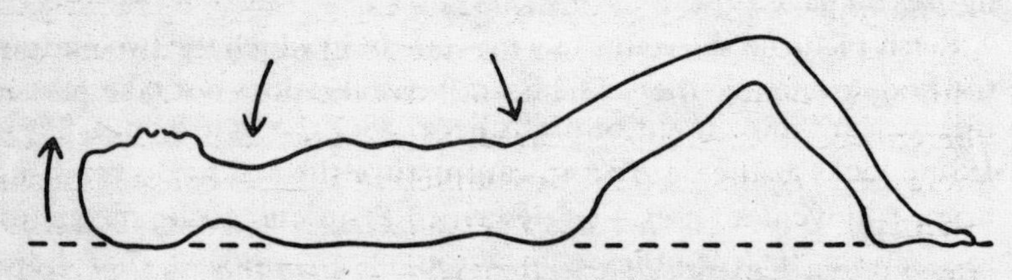
INSPIRATION—BACKWARD MOVEMENT OF PELVIS

in to it. One thing should be clear. The orgasm reflex is not an orgasm. It occurs on a low level of excitation and is a gentle movement. One experiences the reflex as a pleasurable feeling of inner freedom and ease. It denotes the absence of tension in the body.

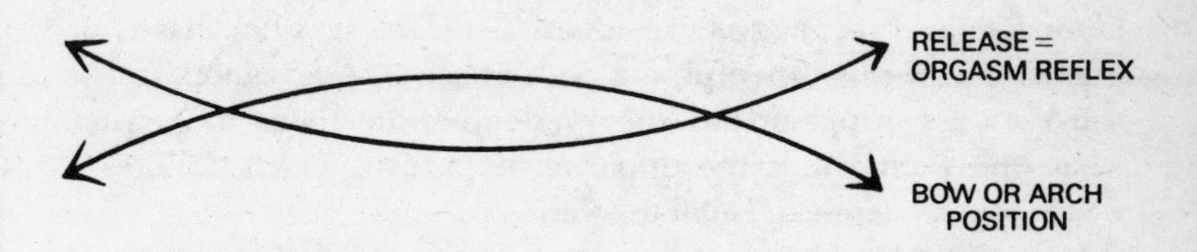

ORGASM REFLEX = RELEASE OF BOW POSITION

The development of the orgasm reflex in the therapeutic situation is no guarantee the patient will have full orgasms in sex. The two situations are radically different. In sex the level of excitation is very high and this makes the giving in more difficult. One has to gain the ability to tolerate this high level of excitation without becoming tense or anxious. Another difference is that the therapeutic situation is geared to support the patient. The therapist is there for him. It is different in a sexual relationship where the sexual partner has a personal interest in the relationship and makes demands. Nevertheless, it is true that if a person is incapable of giving in to the reflex in the supportive atmosphere of the therapeutic situation, it is unlikely he will be able to do so in the more highly charged atmosphere of the sexual encounter.

For this reason bioenergetic therapy does not place as much importance on the orgasm reflex as Reich did. Not that it isn't important or that the therapy doesn't aim at its development, but an equal emphasis has to be placed on the patient's ability to handle stress so that the reflex would function for him in a sexual situation. This is done by getting the charge to flow into the legs and feet, in which case the reflex takes on a different quality.

When the charge moves upward from the ground to the pelvis, it adds an aggressive element to a tender action. Let me say immediately that aggressive doesn't mean sadistic, hard or grasping. It means forceful in a positive sense. Aggression, as the word is used in personality theory, denotes the ability to go after what one wants. It is the opposite of passive, which denotes a waiting for someone to fulfill the want.

In my first book* I postulated two instincts called longing and aggression. Longing is associated with Eros, love and tenderness. It is characterized by the movement of excitation along the front of the body which is perceived as having a tender, erotic quality. Aggression results from the flow of excitation into the muscular system, especially into the large muscles of the back, the legs and the arms. These muscles are involved in standing and moving. The original meaning of the word "aggression" is "to move toward." This action depends on the operation of these muscles.

Aggression is a necessary component of the sexual act for both men and women. In the absence of aggression, sex is reduced to sensuality, to erotic stimulation without climax or orgasm. There is no aggression unless there is an object toward which one moves, a love object in sex, a fantasy object in masturbation.

Again, I should emphasize that aggression does not necessarily have a hostile intent. The intention of the movement can be loving or hostile; it is really the movement that constitutes aggression.

Aggression is also the force that enables us to meet, stand up to and handle stress. If the different character structures were ordered according to the amount of aggression available in each

*Lowen, *The Physical Dynamics of Character Structure*, *op. cit.*, also available in paperback under the title *The Language of the Body*, *op. cit.*

one, the order would duplicate that set forth earlier as a hierarchy of character types. One would have to understand that the aggression of the psychopathic character is a pseudo aggression. His direction is not toward what he wants but toward dominance. Having achieved control, he becomes passive. On the other hand, the masochist is not as passive as he appears. His aggression is hidden. It comes out in his whining and complaining. The oral character is passive largely because of his undeveloped musculature. The rigid character is overaggressive to compensate his inner feeling of frustration.

Now that we have a rational basis for aggression in sex, therapy has to help a person develop his sexual aggressiveness, which is the thrust of the pelvis in both men and woman. Note that I use the word "thrust" instead of "reaching," which was used to describe the reflex.

One can execute a forward movement of the pelvis in three ways: One call pull it forward by contracting the abdominal muscles. However, this has the effect of tensing the front of the body and cutting off the flow of tender and erotic feelings into the belly. It represents, in the language of the body, reaching without feeling. One can push it forward from behind by contracting the muscles of the buttocks or ass. This action tenses the pelvic floor and limits the discharge to the genital apparatus. These are the common ways people move the pelvis in sex. They make the same movements in therapy when one asks them to move the pelvis forward.

The third way of moving the pelvis forward is by pressing down on the ground with the feet. This action will move the pelvis forward if the knees are kept in a bent position. Then, when the pressure on the floor is released, it falls back. This action depends, however, on the person's ability to direct his energy into his feet. In this type of pelvic movement all the stress is in the legs. The pelvis is free from tension and swings, rather than is pulled or pushed.

The energy dynamics of this movement are shown in the following figures which illustrate three basic movements of the human body in relation to the ground: walking, rising, and the pelvis thrust. The principle underlying these actions is one I stated earlier: Action-reaction. If one presses on the ground, the ground presses back, and the person will move. The same principle is operative in a rocket's flight. The energetic discharge from the end of the rocket forces it forward. Here is how this principle works in the three actions listed above.

Walking: Take a position with the feet about six inches apart, the knees bent and the body straight. Shift your weight to the balls of the feet. Press down on the right foot, lift the left foot, and let it swing forward. When you release the right heel, you will step forward onto the left foot. Repeating this process with each foot alternately is walking.

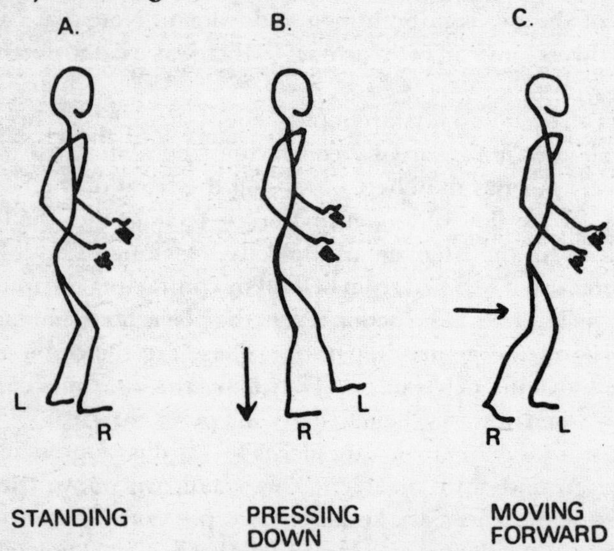

Rising: Assume the same position, but bend the knees more. Shift your weight to the balls of the feet and press down. This time, however, do not lift the left foot or release the heels from the ground. If the heels hold the ground, you will not be able to move forward. Since the resultant force from your action of pressing down must have some effect, you will find that your knees straighten up and you rise to a full standing position.

RISING

A. STANDING KNEES BENT

B. LEANING FORWARD

C. RISING

Pelvic thrust: Assume the same position as in rising. Go through the same procedure as in the second exercise, but do not allow your knees to straighten. You will not rise if you keep the knees bent, and you will not go forward if your heels hold the ground. The only available movement for the resultant force is a forward thrust of the pelvis. If you hold the pelvis locked, you will be in an isometric situation where the force acts on the musculature but no movement is allowed to occur. The movement will not occur if

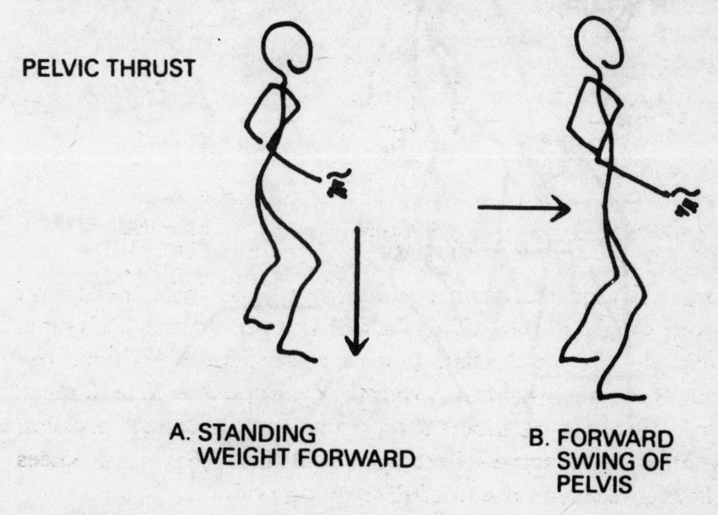

tension in the legs prevents the upward flow of the resultant force, nor will it happen if tensions in the pelvis lock it and prevent any free movement.

Tensions in the pelvic area are released through a variety of exercises and by massaging and kneading the tense muscles. A tense muscle can be palpated either as a knot or as a tight string. I hope to present many of the exercises we use in bioenergetics in a separate study as a manual of bioenergetic exercises. This book is intended to provide a general understanding of the intimate relation between personality and the body.

A variant of the last exercise which I use to free the pelvis also involves falling. I will describe it here, if any of the readers wish to try it (figure, below).

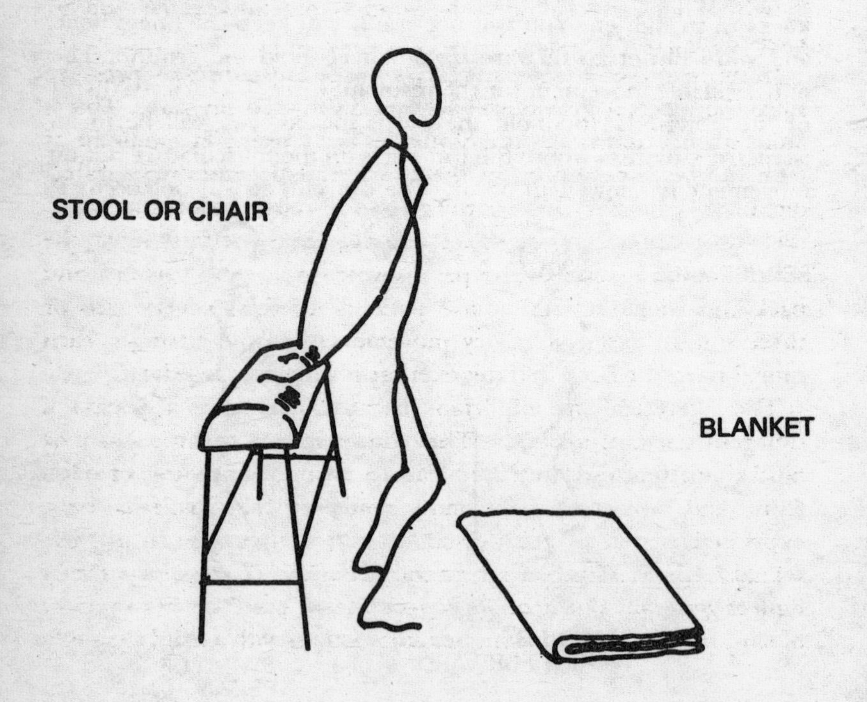

One takes a position in front of a stool or chair that is to be touched for balance only. The feet are six inches apart, and the knees almost fully bent. The body is pitched forward until the heels are *slightly* off the ground. The body weight should then be on the balls of the feet but not on the toes. The body should be arched backward and the pelvis brought forward without strain to form an unbroken arc. In this exercise it is important that one press downward on both heels without, however, letting them touch the floor. This can be prevented by leaning forward and keeping the knees bent. The pressure on the heels stops one from moving forward; the bent knees do not allow a rising to occur.

The person is instructed to hold this position for as long as he can without making it a test of will or endurance. Breathing should be abdominal but easy. The belly should be out, and the pelvis held loosely. When one can't hold the position, one falls forward on his knees onto a blanket.

In this exercise it is not necessary to use any conscious pressure since the force of gravity will act as a downward pressure. This is quite strong, and if the thigh muscles are tense, a fair amount of pain will be experienced in them. When it becomes unbearable, one falls. Generally, the legs will go into vibration before one has to fall. Also, if breathing is relaxed and deep and one stays loose, the vibration will extend to the pelvis, which will move forward and backward involuntarily. I have patients do this exercise two or three times, as the vibratory movements become stronger each time. I have also been told this exercise is a big help to skiers.

The exercises are important because they give a person a different sense of his body. They also help one become aware of blocks and tensions and thus lead to an understanding of one's fears and anxieties. The most common fear patients have expressed is that of being used sexually if they give in to their sexual feelings. This fear can be traced back to a parent or parental figures generally of the opposite sex. "Being used" covers a variety of sins, from a parent having sexual relations with a child to simply getting a kick or charge out of the child's sexuality. The specific fear has to be elucidated, and this can be done analytically or in other ways. In some cases the use of a falling exercise will bring it out.

One young woman was standing on one bent leg, looking down at the blanket, and as she thought about falling, she saw the image of a penis. She then equated the fear of falling with a fear of sexual surrender—to her own feelings. The image of the penis reminded her of her father. He was sadistic, she said. "He spanked and humiliated me. He walked around the house naked without any regard for my feelings." She was most disturbed, she added, by the look in his eyes. "He undressed me with his eyes."

It was unnecessary for her to elaborate. I could understand her problem and sympathize with her. She had no defense except to cut off her sexual feelings. The only way she could do this was by pulling up into the upper half of her body. This involved tightening the diaphragm and tensing the abdomen and pelvis. As a result, she developed falling anxiety.

Falling anxiety, however, was not the only consequence of this defensive action. When a person suffers an insult or injury, his natural response is anger. And it is only when the anger is blocked or inhibited by fear that he takes a defensive position. Inhibited anger turns into hostility and negativity. The individual now feels guilty, and his defensive posture becomes directed against his own hostile and negative feelings, as it is against any further insult or injury. It is not sufficient, therefore, for the person to realize and accept the fact that he is no longer vulnerable to the kind of insult or injury he experienced as a child. This will not substantially affect his defensive posture, since the defense has another function —namely, to hide his hostility.

I pointed out in the third chapter that the two outer layers of the personality, the ego defenses and the muscular armoring, function as monitors and controls over the emotional or id layer of the personality. Every neurotic and psychotic person is afraid of the intensity of his feelings, especially his negative feelings. I explained that these feelings have to be vented or expressed before the core feeling of love can flow freely and fully to the world. This should be done in the therapeutic situation to prevent any acting out of these feelings on innocent persons. It is a consistent practice in bioenergetic therapy to encourage their expression whenever they are appropriate to the immediate therapeutic situation. This would certainly be true of the patient I just described who experienced her father as being sadistic and humiliating. Before we can expect her to give in to her sexual feelings positively, we must allow her to give in to their negative aspect.

It should be recognized that this patient or any other female who has suffered a similar trauma has ambivalent feelings toward men. As a girl and a woman she loves men, and this includes her father, but as a child who was hurt and humiliated by a man she hates all men. In a part of her personality she would like to do to them what they did to her—hurt and humiliate them. She dared not express such feeling as a child, and she dares not do so now as an adult. She also knows such feelings are as destructive to any relationship as they were to her. This places her in a difficult bind from which therapy must help free her. The only way this can be accomplished is by providing an outlet for her negative feelings.

There are several appropriate exercises. One is to give the patient a turkish towel that can be twisted in one's hands. The towel can represent any person. In this case it could be the father, a present boyfriend or me, another representative of the hated male sex. Twisting the towel, the patient can say all the things she would like or have liked to say to her father or to any man. "You're a bastard. I hate you. You humiliated me and I despise you. I could twist your head off your body; then you couldn't look at me with those lascivious eyes." It is obvious the towel could also represent the penis. By twisting it, she can release a lot of hostility against that organ.

This exercise is not done routinely. It has value only when it follows the patient's revelation of a traumatic experience. Such experiences need not be sexual. The exercise can be used to release any hostile or angry feeling stemming from any injury or insult.

An exercise that is specifically sexual and would be more appropriate in the present context is the following: The patient gets on a bed on elbows and knees and digs her or his toes into the mattress. This is the usual male position in intercourse. Now the patient, male or female, socks the pelvis against the bed in a hard driving movement. It can be done with or without vocal utterances. If words are used, they would necessarily be mean, sadistic, hurtful and vulgar.

When a patient lets go in this exercise, he experiences a great sense of release. He gets it out finally and in a manner that is not destructive to himself or others. Vulgarity is appropriate, for the action aims at demeaning the other, but the person feels clean as if he had washed his dirty hands. The clean feeling that ensues is anger, clean anger at the person who inflicted the injury. This anger can then be expressed by hitting the bed with a tennis racket. The hitting is neither demeaning nor punishing. It affirms the right of the patient to respect as an individual and reinforces the feeling of self-respect. No one can respect himself if he cannot or does not become angry at a personal insult or injury.

With each release of a hostile or negative feeling, the falling anxiety diminishes. The same is true of every valid expression of anger. But the falling anxiety is not eliminated by these maneuvers alone. It now exists in its own right as a fear that has to be confronted or faced. One learns to let down without fear not by words but by doing it. And in the process one also learns to stand up for one's respect and one's sexuality against all persons, including the therapist.

I should add that every exercise releases not only suppressed feelings, but also muscular tensions. Falling frees the legs from the strain of having to hold oneself up because of fear. Rocking the pelvis (we do it backward to release muscular tensions associated with suppressed anal sadism) reduces the muscular tensions in the hips and in the pelvic girdle. Twisting the towel and hitting the bed have similiar effects on other parts of the body.

These are typical exercises in self-expression. They are not the only ones we use in bioenergetics, nor are they limited to negative, hostile and angry feelings. Reaching out for contact, touching tenderly and holding are employed to express affection and longing. In the next chapter I will discuss the nature of self-expression and describe some of the ways we treat problems in self-expression. Two closing comments, however, are necessary here.

The emphasis on getting out the negative feelings is based on the clinical fact that a person who can't say no, can't say yes. It is important, therefore, for a person to be able to express a hostile or angry feeling when it is appropriate to do so. I have gone into the philosophic implications of this view in my book *Pleasure: A Creative Approach to Life.* It would be unrealistic to conceive of the human personality as being only positive by nature. It is positive to life, but negative to antilife. Some people are confused, however, and mistake one for the other. Both kinds of forces exist in the world, and it is naïve to think otherwise. If we can distinguish between them, then negativity has a proper place in human behavior.

The seeming overemphasis on bodily expression may lead the reader to believe that words are unimportant in bioenergetic therapy. This is certainly not true of my own work, and I shall talk about the role of words in the final chapter. I don't believe we overemphasize bodily expression. It is emphasized here because in most other therapies it is ignored. Words cannot replace body movement, but by the same token body movement is not equivalent to language. Each has its place in therapy as in life. Many of my patients have some difficulty in expressing themselves satisfactorily through language. Like any other therapist, I work on this problem with them. All my patients, however, have difficulty in fully expressing themselves on a body level, and this problem is the main focus of bioenergetics. I have also found that the body problem underlies the verbal one, though it is not identical with it. It is easier to be fluent about sex than to flow in sex.

IX. Self-Expression and Survival

Self-Expression and Spontaneity

Self-expression describes the free, natural and spontaneous activities of the body and is, like self-preservation, an inherent quality of all living organisms. Every activity of the body contributes to self-expression, from the most mundane, such as walking and eating, to the most sophisticated, such as singing and dancing. The way a person walks, for example, not only defines him as a human being (no other animal walks like man), but also defines his sex, his approximate age, his character structure and his individuality. No two people walk exactly alike, look exactly alike or behave exactly alike. A person expresses himself in every action he takes or movement his body makes.

Actions and body movements are not the only modalities of self-expression. The form and shape of the body, its colorations, hair, eyes, sounds identify the species and the individual. We can recognize a lion or a horse from its picture; no action or movement is involved here. We can even recognize an individual horse from his picture if we know him, as we can recognize an individual person from a picture. Sounds and smells also identify both the species and the individual.

According to this definition, self-expression is not usually a conscious activity. We can be consciously self-expressive or conscious of our self-expression. But whether we are aware of it or not, we are expressing ourselves all the time. Two important points follow from this fact. One is that the self is not limited to the conscious self and is not identical with the ego. The second is that we don't have to do anything to express ourselves. We impress people just by being, and sometimes we impress them more by not doing anything than by trying to be self-expressive. In the latter case we risk creating the impression of a person who is desperate for recognition. And our self-expression may become inhibited by our own self-consciousness.

Spontaneity, not consciousness, is the essential quality of self-expression. Abraham Maslow, in an unpublished paper, "The Creative Attitude," says:

> Full spontaneity is a guarantee of honest expression of the nature and style of the freely functioning organism, and of its uniqueness. Both words, spontaneity and expressiveness, imply honesty, naturalness, truthfulness, lack of guile, non-imitativeness, etc., because they also imply a non-instrumental nature of the behavior, a lack of willful "trying," a lack of effortful striving or straining, a lack of interference with the flow of impulses and the free radioactive expression of the deep person.

It is interesting to note that spontaneity has to be defined in negative terms, as an absence of "willful trying," a "lack of guile," a "lack of interference." Spontaneity cannot be taught. One doesn't learn to be spontaneous, and therapy, therefore, cannot teach it. Since the aim of therapy is to help a person become more spontaneous and more self-expressive, which in turn leads to an increased sense of self, the therapeutic endeavor should be designed to remove the barriers or blocks to self-expression. Necessarily, then, one must understand these blocks. For me that means the bioenergetic approach to the problem of inhibited self-expression.

Comparing spontaneous behavior with learned behavior makes the former's relation to self-expression clear. Learned behavior generally reflects what one has been taught and should be regarded, therefore, as an expression of the ego or superego but not the self. However, this distinction cannot be rigorously applied, since most behavior contains both learned and spontaneous elements. Speaking is a good example. The words we use are learned responses, but speech is more than words or phrases—it includes inflection, tone, rhythm and gesture, which in large part are spontaneous and unique to the speaker. The latter add color to the speech and richness to the expression. On the other hand, no one will argue for a speech that distorts the common meaning of words and ignores the rules of grammar for the sake of spontaneity. A spontaneity divorced from ego control is chaos and disorder, notwithstanding the fact that one can sometimes make sense of the prattle of babies or the mutterings of schizophrenics. A proper balance between ego control and spontaneity would allow an impulse to be expressed in its most efficient form, yet be strongly infused with the life of the person.

While a spontaneous action is a direct expression of an impulse and thus a direct manifestation of the inner self, not all impulsive acting out is self-expressive. Reactive behavior has a spontaneous aspect which is deceiving, since it is conditioned and predetermined by previous experience. Individuals who fly into a rage whenever they are frustrated may appear to be acting spontaneously, but this is belied by the explosive quality of their response. The explosion stems from the blocking of impulses and the piling up of energy behind the block from which it is released by a minor provocation. Reactive behavior stems from an "interference with the flow of impulses" and is an expression of a blocked state in the organism. However, such explosive reactions may have to be encouraged in the controlled therapeutic setting to remove deeply structured blocks.

Bioenergetics is sometimes criticized for this position. There is a naive assumption on the part of many therapists that violence has no rational place in human behavior. I wonder how such a person would respond if his life were threatened! This is a threat that hung over many of my patients in their young years. It is irrelevant to question whether or not the threat would have been carried out. Young children cannot afford to make this distinction. Their immediate and truly spontaneous response is a violent one. Where this response is blocked or inhibited by fear of reprisal, the inner condition for reactive behavior is set. This block will be dissolved not through reassurance and love but only when such reassurance and love supports the patient's right to discharge his violence in the controlled setting of the therapy, not by acting it out in his daily life.

Pleasure is the key to self-expression. Whenever we are truly expressing ourselves, we experience pleasure that may range from the mild to the ecstatic as in sex. The pleasure of self-expression doesn't depend on the environment's response; self-expression is pleasurable in itself. I would ask the reader to think of the pleasure he or she had when dancing to realize how much the pleasure of self-expression was independent of others' reactions. This is not to say a positive response to one's self-expression is without value. Our pleasure is heightened or decreased by the reaction of others. However, it is not created by this response. One doesn't think of others when singing in the shower, yet this activity is self-expressive and pleasurable.

Singing is naturally a self-expressive action, like dancing. But it loses some of this quality when it becomes a performance—that is, when some of the spontaneous impulse to sing is missing. One may derive an ego satisfaction from performance, but when the element of spontaneity is low, the pleasure is proportionately decreased. Fortunately, such a performance would be equally uninspiring for an audience and would not, therefore, tend to be repeated. The same is true of dancing, speaking, writing, cooking or any activity. The challenge to an artist is how to maintain a high standard of performance without losing the feeling of spontaneity in his actions that gives life and pleasure to the activity.

In situations where one can be freely spontaneous without giving any conscious thought to the expression, the experience of pleasure is very high. Children's play has this quality. In most of our actions there is a mixture of spontaneity and control, the control serving to give our actions a sharper focus and a greater effect. When control and spontaneity are harmonized so that each supplements rather than hinders the other, the pleasure is greatest. In such actions the ego and the body work together to produce a degree of coordination in movement that can only be characterized as graceful.

We take pleasure in the good looks of our bodies because they express who we are. We envy the person with fine hair, bright eyes, white teeth, clear complexion, good posture, a graceful manner and so on. We feel these are sources of pleasure for the person and would be so for us. It is a thesis in bioenergetics that the health and vitality of the body are reflected in its appearance. Good looks and good feelings go together.

Spontaneity is a function of the body's motility. A living body is never completely at rest, even in sleep. The vital functions, of course, never stop, but in addition, there are many involuntary movements that occur in sleep. These are more frequent when we are awake and active. They vary in quality and intensity with the degree of excitation. Children are known to become so excited they literally jump. In adults these involuntary movements constitute the basis of our gestures, facial expressions and other body actions. Generally, we are not conscious of this activity which expresses us even more than our conscious actions. It follows, therefore, that the greater the motility of the organism, the more self-expressive it is.

The motility of a body is directly related to its energy level. It takes energy to move. Where the energy level is low or depressed, motility is necessarily decreased. A direct line connects energy to self-expression. Energy ⟶ motility ⟶ feeling ⟶

spontaneity ⟶ self-expression. This sequence also operates in reverse. If an individual's self-expression is blocked, his spontaneity is reduced. The reduction of spontaneity lowers the feeling tone, which in turn decreases the motility of the body and depresses its energy level. Adolf Portmann, a leading biologist interested in the self-expression of animals, comes to a similar conclusion from his studies: "A rich inner life . . . depends largely on . . . that degree of self-hood, that goes hand-in-hand with a rich manner of self-expression."

Portmann's statement suggests an interrelationship of three elements in the personality: the inner life, the outer expression and selfhood. I see each of these as one point of a triangle that requires all three to maintain its form.

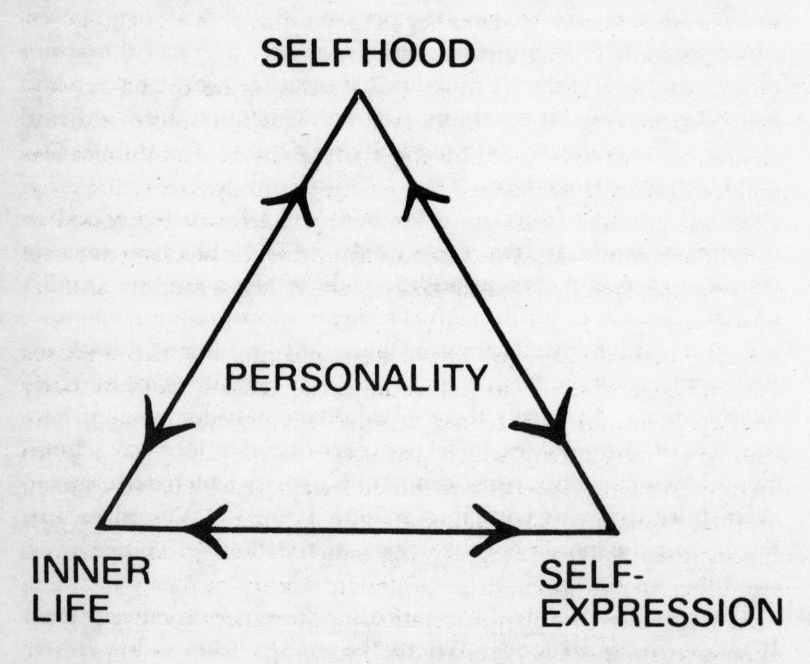

When a person's self-expression is blocked or limited, he may compensate by projecting an ego image. The most common way this is done is through the use of power and the best example of this projection was Napoleon. As he became older, he became even shorter, as his head shrank into his shoulders. He was called the "little corporal," yet his image loomed large over Europe. He was an emperor who wielded great power. I can see the need for such power only as a reflection of a sense of inferiority on the level of self and self-expression. If Napoleon could have sung and danced, he might not have needed to march armies through countries to gain a sense of self which I doubt he ever achieved. Power creates only a larger image, not a bigger self.

Another example of compensation is seen in the person who has to have a big house, an expensive car or a large boat to overcome an inner sense of smallness. What is small is his range of self-expression. He may be rich in money, for that is his ambition, but he remains poor in his inner life (spirit) and in his manner of self-expression.

In bioenergetics we focus on three major areas of self-expression: movement, voice and eyes. Normally people express themselves through each of these channels of communication simultaneously. If we feel sad, for example, our eyes tear, our voice sobs, and our body may convulse. Anger is likewise expressed in body movement, sound and looks. Cutting off or blocking any one of these channels weakens and splinters the emotion and its expression.

In the preceding pages I have discussed many of the exercises and maneuvers we use to reduce muscular tension and free body motility. I would like to say a word here about some of the expressive movements which are used for the same purpose in therapy. We have patients kick, hit the couch, reach out for contact, including touching, sucking, biting and so forth. Few patients can execute these movements gracefully and with feeling. Their actions are either uncoordinated or explosive. Rarely can they combine these movements with appropriate vocal utterances and eye contact to make them more expressive. The blocks against these expressive movements reduce the body's mobility and the person's spontaneity. The blocks can be released only by working with these movements.

Kicking is a good example. To kick means to protest. Since most children were denied the right to protest, as adults they cannot kick with any sense of conviction or with real effect. They need a provocation to release this action explosively. If there is no provocation, their kicking is haphazard and uncoordinated. Sometimes they say, "I have nothing to kick about." But this is a denial, since no person would be in therapy if he felt there was nothing to protest in his life.

Kicking on a bed using one outstretched leg after the other is a whipping action in which, when it is well done, the whole body participates. Tensions in any part of the body interfere with this whipping quality. The legs may move, for example, but the head and torso are immobile. In this case the leg movement is forced and there is no spontaneity. We say the person is afraid to "let go" to the action. Although it is started voluntarily, when a person lets go to the action, it takes on a spontaneous and involuntary quality and becomes pleasurable and satisfying. Using the voice, such as saying no when kicking, adds to the commitment and to the release. What is true for kicking is equally true for the other expressive movements mentioned above.

I have found it necessary to have patients go through these exercises involving kicking, hitting, biting, touching repeatedly to free the movement so that feeling can flow smoothly into the action. Each time they kick or hit the bed, for example, they learn to give in to the movement more fully, allowing more of the body to feel the action. In most cases it is necessary to point out to the patient how he holds against giving in to the movement. For example, a patient will reach for me with his hands while holding back with his shoulders, unaware he is inhibiting the action until I point it out to him. Hitting the bed either with one's fists or with a tennis racket is a relatively simple action, yet few can do it well. They do not stretch enough, they don't arch their backs, they lock their knees, any one of which prevents them from putting themselves fully into the action. Of course, hitting was taboo for most children. Removing the taboo psychologically in the present doesn't help much since it has become structured in the body as chronic tension. With practice, however, the hitting becomes more coordinated and effective, and patients begin to feel a pleasure doing this exercise—a sign they have opened a new area of self-expression.

I have always believed that therapy requires a double approach—one focused on the past, the other on the present. The work on the past is the analytic side, which stresses the *why* of a person's behavior, actions and movements. The work on the present stresses the *how*, how one acts and moves. Coordination and effectiveness of action and movement are for most animals learned qualities, learned in the course of childhood play. But where a child has emotional problems, this learning doesn't take place fully and naturally. To some extent, therefore, every therapy involves a relearning and retraining program. Therapy, in my opinion, should not be an either-or process, either analysis or learning, but a judicious combination of both.

Sound and Personality

The word "personality" has two root meanings. The first derives from *persona* which refers to the mask an actor wore in a play and which defined his role. In one sense, therefore, personality is conditioned by the role an individual assumes in life or by the face he presents to the world. The second meaning is just the opposite of the first. If we break the word "persona" into its component parts, *per sona,* we have a phrase which means "by sound." According to this meaning, personality is reflected in the sound of an individual. A mask is a nonliving thing and cannot convey the vibrant quality of a living organism as its voice does.

One could say, "Pay no attention to the mask, but listen to his sound if you want to know a person." In part this is sound advice—no pun intended. But it would be an error to ignore the mask. The sound does not always tell us what role a person has adopted, although in many cases it does. There is a special manner of speaking that can be identified with roles. Preachers, teachers, servants and sergeants have characteristic ways of speaking that identify them with their profession or vocation. The mask influences and modifies the voice. But there are elements in the voice that the mask does not always touch and that give us different information about the personality.

There is no question in my mind that a rich voice is a rich manner of self-expression and denotes a rich inner life. I believe this is something we all sense about a person, and this sensing is valid, even if unsupported by objective studies. What do we mean by a rich voice? The essential factor is the presence of undertones and overtones that give it a fullness of sound. Another factor is range. A person who speaks in a monotone has a very limited range of expression, and we tend to equate this with a limited personality. A voice can be flat, without depth or resonance, it can be low as if lacking energy, and it can be thin and bodiless. Each of these qualities bears some relationship to the personality of the individual.

So closely is the voice tied to personality that it is possible to diagnose the neurosis of a person from an analysis of his voice. I recommend a careful reading of Paul Moses' *The Voice of Neurosis** to anyone who wishes to understand the relation of the voice to personality. The study of voice has progressed to the point where it can be used in lie detection. This is more subtle than lie detection based on the psychogalvanic reflex in the skin, but the principle is similar in both cases. When a person tells a lie, there is a flatness to his voice that can be detected by an instrument. This flatness, as differentiated from a person's normal voice, indicates a block or holding back of the impulse to speak the truth.

The new lie-detector device is known as a PSE, or Psychological Stress Evaluator. Allan D. Bell, president of the company that markets the device, describes its operation: "There are physiologi-

*Paul M. Moses, *The Voice of Neurosis* (New York, Grune and Stratton, 1954).

cal tremors inherent in the muscles of the human body which are going on all the time when the muscles are in use. Under stress, however, the amount of tremor decreases. The muscles of the voice too exhibit these same tremors, as well as the stress effect. Using the electronic equipment we've devised, you can examine a tape recording of a voice to watch what happens to these tremors. The extent of the tremor is inversely proportional to the amount of psychological stress the person is feeling."

The tremors are what I call vibrations. The absence of vibration denotes stress or holding, whether in the body or in the voice. In the latter it produces a loss of resonance. The relationships are: stress = holding = loss of vibration = flatness of affect or feeling.

I am not an authority on the voice, but as a psychiatrist I pay close attention to it in my work with patients. I use it not only diagnostically to the best of my ability but also therapeutically. If a person is to recover his full potential for self-expression, it is important he gain the full use of his voice in all its registers and in all its nuances of feeling. The blockage of any feeling will affect its expression vocally. It is necessary, therefore, to unblock feelings, something we have been discussing all along; however, it is also necessary to work specifically with the production of sound to eliminate tensions that exist around the vocal apparatus.

To understand the role of tension in the disturbance of sound production, we must consider each of the three elements that go into the creation of sound. These are a flow of air under pressure acting on the vocal cords to produce a vibration, vocal cords that function as vibratory instruments, and the resonating cavities that magnify the sound. Tensions that interfere with respiration, especially those in the region of the diaphragm, will be reflected in some distortion of the quality of the voice. In severe anxiety, for example, when the diaphragm becomes fluttery, the voice becomes very shaky. Generally the vocal cords themselves are free from chronic tension, but with acute strain they become affected and produce a hoarseness. Tensions in the neck and throat musculature that are fairly common affect the resonance of the voice, leading either to chest tones or head tones. The natural voice is a combination of these tones in varying degrees depending on the emotion involved. Such a combination would be a balanced voice.

The lack of a balanced voice is a clear indication of a personality problem. Moses describes two cases he treated which I will quote because he is speaking as an otolaryngologist:

> A twenty-five year old patient spoke in a high child-like voice which caused him great embarrassment. He had completely normal vocal cords adequate to produce a healthy baritone and he could actually sing baritone. But he persisted in speaking in falsetto. Another patient, a young lawyer complained of chronic hoarseness. He used in his voice production an overamount of chest register. The young lawyer had a prominent father who played a leading role in the county's life and his son had a high ideal to live up to. Hence the forced tone to create an illusion which would hide the lack of success in identification with the father's image. Similarly the persistent falsetto of the other patient could be traced to holding onto his mother's apron strings.*

Moses doesn't describe his treatment of these problems, but from his remark we can see it involved some analysis of the patient's background. "In both cases they had to retrace the steps, relearn their lesson in young manhood." I am sure every analyst or therapist could relate many instances from his own practice where an enrichment of the voice followed a successful working through of a personality problem.

John Pierrakos has described one of the ways he works bioenergetically with voice blocks to open up and release the suppressed feelings behind them.

One way to handle these problems directly is to place the

*_Ibid._, p. 47.

thumb of the right hand one inch below the angle of the jaw while the middle finger is placed at the corresponding position on the other side of the neck. The scalene and sternocleidomastoid muscles are grasped and pressure is applied steadily while the patient vocalizes at a high sustained pitch. The same process is repeated several times at the middle point and base of the neck, at different voice registers. Many times this leads to an agonizing screaming which develops into deep sobbing and one can hear real emotional involvement and surrender. The sorrow is expressed in clonic movements and the whole body vibrates with emotion. The voice becomes alive and pulsating and the throat block is opened up. It is striking to discover what is hidden behind the facade of the stereotyped voice. A young woman with an assumed adolescent high-pitched voice, acting the role of the little girl with her father, broke into a melodious mature feminine voice. A man with a flat, dry voice changed his register after this release to a deep masculine voice, challenging his "oppressive father." I was deeply moved when a schizoid female patient who was hiding herself behind an ominous-sounding dry voice, after opening the throat blocks, started singing a melodious, poignant song like a little girl of six.*

Because the voice is so closely tied to feeling, freeing it involves the mobilization of suppressed feelings and their expression in sound. There are different sounds for different feelings. Fear and terror are expressed in a scream, anger in a loud, sharp tone, sadness in a deep, sobbing voice, pleasure and love in soft, cooing sounds. It can be said generally that a high-pitched voice indicates a blocking of the deep notes that express sadness; a low-pitched, chesty voice indicates a denial of the feeling of fear and an inhibition against its expression in a scream. However, it cannot be

*John C. Pierrakos, *The Voice and Feeling in Self-Expression* (New York, Institute for BioEnergetic Analysis, 1969), p. 11.

assumed that the person who speaks in a seemingly balanced voice is not limiting his vocal expression. Balance for this person may represent control and the fear of letting go by voicing strong emotions.

In bioenergetic therapy there is a constant emphasis on letting the sounds out. The words are less important, though not unimportant. The best sounds are the ones that emerge spontaneously. I will describe two of the procedures that can evoke them.

Every baby is born with the ability to cry out. It is the act that establishes the newborn's independent respiration. The strength of that first cry is some measure of the infant's vitality; some cry vigorously, others feebly, but soon most babies learn to cry loudly. Not long after birth they also gain the ability to scream. The scream is a major form of releasing tension whether owing to fear, anger or intense frustration. Many people use the scream for this purpose.

Some years ago I was on an audience-participation broadcast in Boston. One of the listeners phoned in to ask me how to overcome her difficulty of speaking before people. Without knowing the cause of her problem, I still had to offer some advice, and my suggestion to her was to practice screaming. I knew it could only help her. The best place to scream is in a car on a highway with the windows closed. The noise of the traffic is so great that no one could possibly hear. When I finished making this suggestion, I received another phone call. This was from a man who was listening to the program. He said that he was a salesman and that at the end of a day he felt tense and held in from his work. He did not want to return home in this state. The best way he had found to relieve it was to scream in his car. He said it helped greatly, and he was surprised anyone else had thought of it. Since then, I have had several people tell me they have used this technique with similar results.

Unfortunately, many people are unable to scream. Their throats are too tight to allow it to come through. One can palpate the extremely tense muscles at the sides of the throat. This tension can be released and a scream elicited, if pressure is applied to these muscles, specifically to the anterior scalene muscle at each side of the neck. Pierrakos used this maneuver as we saw earlier, but since it is so important, I will also describe how I do it. The patient, lying on the bed, is asked to make a loud sound. Then, with my thumb and middle finger, I apply a medium pressure to these muscles. The initial pain is generally strong enough to shock the patient into a scream, especially since he is already making a loud noise. The pitch spontaneously rises, and the scream erupts. Surprisingly, while the patient is screaming, he feels no pain although the pressure is continuing. Often the screaming will continue long after I have removed my fingers. If the patient doesn't scream, I stop the pressure since the holding against the scream will only intensify.

Effective as this procedure is in eliciting a scream, it does not release all the tensions around the mouth and throat that affect voice production. When the voice of a person is free, it comes from his heart. He is a person who speaks from his heart. This means that the channel of communication from the heart to the world is open and free of obstructions. If we look at this channel anatomically, we will find three areas where chronic tensions can form rings of constriction, narrowing the channel and impeding the full expression of feeling. The most superficial ring can form around the mouth. A tight or closed mouth can effectively block all communication of feeling. Compressing the lips and setting the jaw are the way one can clamp down to shut off any sound from breaking through to the outside. We speak of people with this attitude as being "tight-mouthed."

The second ring of tension forms at the junction of head and neck. This is a critical area because it represents the zone of transition from voluntary to involuntary control. The pharynx and mouth are in front of this zone, the esophagus and trachea behind it. The organism has conscious control of anything that is in the mouth or pharynx; one has the choice of whether to swallow it or spit it out. That choice is lost when the substance, food or water, for example, passes through this area and enters into the esophagus. From this point downward the involuntary system takes over, and conscious control is gone. The biological importance of this transition zone is evident, for it allows an organism to taste and then reject any substance that is unacceptable or unsuitable. Its psychological importance, though less evident, is also clear. By not swallowing an unacceptable or injurious element the psychological integrity of the organism can be maintained.

Unfortunately the psychological integrity of children is often violated by forcing them to swallow "things" they would otherwise reject. "Things" refer to food, medicine, remarks, situations and so on. I am sure we have all had experiences of this sort. My mother used to make me drink castor oil mixed with orange juice. The concoction was extremely unpleasant, and for many years I couldn't stand the taste of pure orange juice. We all have had to swallow insults or derogatory remarks, and many of us have been forced to "eat our words." One of my patients told me an interesting story her mother had recounted proudly. The mother would put some cereal into the baby's mouth, and before the child could spit it out, she forced her breast into the baby's mouth so that it had to swallow the food in order not to choke.*

The effect of such procedures is to create a ring of tension at this critical junction. This tension constricts the passageway from the neck to the oral cavity and represents an unconscious defense against being forced to swallow any unacceptable "thing" from outside. At the same time it is an unconscious defense or holding against the expression of feelings one fears may be unacceptable to others. Necessarily the constriction interferes with respiration by narrowing the opening for the passage of air. It contributes, therefore, to anxiety. The location of this ring of tension is shown in the following figure:

*How many of us have been forced to swallow tears and our protests because their expression was not acceptable.

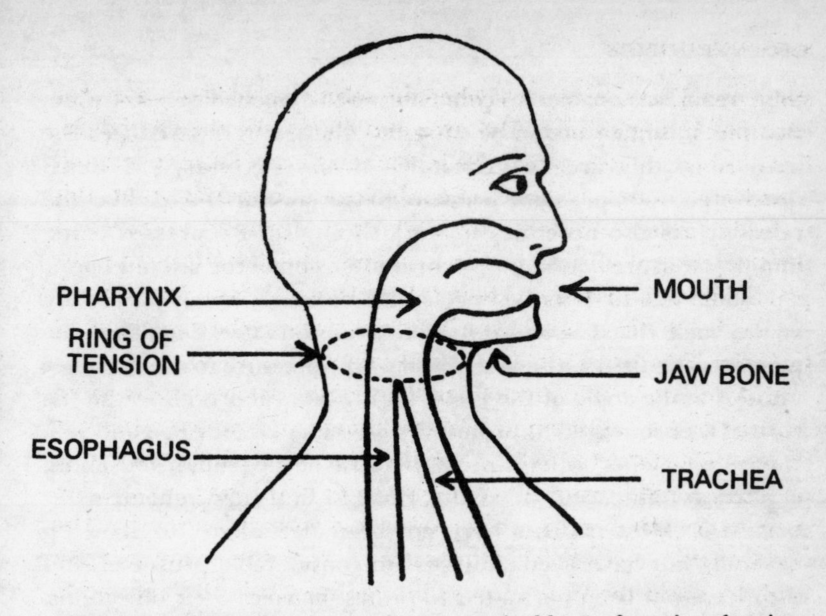

This ring of tension is not an anatomical but a functional unity. Many muscles take part in its formation, and several structures, such as the jaw and tongue, in its operation. The lower jaw plays a special role, for by setting the jaw, one effectively locks the tension in place. Setting the jaw, regardless of its position, is equivalent to saying, "They shall not pass." It functions in this respect like the portcullis of a castle which keeps undesirable people out but also encloses those on the inside. When an organism needs more energy, as it does when tired or sleepy, the portal must be opened wide to permit a fuller breath, which is what we do when we yawn. In the yawn the ring of tension which includes the muscles that move the jaw are temporarily released with the result that mouth, pharynx and throat open wide to let in the air one needs.

Because of its strategic location as the portcullis for the personality, the tension in the muscles that move the jaw is the keystone to the holding pattern in the rest of the body. Considerable work is done in bioenergetics to release this tension, which is present to different degrees in all persons. It was the first area that Reich focused on in his therapy with me. Reich constantly emphasized the necessity to drop the jaw. When I dropped my jaw, the scream was enabled to come out when I opened my eyes wide. But the voluntary action of dropping the jaw rarely reduces the tension in this area significantly. It was necessary, as Reich discovered, to apply some pressure to the jaw muscles to effect the release. It is also necessary to work through the repressed biting impulses that are bound in the chronic tension of the jaw muscles.

I would like to describe one simple maneuver involving the use of the voice that I use to reduce this tension. Standing above the patient as he lies on the bed, I will apply pressure to the masseter muscles at the angle of the jaw. This is a painful procedure, so the patient is encouraged to protest. I suggest he kick the bed and yell, "Leave me alone," when I press. Because of the pain, his response is often genuine, and he is surprised to find how vehement his protest is. Most patients have not been "left alone" to grow up naturally but have been subjected to considerable pressure. And they have not been permitted to protest or voice their objections. For many patients it is a new experience to let their voice and actions express strong feeling.

I do not wish to give the impression that pain is an essential part of bioenergetic work. Many of the procedures are very pleasurable, but pain cannot be avoided if one wants to free himself from chronic tensions. As Arthur Janov points out in *The Primal Scream,* pain is already in a patient. Crying and yelling are one way to release the pain. The pressure I apply to a tense muscle is not that painful in itself. It is minor when compared to the tension in the muscle and would not be experienced as painful by a person whose muscles are relaxed. My pressure, added to the tension in the muscle, will exceed its pain threshold, but it will also make the person conscious of his tension and lead to its release.

I mentioned above that there are three areas where a ring of tension can develop that will obstruct or constrict the passage from the chest to the outer world. The first is around the mouth; the second at the junction of head and neck. The third is at the junction of neck and thorax. The ring of tension that develops in this area is also functional in nature and involves mostly the anterior, middle and posterior scalene muscles. This ring of tension guards the opening to the chest cavity and so to the heart. When chronically contracted, these muscles elevate and immobilize the upper ribs, constricting the opening to the chest. Since this also interferes with the natural respiratory movements, it seriously affects voice production, particularly in the chest register. In working with the voice, one has to be aware of this area of tension.

Let me add here that every sound has a place in self-expression. Laughter is as important as crying, singing as wailing. I often ask patients to make purring, cooing and calling sounds to help them feel the pleasure of vocal expression as they must have felt it sometime in their babyhood. But how difficult it is for many people to identify with the baby they were and the baby they still are in their hearts.

The Eyes Are *the Mirrors of the Soul*

Eye Contact

On the first page of the textbook on ophthalmology I studied in medical school was the statement "The eyes are the mirrors of the soul." I was intrigued by the statement, which I'd heard before, and anxious to learn more about the expressive function of the eyes. But I was sadly disappointed. The book contained no further reference to the relationship between the eyes and the soul or between the eyes and feeling. The anatomy, the physiology and the pathology of the eyes were thoroughly described in a mechanistic way, as if the eye were a machine like a camera rather than an expressive organ of the personality.

I suppose the reason why ophthalmology ignores this aspect of the eye is that as a strictly scientific discipline it has to deal with objective data. The expressive function of the eye is not subject to objectification or measurement. But this raises the question whether an objective scientific view could fully comprehend the functioning of an eye or for that matter a human being.

Psychiatrists and other students of personality cannot afford this narrow view. We must see a person in his expressive nature and how we look at him will determine not only how we understand him, but how he responds to us.

Body language contains the wisdom of the ages. I have no doubt that the statement about the eyes being the mirrors of the soul is true. This is our subjective impression when we look into certain eyes, and I believe it corresponds to the expression we see. This soulful quality is particularly evident in the eyes of a dog or a cow. Their soft brown eyes are like the earth when these animals are relaxed. Their soulful expression is associated, in my mind, with contact, with the sense of belonging or being part of life, nature and the universe that I described in Chapter II.

Each kind of animal has a special look in its eyes that reflects its special quality. Cat's eyes, for example, have a quality of independence and distance. The eyes of a bird are different. Yet the eyes of all animals are capable of expressing feeling. When one has lived with a cat or a bird for some time, one is able to distinguish different expressions. One can tell when the eyes become heavy with sleep or bright with excitement. If the eyes are the mirrors of the soul, then the richness of an organism's inner life must be reflected in the range of feeling visible in the eyes.

In a more prosaic way we can say the eyes are the windows of the body since they reveal the inner feeling. But like all windows, they can be shuttered or open. In the first case they are impenetrable; in the second, one can see into the person. They can have a vacant or distant look. Vacant eyes give one the impression that "no one is there." This look is commonly seen in the eyes of schizoid people.* Looking into such eyes, one gets an impression of inner emptiness. Distant eyes indicate the person is far away, off somewhere. We can bring him back by gaining his attention. His return coincides with the contact established between his eyes and our own as he looks at us and his eyes focus on us.

*Lowen, *The Betrayal of the Body*, *op. cit.*, contains a fuller description of the eyes of the schizoid individual.

Eyes light up when a person is excited and dull when the inner excitation fades. Conceiving of eyes as windows (they are more than that, as we shall see) allows us to postulate that the light which shows in them is an inner glow emanating from the fires that burn in the body. We speak of burning eyes in the face of a zealot who is consumed by an inner fire. There are also laughing eyes, sparkling eyes, twinkling eyes, and I have seen stars in a person's eyes. Most commonly, however, one sees sadness and fear in people's eyes when the shutters are open at all.

While the expressive aspect of the eye cannot be dissociated from the circumocular region and the total face, the expression is largely determined by what goes on in the eye itself. To read this expression, one should look softly at the eyes of a person, not staring or penetrating but allowing the expression to come through. When this happens, one gets an impression of a feeling. One senses the other person. I rarely question my impressions, for I trust my senses.

Among the feelings that I have seen expressed in people's eyes are the following:

Appealing—"Please love me."
Longing— "I want to love you."
Watchful— "What are you going to do?"
Distrustful—"I can't open to you."
Erotic— "I am excited by you."
Hateful— "I hate you."
Confused— "I don't understand."

Many years ago I saw a pair of eyes I will never forget. My wife and I were riding in a subway car, and both of us simultaneously looked into the eyes of a woman sitting opposite us. The contact with her eyes gave me a feeling of shock. Her eyes had such a look of evil I almost shuddered with horror. My wife had an identical reaction, and as we discussed it afterward, we agreed we had never seen such evil-looking eyes. Prior to that experience I didn't believe it was possible for eyes to look evil. The incident evoked the memory of stories I'd heard in my youth of the "evil eye" with its strange, frightening powers.

The physiological processes that determine the expression of eyes are unknown. We do know that the pupils widen when one is in pain or fear and narrow with pleasure. The narrowing of the pupil increases the focus. Widening the pupil enlarges the field of peripheral vision while reducing the sharpness of focus. These reactions are mediated by the autonomic nervous system, but they do not explain the subtle phenomena described above.

The eyes actually have a double function; they are an organ of vision and also of contact. When the eyes of two people meet, there is a sensation of physical contact between them. Its quality depends on the look in the eyes. It can be so hard and strong it feels like a slap in the face or so soft it feels like a caress. It can be penetrating, disrobing and so forth. One can look into a person, through him, over him and around him. Looking involves an aggressive or active component that can best be described as a "taking in" with the eyes. Contact is a function of looking. Seeing, on the other hand, is a more passive process in that one allows the visual stimuli to enter the eye and give rise only to an image. In looking, a person actively expresses himself through the eyes.

Eye contact is one of the strongest and most intimate forms of contact between two people. It involves the communication of feeling on a level deeper than verbal because eye contact is a form of touching. For this reason it can be very exciting. When, for example, the eyes of a man and a woman meet, the excitation can be so strong that it runs through the body to the pit of the belly and into the genitals. Such an experience is described as "love at first sight." The eyes are open and inviting, and the look has an erotic quality. Whatever the feeling conveyed between two pairs of eyes, the effect of their meeting is the development of an understanding between two people.

Eye contact is probably the most important factor in the relation of parents and children, especially in the relationship of a mother to a baby. One can observe how a nursing infant regularly looks up to make contact with its mother's eyes. If the mother responds lovingly, there is a sharing of the pleasure in the physical closeness that reinforces the infant's sense of security and faith. However, this is not the only situation where children seek eye contact with their mothers. Every time a mother enters a child's room its eyes will rise to meet hers in either pleasurable or fearful anticipation of what the contact will bring. A lack of contact owing to a mother's failure to meet the child's eyes is experienced as rejection and leads to a sense of isolation.

In whatever way a parent looks at a child, that look will affect the child's feelings and may profoundly influence its behavior. Looks, as I have said, are far more potent than words. Often they belie the words. A mother may tell a child she loves it, but if her look is cold and distant and her voice flat or hard, the child will not get the feeling of being loved. It may actually feel just the opposite. This will produce a state of confusion, which is neurotically resolved when the child, in his anxiety to believe the words, turns against his own sensing. It is not just hateful looks that are damaging to a child's personality; seductive looks by a parent are even more difficult to cope with. A child cannot easily become angry at such a look because the parent may justify it as affection. A seductive or erotic look from a parent to a child will also excite the child's sexuality and lead to the formation of an incestuous bond between them. I am sure most incestuous relations in a family are based more on looks than on actions.

Many people avoid eye contact because they are afraid of what their eyes will show. They are embarrassed to let another person see their feelings, and so they either avert their gaze or look in a fixed manner. Staring is used to avoid or discourage contact. The important point is that there is not contact unless there is a communication or exchange of feeling between the parties. The feeling need not be more than a recognition of the other person as an individual. In this connection I would mention that some primitive people use the expression "I see you" as a form of greeting. Since eye contact is a form of intimacy, it may have a sexual implication, particularly when the parties are of the opposite sex. One does not "recognize" another individual unless one acknowledges his or her sex.

Because the eyes are such an important avenue of communication, many of the newer types of group therapy encourage eye contact between the members in special exercises. We use similar exercises in bioenergetic group therapy. Most patients find them very helpful because they bring feeling into their eyes, which then makes the person feel more alive. When people are closed off, their eyes are equally closed, and they do not take in their environment in a feeling way. They see it, of course, but the seeing is without excitement or feeling.

Eye contact with the patient is something I constantly strive to establish. Not only does it help me know what is going on from moment to moment, but it provides a deep assurance to the patient that I am with him. When eye contact is used as part of a group exercise or individual therapy, it must be done with some spontaneity to guarantee that it is an honest expression. This can be achieved by making the contact brief—a look, a touch, a flash of understanding, and then one turns away. Maintaining eye contact beyond a brief period is unnatural and a strain. The looking becomes forced and mechanical.

The Eyes and Personality

The eyes are the soul's mirrors because they directly and immediately reflect the energy processes of the body. When a person is energetically charged, his eyes are bright—a good sign of his state of health. Any depression of a person's energy level dims the luster of his eyes. In death the eyes glaze over. There is also a relationship between the charge in the eyes and the level of sexuality. I am not speaking of genital excitation, which also has an effect on the eyes. Sexuality is a total body phenomenon and denotes the degree to which a person is identified with his sexual functioning. In a person with a high degree of sexuality the energy flow is full, and the peripheral points of contact with the world are in a charged state. These points, as I mentioned earlier, are the eyes, the hands, the genitals and the feet. This does not mean the genitals are excited. That happens when feeling or energy becomes focused on this organ. The connection between eyes and sexuality is expressed in the phrase "bright-eyed and bushy-tailed."

Being identified with one's sexuality is an aspect of grounding. Any activity or exercise that increases the feeling of being grounded increases the charge in the eyes. We can affect the overall functioning of the eyes by strengthening a person's contact with his legs and the ground. The various grounding exercises are helpful in this regard. Many patients have reported that after they have worked strongly with their legs, their vision improved to the extent that objects in the room seemed clearer and brighter. When a person doesn't have his feet on the ground, he doesn't see clearly what is going on around him—he is blinded by his illusions.

These considerations support the proposition that the degree of energy charge in the eyes is a measure of the strength of the ego. The individual with a strong ego has the ability to look directly into the eyes of another. He can do this easily because he is sure of himself. Looking at another person is a form of self-assertion, just as looking itself is a form of self-expression. We are all naturally aware of these facts, and it is surprising, therefore, that there is so little reference to the eyes in most discussions of personality.

The next step in our understanding of the relationship between eyes and personality is to relate the look in the eyes to the different character types. Each character structure has a typical look that may not always be perceived by an observer but that is, nevertheless, common enough to serve as a diagnostic criterion. Certainly this is true of the schizophrenic individual whose eyes have a "faraway" look. Reich commented on it, and I described it in *The Betrayal of the Body*. One has only to see this look in a person's eyes to know he is "off" or can "go off."

Let me emphasize, in outlining the looks I associate with the different character types, that they are not continually present and that an occasional look is not significant in this respect. What we are seeking is the typical look.

Schizoid character: The typical look can be described as vacant or unexpressive. It is the absence of feeling in the eyes that characterizes this personality. When a schizoid looks at you, you immediately sense a lack of contact.

Oral character: The typical look is appealing—an appeal for love and support. It may be masked by an attitude of pseudo independence, but it comes through often enough to distinguish this personality.

Psychopathic character: Two looks are typical of this personality, corresponding to the two psychopathic approaches or attitudes. One is the compelling or penetrating look seen in those individuals who have a need to control or dominate others. The eyes fix you as if to impose their owner's will. The other is the soft, seductive or intriguing look that beguiles the person to whom it is directed into giving himself over to the psychopathic individual.

Masochistic character: The typical look is one of suffering or pain. However, this is often masked by an expression of confusion. The masochist feels trapped, and he is more in touch with this feeling than his underlying sense of suffering. In the sadomasochistic personality—that is, in those individuals who have a strong sadistic element in their makeup—the eyes are small and hard. This can be explained as a reversal of the normal masochistic eye, which is soft and sad.

Rigid character: This personality generally has fairly strong, bright eyes. When the rigidity is marked, however, the eyes become hard without losing their brightness. The hardness is a defense against the sadness lying below the surface of the rigid character and related to the feeling of frustration in love. Unlike the masochistic character, the rigid individual compensates with a strong aggressive attitude that brightens both his manner and his eyes.

At this point I could add some comment about my own eyes which would be revealing. I always used to think my right eye was the stronger. It has a more determined look with which I identified. Some years ago, on the occasion of a driving test, I was surprised to learn this eye was the weaker of the two. My left eye had always impressed me as being weak, because it would tear more quickly and more copiously in a sad situation or under a strong wind. Now I realize it was this quality in my left eye that preserved its visual acuity, while my seemingly strong right eye was under the strain of defending against an inner feeling of sadness which the left eye was free to express. This was a personal experience that made me realize how closely the expression of feeling in the eye is related to and affects the visual function.

I have never worn glasses and still don't despite the fact that I am long past the age when glasses for reading supposedly are mandatory. When I was fourteen, however, glasses were prescribed for me. In a routine eye test at school I misread one or two letters on the lower line of the chart. At the clinic I was given a more thorough eye examination, and the prescription of glasses was the result. I was never told what my eye disturbance was. I had never experienced any difficulty at school or elsewhere. I guess now that I was farsighted. That accords with what I know of my personality, but it gave me no trouble in close work.

I got the glasses, but I refused to wear them except for reading. And carried them in my briefcase. I was strongly opposed to the idea of glasses. In my youth, they had a negative connotation. People with glasses were called four-eyed. I suppose that as a result of this attitude, I lost the glasses in the first week. My mother who was overconcerned with my health, insisted I go back for another pair. I couldn't resist her in those days, so I went. But I couldn't hold onto the second pair of glasses either. They, too, disappeared within a week. My parents couldn't afford another outlay, and so, despite her concern, my mother gave up on glasses for me.

I attribute my present good vision to a habit I had of reading and studying in the sunlight, plus the help I got from therapy in being able to cry and express feelings more openly. I loved the sun and the bright clear light of a sunny day. I used to play a lot of tennis on clay courts, where I was exposed to the bright light of the reflected sun. I didn't realize how valuable this was until I learned some years ago that looking at the sun and visualizing one's self (with eyes closed) in a pleasant, sunny atmosphere are techniques which some practitioners of the Bates method use in treating myopia. In retrospect, I *see* I had a need to see sharply and clearly. For me, seeing is believing, and I would describe myself as a visually oriented person which may account for my interest in bodily expression.

Head and Eye Problems and Bioenergetics

Myopia is the most common eye disturbance—so common it is almost statistically normal. In this respect it can be compared with lower-back pain and depression which many authorities regard as normal for our culture, when not disabling. It seems to me we are becoming so crippled, emotionally and physically, that we tend to regard the state of health as an abnormality. Unfortunately, it *is* becoming a rarity.

Many people who wear glasses are aware that while the glasses improve their vision in a mechanical sense, they interfere or block expression and eye contact. When I work with patients, I always ask them to take off their glasses so I can read the expression in their eyes and make contact with them. In some cases, however, the patient sees me only as a blur, and this poses a problem. I offer a compromise when necessary by letting the patient wear his glasses when talking to me but remove them when we work physically. Contact lenses have the same effect as glasses in a less obvious way.

Myopia, I am convinced, is a functional eye disorder that has become structured in the body as a distortion of the eyeball. It doesn't differ from other bodily distortions that are the result of chronic muscular tensions. In many cases these distortions are significantly reduced as the tensions are released. I have seen considerable changes produced in people's bodies by bioenergetic exercises and therapy. And I know one person who completely overcame his myopic condition through the Bates method. One of the difficulties in working with the myopic eyes is that the tense ocular muscles are not accessible to palpation and pressure. The difficulty with the Bates method is that it requires a commitment to an intensive program of eye exercises that most people seem unable to make. If we make allowance for such practical difficulties, the fact remains that myopic eyes can be improved. I have seen such improvement occur in the course of a dramatic therapy session. Unfortunately, it was temporary, and the gain was not fully held. Nevertheless, many patients report some sustained vision improvement as a result of bioenergetic therapy.

Bioenergetics deals with body structure and seeks to comprehend that structure dynamically in terms of the forces that create it. Reich has stated that structure is frozen motion, and while this is a broad and philosophic statement, it has a practical application in cases where the structure develops as a result of what is generally called psychological traumas. This is true of the myopic eye which is wide open and fixed. There is little mobility in the eyeball. The eye muscles are contracted and tense. If we can restore mobility to the eye, we can substantially reduce its myopic condition. To do this, however, one must understand its expression. The wide-eyed look and the slightly bulging eyeball typical of myopia is an expression of fear. Extreme fear would cause this look in any person. The individual with myopia, however, does not feel any fear, nor is he aware of any connection between his eyes and that feeling. The reason: The myopic eye is in a partial state of shock, thus blocking out any emotion from registering in that organ.

It is not difficult to explain the fear. When a child encounters a look of rage or hatred in its mother's eyes, its body will experience a shock, particularly in its eyes. Such looks by a parent are the equivalent of a fist in the face. Many mothers are not even conscious of the looks they give children. I saw a mother in my office look at her daughter with such a black rage in her eyes that it frightened me. The daughter paid no attention; it may have been a commonplace occurrence for her, and the mother seemed oblivious of the look. But I could imagine how the daughter's personality problem was related to this look. The girl was myopic. She had long since blocked out any awareness of her mother's expression, but her eyes were wide with fear.

Every fear is a momentary shock to the organism. Both fear and shock produce a contraction in the body. Generally, the body rebounds from this state of contraction in some violent outburst—crying, screaming or anger. These reactions release the body from shock and fear and the eyes then return to their normal condition. What if this release does not occur? This could happen when the mother's anger or hatred is further provoked by the child's crying, screaming or temper, or when the mother's hostility is repeatedly experienced by the child.

I had personally experienced such a shock at the age of nine months, as I recounted earlier, and it had a lasting effect on me. Fortunately, it was not a repeated occurrence. My mother looked at me mostly with an affectionate gaze, for I was "the apple of her eye." Not all children are so fortunate. If a child constantly anticipates a hostile look from a parent, its eyes will tend to remain wide open in fear. Wide eyes, as I said earlier, enlarge the field of peripheral vision but reduce central vision. To regain its visual acuity, the child will forcibly constrict its eyes, creating a condition of rigidity and strain. There is another element. Frightened eyes tend to roll upward. This tendency, too, must be overcome by an effort of will if the child is to maintain its ability to focus. Now the strain of these efforts cannot be maintained indefinitely. At some point the eye muscles tire, and the child gives up the effort to look out.

Myopia sets in when this compensation breaks down. This will depend on many factors, including the available energy of the child and the amount of stress in the home. In many cases the decompensation sets in between the ages of ten and fourteen when the child's developing sexuality reactivates old conflicts and creates new ones. The attempt to maintain a sharp vision collapses, and the eyes become wide again with fear, but fear of a nonspecific nature. A new defense is erected on a lower level. The muscles at the base of the head, particularly in the occipital region and around the jaw, become contracted to cut off the flow of feeling to the eyes. This ring of tension is found in all cases of myopia. Psychologically the child retreats into a smaller, more confined space, shuttering out the disturbing elements in its world.

Because the myopic eye is in a state of shock, special eye exercises like the Bates method while helpful and necessary, are not the full answer to the problem. Their value would be greatly increased if the tensions were dissolved to allow more energy and excitation to flow into the eyes. Most important is to evoke the underlying fear so that it can be experienced and released. This is the basis of the bioenergetic approach to myopia. It is limited only by the fact that most patients have so many other problems and related tensions requiring attention that we cannot give the eye problem the time it needs.

It should be recognized from what I have said about the different defensive attitudes that there are cases where myopia does not develop, though the conditions for its occurrence are present. I have seen patients whose life experience involved equal or greater amounts of fear but who did not develop myopia. I don't believe the difference is due to heredity. When the shock to the child from parental hostility or rejection is more severe, the total body becomes affected. A degree of paralysis develops that reduces all feeling on a deeper level and limits all forms of self-expression. This is seen in schizoid individuals. Their energy level is decreased, their breathing severely restricted and their overall motility low. The conflict is removed from the area of the eyes to the total body. The eyes are seemingly spared because the individual has shut out his total interpersonal world, not just his visual one. But while the eyes of the schizoid may not be myopic, neither are they charged or expressive. The visual function is retained by dissociating it from the function of emotional expression.

The bioenergetic therapy for eye problems is both general and specific. Generally, as with problems of motility and vocal expression, the patient's energy level must be raised by fuller and deeper breathing. Not only does this increase body sensation and feeling, but it provides the extra energy needed to charge the peripheral points of contact with the world, including the eyes. Breathing has a positive effect on the eyes. After sustained deep breathing through the various exercises the eyes of most patients are noticeably brighter. Patients themselves often comment on their improved vision, as I mentioned earlier. Grounding exercises also help this process.

The specific therapy of eye disturbances requires a knowledge of the pathways of energy flow into the eyes. There are two such pathways which I will describe and picture in a figure. One is along the front of the body, from the heart through the throat and face and into the eyes. The feeling associated with this flow is longing for contact, a reaching out through the eyes to sense and touch. It gives rise to a soft, appealing look. The second is along the back and up over the top of the head to the forehead and eyes. This flow provides an aggressive component to looking. It can be best understood by the expression "to take in with one's eyes." In normal looking these two components are present in different degress. If the tender component related to longing is cut off, the look will be hard and even hostile. It may be so strong as to push the other person away. If the aggressive component is weak, the look will be appealing, but it will fail to touch the other person. Both components are needed for good eye contact.

The figure below shows the two pathways described above, plus a third at the base of the brain that connects the visual centers directly with the retina. Although there is no objective proof of these pathways at this time, their existence is supported by subjective experience and clinical observation. Many patients

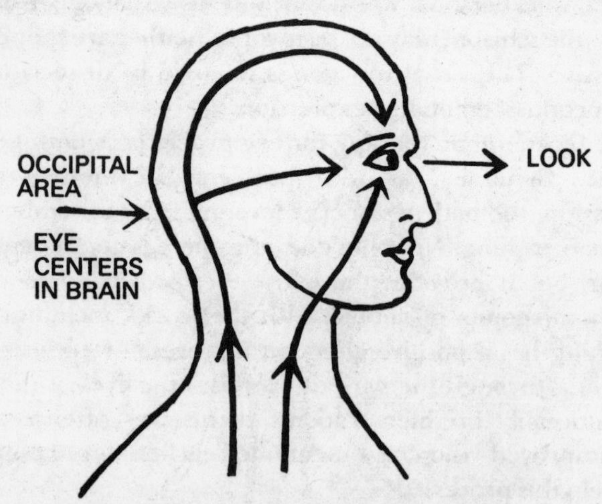

PATHWAYS OF ENERGY CHARGE TO EYES

report feeling a movement of charge into their eyes along these pathways as a result of the various bioenergetic procedures. These sensations are corroborated by seeing the patient's eyes become brighter, more charged and more in contact. When these pathways are open and the charge flows freely and fully into the eyes, they are relaxed. The individual is in a state of pleasure manifested by a smooth forehead, lowered brow, narrow pupils and focused vision.

In the following diagram we see the withdrawal of energy from the eyes caused by fear. This energetic withdrawal produces the typical fear expression. As the aggressive component is pulled back along its pathway, the brow is raised and the eyes open wide. If the fear is intense, one may actually feel his hair stand up and the back of his neck tighten. As the tender component is withdrawn, the jaw drops and the mouth opens wide. If the experience is momentary, the energy streams back to the eyes and the features relax. However, if the fear becomes structured in the body as a chronic state of apprehension, the energy is locked in the ring of tension around the base of the head. Now the person must make a conscious effort to focus his eyes which imposes a severe strain on the eyeball and the ocular muscles. Part of this effort involves setting the jaw to overcome the feeling of being frightened. By

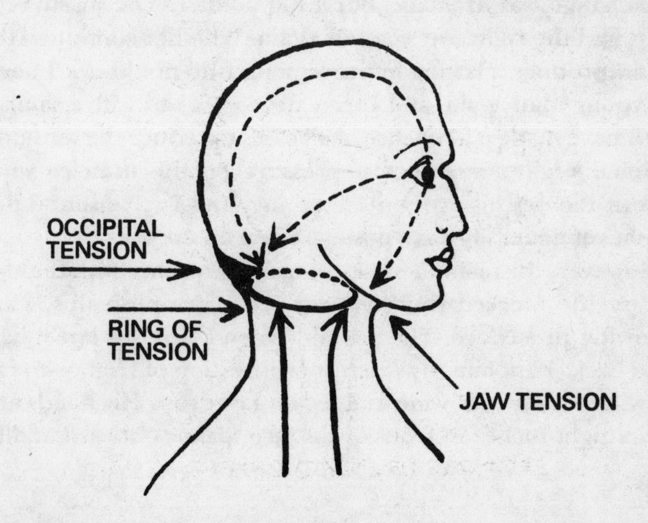

setting his jaw, the person says, "I am not going to let myself be afraid." However, this effort creates an internal conflict between the feeling and the attitude, which increases the muscular tension.

Some years ago I worked briefly with a young man who was cross-eyed. He saw with only his left eye. The vision of the right eye, though normal, was suppressed to avoid a double image, since he could not focus both eyes. As a child he had had two operations to correct this condition, but they had failed to produce any lasting change. Not only was the right eye turned outward, but the right side of his face was slightly twisted. Palpation revealed a severe muscle spasm on the right side of the occipital area. This young man was the son of a psychologist who was participating in a professional bioenergetic workshop. He had come to videotape the proceedings. My intervention was experimental. I was interested to learn whether or not I could affect his strabismus by releasing the tension at the back of his head. I applied a firm pressure with my fingers to the spastic muscles for about thirty seconds, and I felt the muscles relax. Several doctors who were watching the procedure as the young man lay on the bed were amazed to see his eyes become straight. The young man turned to me and said he had single vision with both eyes, and I, too, noticed that both were in focus. The change was dramatic, but it did not last. The spasm returned later, and the right eye went off again. Whether continued therapy would produce a lasting improvement, I do not know. I never saw the young man again, and I have never worked with a similar case. But I have made it a practice in all cases to reduce the tension in the occipital region by selective pressure on the muscles while the patient focuses his eyes on the ceiling, and I have found that this maneuver generally has a positive effect on the eyes.

However, the main therapeutic task in working with the eyes is to release the blocked fear in them. To accomplish this, I use the following procedure. The patient lies on a bed, his knees bent and head back. I ask him to assume an expression of fright—to raise his brow, open his eyes wide and let his jaw drop. His hands are held about eight inches in front of his face, palms outward and fingers spread, in an attitude of protection. I then lean over the patient and ask him to look directly into my eyes, about a foot above his own. Despite the fact that the patient is in a position of vulnerability and has assumed an expression of fear, few allow themselves to feel frightened. Often the patient looks at me with a smile on his face, as if to say, "There is no reason to be afraid. You will not hurt me because I am a good boy." To get past this defensive denial, I apply pressure with my thumbs to the risorius muscles on both sides of the wings of the nose. This prevents the patient from smiling and removes the mask from his face.

If it is done correctly (and I might add that it is a maneuver requiring considerable skill and experience), it often evokes a feeling of fear and may elicit a scream, as the defense against the fear gives way. Having the patient make a sound before the pressure is applied will aid the release of the scream. I remove the pressure when the scream starts, but in many cases the screaming will continue after the pressure is withdrawn, as long as the eyes remain wide open. The reader will recall what happened to me in my first session with Reich. He didn't need to use any pressure to release the scream. However, there are very few patients who will react spontaneously to an expression of fear by screaming. Some do not react even when pressure is used. In their case the defense against fear is more deeply ingrained.

I suppose to the patient my eyes look strong and maybe hard when I apply the pressure. I feel them soften as the patient begins to scream, because I empathize with him. After the scream I generally ask the patient to reach out and touch my face with his hands. I have found that the scream releases the fear and opens the way for tender and loving feelings. As we look at each other, the person's eyes often melt and fill with tears, as the longing for contact with me (as surrogate for his mother and father) wells up in him. The procedure frequently ends in a close embrace, with the patient sobbing deeply.

As I mentioned, this procedure does not work all the time. Many patients are too frightened of their fear to allow it to surface. When it does, the effect is dramatic. One patient told me that as she was screaming, she saw her father's eyes looking at her angrily as he was about to beat her. Another said he saw his mother's furious eyes in a recollection reaching back to the time he was a year old. One woman felt so liberated by the release of her fear that she jumped off the bed and ran to hug her husband, who was in the room with her. One man who had been in therapy for some time felt so shaken by the experience of his terror that he left my office in a state of collapse. He immediately went home and slept for two hours. I heard from him as soon as he awoke. He called to tell me he had such a feeling of joy as he had never known before. The joy was a rebound following the release of his terror.

There are a number of other procedures which can be used to mobilize feeling in the eyes. One is important to describe—an attempt to bring the patient out through his eyes by having him contact mine. In this procedure the patient is also lying on the couch in the same position. I lean over and ask him to reach up and touch my face with his hands. I place my thumbs on his brows and with a gentle, soothing movement try to remove any expression of anxiety or concern that would cause a knitting of the brows. As I look softly into his or her eyes, I often see a little child looking out at me from behind a wall or through an opening, wanting to come out but not daring to. This is the child kept hidden from the world. I may say to him, "Come out and play with me. It's all right." It is fascinating to watch the response as the eyes relax and feeling flows into and through them to me. That little child wants desperately to come out and play but is scared to death it will be hurt, rejected or laughed at. It needs my reassurance to venture forth, especially my loving touch. And how good it feels to come out and find oneself accepted!

An experience such as the above may be the first time in a very long while that the patient has revealed and acknowledged the hidden child in him. But once the acknowledgment is consciously made, the way is open to analyze and work through all the anxieties and fears that have forced the child to hide and bury his love. For the child is loving, and it is love we dare not express in action through our eyes, in our voices and with our bodies.

All these reactions are noted and discussed; they are the best grist for the analytic mill, since the experiences are immediate and convincing. Much depends of course, on the sensitivity of the therapist and on his freedom to make contact, to touch and be touched, particularly on his ability to stay free of any emotional involvement with the patient. A situation of this kind can easily lead a therapist to unloading on the patient his own need for contact. If this happens, it is a tragic error. Every patient has all he can do to accept and cope with his own needs and feelings. To have to handle the personal feelings of a therapist adds an impossible obstacle to the recovery of his self-possession. He will respond to the therapist's feelings to escape his own; he will see the therapist's need as greater than his own, and in the end, he will lose the sense of his own self as he did when a child and was caught in the conflict between his needs and rights and those of his parents. A patient pays to have the therapeutic session oriented solely to his problems, and it is a betrayal of trust for a therapist to take advantage of the situation for his personal benefit.

One other cautionary note must be sounded, even though it may be repetitious. Regardless of how much a patient regresses in the course of a session to an infantile state, he or she is still an adult and fully conscious of that fact. Touching between adults always has an erotic or sexual connotation. One doesn't touch a neuter body; one touches a man or a woman. This is only natural. But if one is aware of a person's sex, one is also conscious of his or her own sexuality. However, sexuality does not mean genitality. Most patients are consciously aware I am a man when they touch me. Some may push this awareness to the back of their minds, but it is there nonetheless. Then how is this situation handled?

It is a matter of principle with me, and a rule in bioenergetic therapy, that there is no sexual acting out with patients. This can so easily happen in subtle ways and sometimes overtly. The therapist has to be constantly on guard against this possibility. I know that many female patients have developed sexual feelings toward me. Many have told me so. That is as far as it goes. My feelings are not their concern, and it would be a gross fault to intrude them into the therapeutic situation. We can, if advisable, talk about them, but if I cannot keep them to myself, I cannot do good therapy. A therapist must be able to contain his feelings—that is, to have self-possession.

I have talked about letting go. Containment is equally important and is equally stressed in bioenergetics. It will be one of the themes in my next and final chapter. The containment is conscious and voluntary which presupposes an ability to let go. If one can't let go because the holding is unconscious and structured in the body, one can't speak of containment as a conscious expression of the self. The person doesn't contain; he is contained.

Headaches

The subject of headaches belongs in a chapter on self-expression because some are caused by eye strain and all, in my opinion, are related to blocks in self-expression. I am not an authority on headaches, but I have had considerable experience treating them in my patients and others. The bioenergetic understanding of tension provides a good base for the attempt to comprehend this problem.

On a number of occasions I have demonstrated in public how one can relieve a headache by dissolving muscular tension. At public lectures I have asked if anyone in the audience had a headache. Usually there was at least one and I would ask him to come up before the audience so I could try to take his headache away. The procedure is very simple. The person sits on a chair, while I palpate for tension at the base of the head in the occipital region, on top of the skull and in the frontal area. Then, with my left hand holding his forehead, I massage the tense muscles at the back of his head and in the occipital area with my right hand. After a minute or so I reverse my hands. With my left hand holding the back of his head, I loosen the frontal area with my right. In the next step, I encircle his scalp with both hands, my fingers on top of his skull, and move the scalp gently from side to side. At this point I explain to the audience that I am unscrewing the tight lid on his head. So far this procedure has worked without fail, and the person remarks, in response to my question, that his headache is gone.

This maneuver, however, works only with a tension headache. A migraine headache is a different proposition and requires a different approach. I shall explain the difference in a moment.

I discovered the above maneuver quite by accident. Many years ago I was visiting some relatives I hadn't seen in a long time. They were curious about the kind of psychiatric work I did which involved the body. I explained the role of muscle tension in emotional problems, but I thought it would be more helpful if I demonstrated my approach. After telling them most people have considerable tension in the back of the neck at the base of the head, I went over to my cousin, put my hands on his head and gently massaged the area. He had some tension there, but I made no special reference to it. And that was all. When we returned home, my wife sent the hostess a thank-you note. Two weeks later I received a reply: "I don't know what you did to my husband, but you relieved him of a headache he has had for the past fifteen years."

The tension at the base of the head is comparable to the tension in the lower back. They are generally found together in the same person, and both express the need to maintain control. The upper tension is the somatic equivalent of the psychological commandment "Don't lose your head." This means "Don't ever let your feelings get out of control." The lower tension has the same significance for sexuality. It would correspond to the commandment "Don't let your ass run away with you." Most of us are committed to control.

Let me return to the figure of the preceding section to portray my ideas about the cause of some headaches.

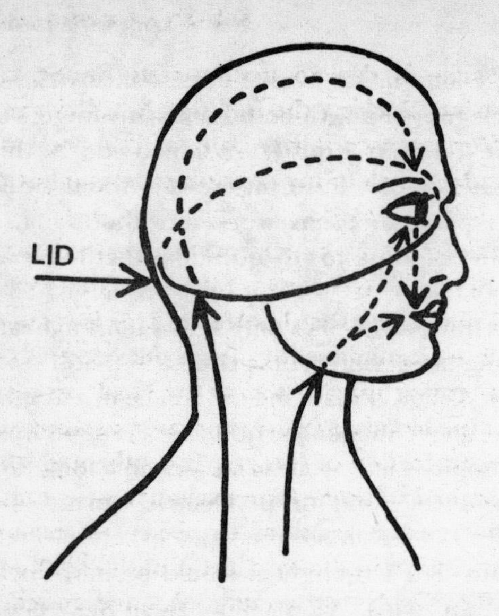

This figure shows the pathway of the flow of energy or excitation up the back of the neck and over the top of the head to the eyes and, though not shown, to the upper teeth. This flow carries the aggressive component of all feelings. It is necessary in such actions as looking out and speaking out. If we place a lid on our aggressions, a pressure inevitably builds up against the lid, creating a headache.

The lid is a figurative concept, but in some cases the whole top of the head is tense so it acts like a lid. In these cases a headache is experienced over the whole head. In other cases there is a band of tension around the head at forehead level that blocks aggressive impulses from getting through. Pressure builds up around the band, and the pain is generally felt through the forehead and sometimes at the back of the head. When these tensions are released, the headache vanishes.

It is also possible to remove the headache by expressing the blocked feeling. However, it is rare for a person with a headache to know what is bothering him. When a conflict is conscious, one is aware of the feeling. This means it has reached the surface of the mind. One may get a tight head, but it is not the same thing as a headache. A headache is due to unconscious forces; both the feeling and the tension blocking the feeling are below the level of consciousness. All one senses is the pain of the pressure. This explains why a headache, as in my cousin's case, can persist for a long time.

A migraine headache, in my experience, stems from a blocking of the feeling of longing. This feeling is mainly carried through the arteries. I pointed out in my first book that Eros is related to the flow of blood which transmits feelings from the heart. It is known medically that in migraine the arteries in the head are constricted and the pressure of the blood causes the intense pulsating pain.

But while the erotic feeling of longing flows through the blood channels, it is not limited to them. The excitation or energy charge passes upward through the front of the body as shown in the figure—seeking expression in the eyes, the mouth and through the reaching out of the hands for contact. I have found in this condition that there is an area of severe muscular tension on one side of the neck just below the angle of the jaw. Slight pressure on this area will produce a shooting pain to the back of the eye. This tension is always on the side of the headache, but why it becomes focused on one side I do not know.

Migraine headaches have proved responsive to psychotherapy. I worked with one migraine sufferer for many years and was able first to reduce the frequency and intensity of the headaches and finally to eliminate them. At times I was able to free this patient from a very severe attack by helping her release her feelings in crying and screaming. At other times when the attack had lasted for many hours, this procedure reduced the intensity but did not remove the headache. However, after a night's rest following a session, the headache would invariably be gone. It was always necessary for the crying to be accompanied by tearing to remove the pain from behind the eye.

This patient had great difficulty in expressing any feeling of longing for closeness and contact. She was embarrassed and found it frightening to touch my face with her hands in a soft, feeling way.

She was also greatly inhibited sexually, as one would expect from such a severe block to any expression of longing. She used to get attacks before going out if she had any feeling for her date. They were more severe whenever I was away on a trip or vacation. Talking to me on the phone helped, and she often called me long distance. She had, of course, made a strong transference to me of feelings she had had for her father that she could not acknowledge. Working out the transference problem analytically and opening up her longing for closeness to her father were necessary to remove the cause of the headaches. But only when she gained the ability to express these feelings in her eyes and in her voice was I sure she would remain free of this tormenting condition.

Every migraine sufferer has a sexual hang-up which has nothing to do with sexual activity. I have known many migraine patients who were sexually active. The headache stems from a blocking of the tender and erotic component of sexuality. The feeling goes to the head instead of to the genital apparatus, where it could be handled and discharged. The head end of the body does not provide this outlet. Crying and screaming will release the immediate tension, but they are not the solution to the problem. The ability to have an orgasm is.

One of my patients said the migraine is aptly named because the feeling runs against the grain. I have long felt that this is a valid observation. Reversing the direction should help the migraine sufferer. This can be done through the grounding exercises; these will not help when an attack is in full swing, but I have found they are very useful either when the person senses an attack coming on or when it has just started.

The fear of letting down into the ground and into one's sexuality is tied up with falling anxiety. I mention this because of the nausea that invariably accompanies a strong migraine attack—a nausea produced by a diaphragmatic contraction tied to the fear of letting down.

However effective I or other bioenergetic therapists are with our physical approach, no personality or emotional problem can be worked through without first expanding the consciousness of the patient to include an understanding of his problems. But understanding is not an intellectual operation alone. For me it means standing under or empathizing from below. It involves going to the roots of a situation and sensing the forces that influence and shape feelings and behavior.

X. Consciousness: Unity and Duality

Expanding Consciousness

In the past decade an increasing interest has developed in what is called the expansion of consciousness. The focus on expanding consciousness is part of the new humanistic approach to psychology which grew out of sensitivity training, the encounter movement, gestalt therapy, bioenergetics and other modalities for enlarging the awareness of self and others. Since bioenergetics contributed to this development and belongs to the humanistic approach, it is important to understand the role of consciousness in bioenergetic therapy and how it is expanded through such therapy.

We should recognize, however, that this idea is not new in human culture, for culture is the result of man's continual effort to expand his consciousness. Every step in the growth of culture—whether in religion, the arts, natural science or government—represented an expansion of consciousness. What is new is the conscious focus on the *need* to expand consciousness. This development suggests to me that many people experience the present culture as confining and constricting and feel psychically suffocated by its increasingly materialistic orientation. People sense a desperate need to bring some fresh air into their minds and lungs.

Desperation is the most powerful motivation to change, but it is not the most reliable one.* We know very little of the nature of consciousness, and in our desperation to make a change we easily make the wrong change. Too often the desperate person leaps from the frying pan into the fire. It is naive to assume that change is always for the better. People, as well as cultures, can go downhill as well as up; the course of history records periods of devolution as well as evolution. It is almost invariably true that the reaction to any situation goes to the opposite extreme, after which there is a slow integration of the two positions to start a new upward movement.

If our present culture and the consciousness it represents can be described as mechanistic, then the reaction against it will lead to mysticism. These terms need some definition. The philosophy of mechanism rests on the assumption that there is a direct and immediate connection between cause and effect. Since this assumption underlies our technological-scientific world view, it can be described as mechanistic. A simple example of mechanistic thinking is to regard crime as a direct result of poverty. There is, of course, a relationship between crime and poverty, a relationship expressed in the saying "Poverty breeds crime," but to assume that poverty *causes* crime is naïve; it overlooks the complex and subtle psychological factors influencing behavior. The failure of this thinking is shown in the mounting crime rate that occurs in periods of economic prosperity.

The mystical attitude denies the operation of the law of cause and effect. It sees all phenomena as manifestations of a universal consciousness and negates the importance of the individual consciousness. In a world where the law of causality is an illusion, action has no meaning. The mystic is forced by his belief to withdraw from the world. He turns inward to find the true

*Lowen, *The Betrayal of the Body*, *op. cit.*, has a full discussion of the psychology of desperation.

meaning of life, and then, it is true, he discovers his oneness with all life and the universe. Or, at least, that is what he is constantly struggling to achieve, for life does not permit a total withdrawal from the world that sustains it, except through death. Neither the mystic nor any being can fully transcend his bodily existence.

In our present state of reaction against the mechanistic philosophy of our culture we can easily be misled into believing that mysticism is the answer. And very many people have indeed turned to mysticism to free their consciousness from the stranglehold of the mechanistic view of life. I don't believe this is a way upward. It is not that the mystic is wrong, for there is some truth in his position. But, then, neither is the mechanist wrong, for his science has shown that in certain situations—namely, closed systems where all the variables can be controlled or determined—the law of cause and effect does work. Life, however, is not a closed but an open system; all the variables affecting human behavior can never be known or controlled, so the law of causality is not fully applicable. On the other hand, there is a mechanism to life, as well as a dynamism, and if I plunge a knife into your heart, you will surely die, for I will have destroyed the ability of the heart to perform the mechanical function of pumping the blood.

If neither is wrong, then both are only partially right, and we have to see what the whole truth is and how each fits into that picture. Let me put it this way. There is an objective validity to the mechanistic position. In the world of objects or things, especially material things, the law of cause and effect seems to apply. The mystic can claim a subjective validity, for he is describing a spiritual world where objects do not exist. But both worlds exist, for neither negates the other, and a normal human being is in touch with both, experiencing himself both as subject and object. I don't believe this is uniquely human—the higher animal organisms seem to function in both worlds, too—but what *is* unique to man is his consciousness of the polarity in the two positions. Also unique to man is the possibility of splitting the unity of inner and outer as he finally split the unity of the atom, creating the objective terror of the nuclear bomb, which is the substantiation of the subjective, world-destruction terror of the schizophrenic personality.

A simple diagram can show these relationships more clearly than words. We will represent the organism, man, by a circle with a center or nucleus. Impulses originating at the center or core as energy pulses flow outward as waves to the periphery of the circle

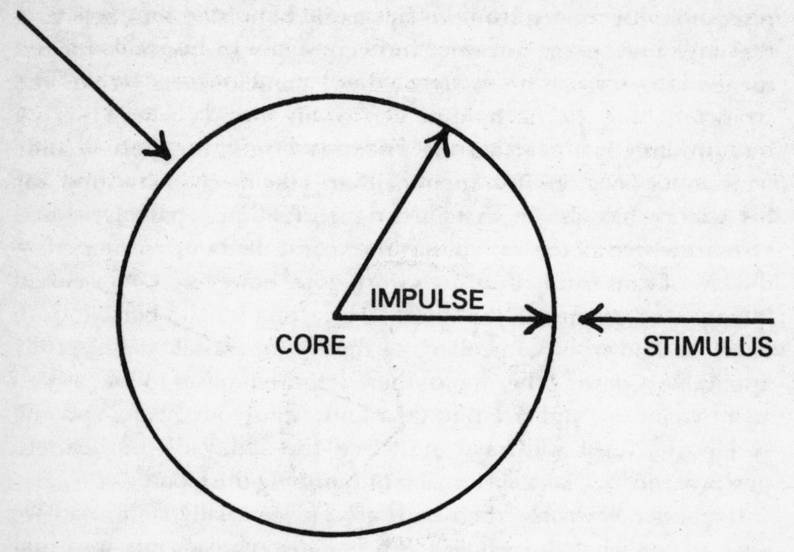

when the organism interacts with the environment. At the same time stimuli arising in the outer world impinge on the organism, which will respond to some of them.

Looking at this figure, we are reminded of a single-celled organism enclosed by a special, semipermeable membrane represented in the figure by the circle. The human organism begins life as a single cell, and although that cell multiplies astronomically to create a person, the person in his energetic unity retains a functional identity with the single cell that was his origin. A living membrane surrounds each organism, creating its individuality by setting it apart from the world. But the membrane is not a wall; it is selectively permeable, allowing an interchange between the individual and the world.

In his healthy state, an individual perceives the contact between his core and the outer world. Impulses from his pulsating core (heart) flow into the world, and events in the external world reach and touch his heart. As a responsible entity he feels one with the world and with the cosmos. He doesn't just reach in a mechanical way, as conditioned behavior theory would have us believe, but responds with feeling from his heart and out of the uniqueness of his individual being. But since he is conscious of his individuality, too, he is aware that his responsive and spontaneous actions affect the world and the people in it *causally* and he can take the responsibility for those actions. For causality does operate; if I say or do something that hurts you, I must take the responsibility for the pain I cause you.

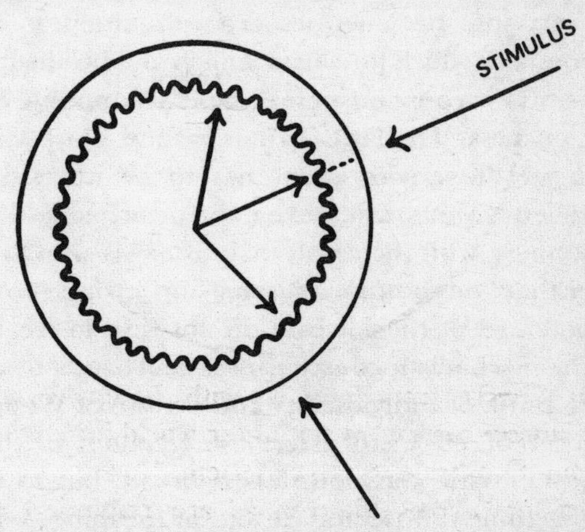

This normal situation is disturbed when man becomes "armored" as Reich described it. In the above diagram that armoring is represented by a jagged line lying below the surface or membrane of the organism. In effect the armoring splits the feelings of the core from the sensations at the periphery. In doing so it splits the organism's unity and the true unity of its relationship to the world. He now has inner feelings and outer reactions, an inner world and an outer world with which to identify, but because of the split, the two worlds are not together. The armoring is like a wall, and the person can be on one side or the other but not on both at the same time.

I believe we are now in a position to understand the problem of mysticism vs. mechanism. Both attitudes are the result of an armored state. The mystic lives in the inner world and has dissociated himself from the events in the outer. For him the law of causality is irrelevant; all that matters is to *try* to stay in touch with his pulsating core. If he attempts to get involved in the world of objects, he will have to cross to the other side of the wall and so lose contact with his center. The mechanist, who is on the other side of the wall, has lost contact with his center. All he senses or sees is how he reacts to events in a causal way, and so he believes life is merely a matter of conditioned reflexes. Since objects and events determine his reactions, his energies are committed to manipulating an environment which he senses is alien and hostile to his being.

The mystic consciousness is the exact opposite of the mechanistic consciousness. The latter is narrow and sharply focused, for each object in the environment has to be isolated in order to be controlled. Events, too, have to be detached and studied as special happenings, with the result that history is seen as a series of events rather than the continous striving and struggles of people to realize the potential of their lives. I do not wish to create the impression that the mechanistic consciousness is all bad; it developed out of the strong sense of individuality and egoism of Western man through centuries of effort to assert the freedom of the individual. By contrast, mystic consciousness is broad, but so broad in its final form as to be diffuse and devoid of meaning. I suppose we could say simply that where the mechanistic consciousness doesn't see the forest for the trees (since it is intent on cutting them down), the mystic consciousness doesn't see the trees for the forest. I am reminded of some human beings who are so "in love" with *people* that they cannot see or respond to the person in front of them. Another analogy suggests itself. The mystic, walking with eyes wide open to the wonder of the universe, doesn't see the stones on his path and stumbles over them. But no matter. The mechanist, looking intently for the stones that might trip him up, fails to see the beauty of the sky.

One cannot resolve this conflict by trying to do both—look down, look up, look down. One has to become an acrobat to scale the wall so repeatedly. The only way is to tear the wall down, remove the armoring or release the tensions, which is what bioenergetics is all about. So long as the wall is up, the person is split into mysticism and mechanism, for every mechanist is a mystic within and every mystic is a mechanist on the surface. Fundamentally they are the same, turning a garment inside out doesn't change it. This explains why a great scientist like Erwin Schrödinger turning inward to his feelings in *What Is Life?* thinks mystically.

Thinking that is neither mechanistic nor mystical is called functional thinking. I regard the concept of functional thinking, as elucidated by Reich, as one of the great achievements of the human mind. It is particularly helpful to an understanding of consciousness.

Let us start by thinking of consciousness as a function, not a state, like the function of talking, for example. One can talk or be quiet, depending on the need, so one can be conscious or not depending on the situation. It is interesting to note how closely consciousness is tied to subvocal speech which we do most of the time in the name of thought. It is also interesting to speculate that in talking, we convey information to others, whereas consciousness is concerned with our receiving information. There is a close connection between consciousness and paying attention, for the more attention we pay to something, the more conscious we are of it.

But if consciousness is a function, it has the connotation of an ability. Expanding consciousness makes no sense unless one thinks of it as increasing one's ability to be conscious. Shifting attention from one thing to another doesn't expand consciousness, for in the process of seeing the new, we cannot see the old. Consciousness is like a searchlight that illuminates one aspect of a field so that we can see it clearly but that, in the process, makes the rest of the field seem darker. Shifting the light doesn't increase or expand consciousness since the first area now becomes dark and one's field of vision (seeing or understanding) hasn't changed. Nevertheless, the mobility of the light is a factor in consciousness. A person whose eyes are fixed on only one aspect of life has a more limited consciousness (ability) than a person who can move his eyes about to see many different things.

Comparing consciousness with a light allows me to introduce a number of factors that measure the function of consciousness. Obviously a bright light is more revealing than a dull one. Similarly with consciousness: A person with a brighter vision, more acute hearing, keener smell, better taste—in other words, a higher degree of perceptual sens-ibility—has a higher degree of functioning consciousness than an individual whose sense-ability is reduced. The depth or penetrating quality of a light, which is a function partly of intensity of illumination and partly of focus, corresponds to a similar factor in consciousness. There are farsighted people psychologically who think deeply and see ahead. This reflects a quality of their consciousness. And it would be a handicap if the person also couldn't see what was in front of his nose. Finally, there is the ability to broaden or narrow the field of perception, to be able to move freely between the mechanistic and the mystical vision owing to the absence of a wall.

When expressed this way, it is not difficult to see that the function of consciousness depends on the aliveness of the person and that it is directly related to emotional health. More important, however, is the conclusion that the ability to be conscious is tied to the energetic processes of the body—namely, to how much energy a person has and how freely it can circulate. Consciousness reflects the state of inner excitation; in fact, it is the light of the inner flame projected on two screens—the surface of the body and that of the mind.

One further analogy may help clarify these relationships. We can compare what happens in consciousness with a television set. A television set consists of an apparatus for receiving signals, an amplifier, a source of energy (electrons) which is projected on a sensitive screen. When the set is turned on and tuned in to receive the incoming signals, the screen lights up and shows a picture. The brightness and clarity of the picture are determined by the strength of the electron flow and the sensitivity of the screen. Similar factors operate in consciousness—namely, the energy charge of the impulses flowing from the core and the sensitivity of the two surfaces, that of the body and that of the mind. We say that people are thick-skinned or thin-skinned depending on their sensitivity. A body without a skin cannot screen incoming stimuli, and the person is thus hypersensitive and vulnerable to every breeze that blows. Such a state is an extremely painful condition.

A TV set is a mechanical device, but because there is a mechanical aspect to the body's functioning, it is possible to make such comparisons. However, a body has its own energy and an ego or will that can direct this energy to suit its needs. We can direct our consciousness to one part of the body or another at will. We do this by focusing attention on the part. I can look at my foot for instance, and get an image of it, move it and sense it kinesthetically or let energy and feeling flow into it, in which case it may tingle and vibrate. Only then am I conscious of my foot as an alive and sentient part of my being. There are different levels of consciousness that require clarification.

I have discussed this phenomenon earlier in this book, showing how one can direct attention to the hand and so increase the charge in it. By the same token, when the hand, foot or any other part of the body becomes energetically charged, attention is drawn to that part, and consciousness of it increases. The increased charge puts the part in a state of tension (tention), it is at-tention. This is not the chronic tension in a contracted or spastic muscle, but an alive, positive state that could lead naturally to response and release. In the musculature it is called a set or readiness for action. In the penis it is the condition for expressing sexual love.

Although we can direct our attention by an act of will, which implies the ego has some measure of control over the flow of energy in the body, most of the time our attention is captured by an external or internal event. I have pointed out many times that the will is generally an emergency mechanism. If our responses are spontaneous, the peripheral parts of the body that are in contact with the world must be relatively charged at all times and in a state of readiness to respond. This is to say that when we are awake, we are normally in a relative state of at-tention or alertness. In other words, we are conscious. It also follows that the range of our consciousness is proportionate to how much of the body is charged, while the degree of consciousness depends on the intensity of the charge. In sleep, when the charge is withdrawn from the surface of the body, our range of attention and consciousness drops to zero. This also happens when one blacks out.

I have mentioned that there are levels of consciousness. The consciousness of an infant is on a different and lower level from an adult's. An infant has a greater body consciousness than an adult, but it is less defined and less refined. An infant is sensitive to more body sensations but less aware of specific feelings such as emotions or thoughts. Consciousness becomes sharper with the growth and development of the ego, which itself is a crystallization of consciousness. I see the levels of consciousness, therefore, as being coterminous with the hierarchy of personality functions as I have described them earlier. These are shown in the diagram as levels of consciousness.

Consciousness of body processes is the deepest and broadest level of consciousness. These processes are rhythmic breathing, the vibratory state of the musculature, involuntary and spontaneous actions, streaming sensations and the pulsatory expansion and contraction of the cardiovascular system. We are generally conscious of the latter only in states of high excitement or in the state of mysticism. This is the level on which we *feel* our identification with life, nature and the cosmos. Among primitive people this consciousness has been described as participation mystique, denoting a mystical identification with natural and universal processes. At its extreme one loses the sense of one's unique individuality, as the boundary of the self becomes so

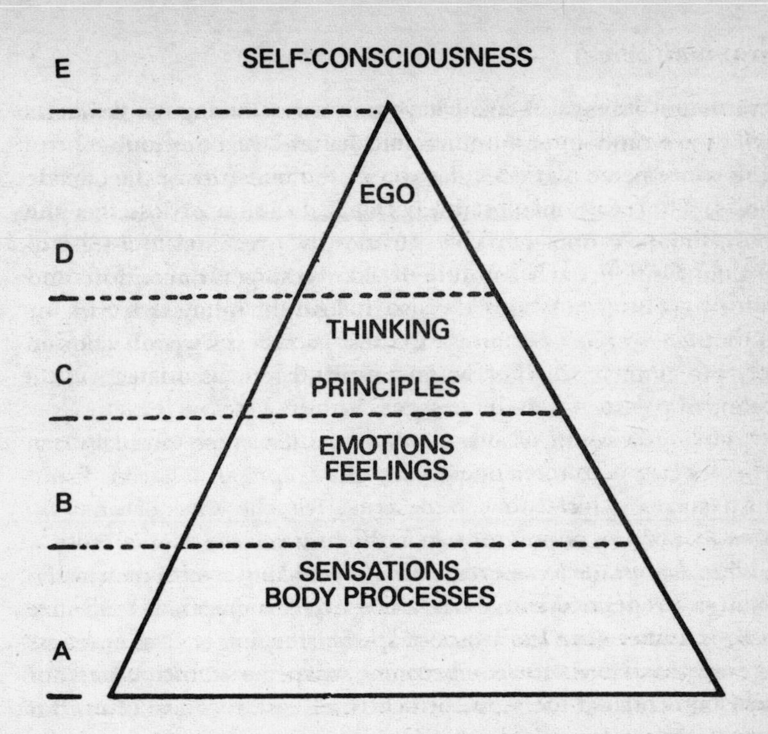

RISING LEVELS OF CONSCIOUSNESS

nebulous that it no longer differentiates the self from the environment. It is also the level of infantile consciousness, which, however, has an opposite direction from mystical consciousness. The former is growing toward a differentiation of the self, while the latter is moving toward undifferentiation.

The next level of consciousness in my thinking involves the perception of specific emotions. A very young infant does not feel angry, sad, frightened or happy. These emotions depend on some degree of awareness of the external world. Anger, for example, implies a directed effort against a "hostile" force outside the organism. A very young infant will struggle against a restraining force, but its actions are random and undirected. It lacks the conscious control of its movements and does not yet sense the nature of the outside forces. The emotion of sadness implies a sense of loss that the young infant cannot perceive. It cries as a reaction to a state of tension arising from a painful condition (hunger, discomfort, and so forth). This is not to say there is no loss; the infant that cries for its mother is crying because it has lost its necessary connection to her, but until it sees her as an outside agent associated with a feeling of pleasure, it does not sense the loss.

Consciousness unfolds like the bud of a flower, so gradually one cannot perceive the changing. Yet our consciousness can distinguish stages, which we can describe for the sake of analysis. Memory plays an important role in the function of consciousness.

When does a child become conscious of its thinking or think consciously? Though I cannot give an exact answer to this question, I am sure there is a time when these aspects of the function of consciousness become operative. It seems to me that the consciousness of thinking is related to the use of words, at least, for most of us. But since words arise in social relationships and are used in the communication of information, this stage of consciousness is associated with a growing awareness of the social world. As this world enlarges, one's own space diminishes in comparison, and one's position (ego, individual) becomes more defined.

Thinking consciously or objectively gives rise to a consciousness of the ego. One sees oneself as a conscious actor in the world with a choice of behavior. The important choice is whether to tell the truth or to be deceptive.* This choice means that consciousness can turn back on itself to be aware of the self as an objective factor in one's thinking. To put it simply, one can think about one's thinking. This development creates the duality that characterizes modern consciousness. A person is both subject and object, conscious of being an actor but also of being acted on.

*Lowen, *Pleasure, op. cit.*, discusses the role of deceit in forming the ego.

On the ego level consciousness is dual but not split. Splitting occurs when consciousness transcends the personality, giving rise to self-consciousness. This is not the same as being conscious of the self, but a pathological state where consciousness becomes so intensely focused on the self that movement and expression are painful and difficult. Such a state of consciousness, while not infrequent in schizophrenia, may happen momentarily to an average person. The intensity of the focus narrows consciousness to the point where there is the risk of it breaking or fading out, which is extremely frightening.

The above analysis makes one thing clear: As consciousness rises to higher levels, it does not expand but narrows to increase its focus and its ability to discriminate. On the other hand, as consciousness deepens to include feelings, sensations and the bodily processes that create them, it becomes broader and more extensive. To dramatize this difference, I shall use two very general terms—head consciousness and body consciousness—to represent the peak and the base of the triangle respectively.

Many people, especially those who are characterized as intellectuals, have mainly a head consciousness. They think of themselves as being very conscious persons, and they are, but their consciousness is limited and narrow—limited to their thoughts and images and narrow because they see themselves and the world only in terms of thoughts and images. They communicate their thoughts easily, but they have great difficulty in knowing or expressing what they feel. They are generally unaware of what goes on in their bodies and by the same token, they are unaware of the bodies of those around them. They talk about feelings but neither sense nor act on them. They are only conscious of the *idea* of the feeling. Of such people it might be said that they don't live life, they think their way through it. They live in their heads.

Body consciousness is at the opposite pole. It is characteristic of children who live in the world of the body and its feelings and of adults who retain a close connection to the child they were and still are inside. A person with body consciousness knows what he feels and where he feels it in his body. But he can also tell you what you feel and how he sees it in your body. He senses you as a body and responds to you as a body; he is not misled by the "emperor's new clothes."

There is a big difference between being conscious of the body and having a body consciousness. One can be conscious of the body with a head consciousness, and this is true of so many people who engage in physical culture (attendance at the health spas, for example, to improve their figure) or in professional athletics and the performing arts. The body is seen then as the instrument of the ego, not as the true self. I have worked with a number of these people in bioenergetic therapy and have long since got over my surprise at how little they are in touch with their bodies.

I do not claim that body consciousness is superior to head consciousness, although the reverse position is not uncommon. I have little regard for a dissociated head consciousness, but I respect very highly a head consciousness that is fully integrated with body consciousness. Similarly, I regard a body consciousness alone as an immature level of personality development.

Bioenergetics, of course, aims to expand consciousness by increasing a person's body consciousness. In doing this, it cannot afford to (and does not) neglect the importance of head consciousness. Consciousness can, however, be heightened in bioenergetic therapy through the use of language and words. We must recognize, though, that our culture is predominately a "head" culture and that we are sadly lacking in body consciousness.

Body consciousness occupies a mid-position between head consciousness and the unconscious, and thus it serves to connect and orient us with the mysterious forces in our nature. We could simplify the following figure to show this relationship.

Whereas head consciousness has no direct connection with the unconscious, body consciousness does. The unconscious is that aspect of our bodily functioning we do not or cannot perceive. Thus, while we can become conscious by an effort of attention of our breathing and in some states of our hearts, we cannot become

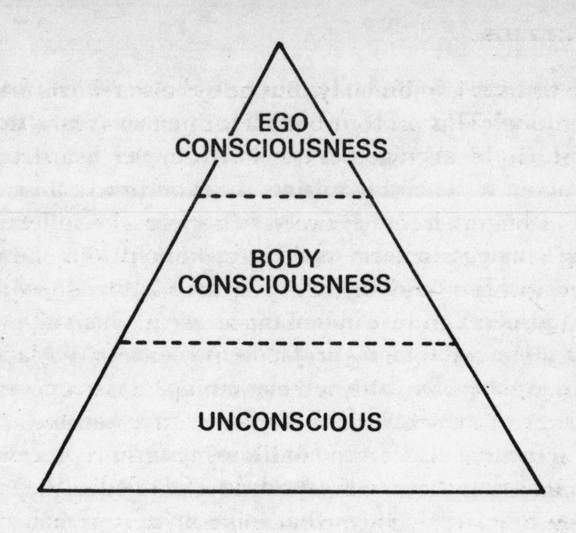

conscious of the action of our kidneys, let alone of the subtle reactions occurring on the tissue or cellular levels. The very vital process of metabolism is beyond perception. So much of our life takes place in a dark region where the light of the conscious mind cannot shine. And since mind consciousness is a pure light, it is afraid of the dark.

On the level of head consciousness the world is a series of discontinuities, of unrelated events and causes. It is the essential nature of mind or ego consciousness that it creates dualities and splits the essential unity of all natural functions. This is beautifully expressed by Albert Camus in a poetic way: "As long as the mind keeps silent in the motionless world of its hopes, everything is reflected and arranged in the unity of its nostalgia. But with its first move, the world cracks and tumbles: an infinite number of shimmering fragments is offered to the understanding."* The intrusion of the conscious mind has a disruptive effect. The theoretical problem is how to reconstruct that unity consciously.

*Albert Camus, *The Myth of Sisyphus* (New York, Vintage Books, 1955), p. 14.

Because this can't be done, Camus calls the world "absurd." But need it be done? This problem, which torments so many thinkers, doesn't disturb the average person. I have never heard a patient complain about it. Their complaints focus on practical issues and conflicted feelings. I have never seen a patient who suffered from "existential" anxiety. In every case I have worked with, the anxiety could be related to a "choking in the narrows." Why do we assume that consciousness can provide all the answers, when all evidence shows that it creates as many problems as it solves? Why are we so arrogant as to believe we can know everything? It is not necessary.

The answer to these questions is that we have become afraid of the dark, of the unconscious and of those mysterious processes that maintain our being. Despite every advance of science, they remain mysterious, and I am content that some mystery remains in our lives. A light without shadows is a painful glare. If we can light up everything, we risk creating a "whiteout" that would destroy consciousness. It could be like the flash of light in the brain of an epileptic that precedes the convulsion and the blackout. As we continue to heighten consciousness at the top of the pyramid, we can easily pass over to the state of self-consciousness and become immobilized.

Bioenergetics proceeds differently. By expanding consciousness in a downward direction, it brings the individual closer to the unconscious. Our aim is not to make the unconscious conscious, but to make it more familiar and less frightening. When we descend to that border area where body consciousness touches the unconscious, we become aware that the unconscious is our strength, while consciousness is our glory. We sense the unity of life and realize that life is the meaning of life. We may even descend further and allow the unconscious to envelop us as in beautiful sleep or ecstatic orgasm. We then become renewed in the deep wellsprings of our being and can rise to a new day with a heightened consciousness that does not need to hold onto its ephemeral light because of fear of the darkness.

Words and the Heightening of Consciousness

In 1949 Reich changed the name of his form of therapy from character-analytic vegetotherapy to orgone therapy. Orgone was the name he gave the primordial cosmic energy. This change coincided with his belief that words could be dispensed with in the therapeutic process, since significant improvement in personality could be effected by direct work on the body's energy processes. Orgone therapy also involved the use of the orgone energy accumulators to charge the body.

I reported in the first chapter that Reich had been able to help some patients develop the orgasm reflex within a very short time, but that it did not hold up in the post-therapy period. Under the stress of daily living the problems reappeared, and the patient's ability to give in to his body collapsed. But what exactly does "working through one's problems" mean? We use this term glibly without spelling out its dimensions.

Analytically speaking, a problem is worked through when a person *knows* its what, how and why. What is the problem? How does it affect my behavior in life? Why do I have this problem? The technique of psychoanalysis aims to provide answers to these questions. Why, then, hasn't it worked more effectively? The answer is that there is a fourth factor, an economic or energetic factor. Reich showed that unless there was a change in the sexual functioning of a patient or in his energy economy—that is, unless he had more energy than he discharged more fully—a patient did not improve significantly.

Knowing is not enough. We all are familiar with people who know something about the what, how and why of their problems without being able to change their emotional responses. So many books have been written on psychology that a fairly comprehensive knowledge about personality problems is readily available. These books rarely help a person work through his problems, even when they provide complete information about their what, how and why.

The reason is that knowing is a function of head consciousness which does not necessarily penetrate and affect body consciousness. Of course, it *can* affect body consciousness. This happened in the early days of psychoanalysis, before people became psychologically sophisticated. Then the patient who learned through the interpretation of a dream that he had an incestuous involvement with his mother was emotionally upset and physically stirred by this knowledge. It had an *impact* on him, to which he responded with his total being. It was an effective insight. Today patients talk glibly of their hatred of their mothers or the rejection they experienced by their mother without any strong emotional or energetic charge to their words.

It was precisely this situation, talking about feelings, but not feeling, that led Reich to first develop the technique of character analysis and then the techniques of body "dearmoring." And we are still caught up in the mystique of words, as if saying it changed things. I think it goes even further. We often use words in order not to change anything. We feel safe so long as we can talk about it, for talking reduces the need to feel and to act. Words are a substitute for action, at times a very necessary and valuable one, but at others they are a block to the life of the body. And when words are used as substitutes for feeling, they abstract and diminish life.

There is always the danger in relying on words that they do not express the truth of the person. People lie deliberately. They cannot do so on the body level since the masking of a feeling betrays the insincerity. I do not often encounter people in therapy who consciously lie to me, although this does happen. But there is the matter of self-deception, when a person makes a statement that he thinks is true but that does not accord with the truth of his body. People often say, "I feel fine," when even a cursory look reveals they appear tired, sad or dejected. It may not be a deliberate lie; often it is a façade they erect with words, more to convince themselves than others.

Who would dare proclaim he believes all the words people say? Such a person would be consummately naïve or foolish. Every therapist distrusts a patient's words until he gets behind the façade or the defenses the patient has unconsciously erected against self-disclosure.

It is therefore understandable why Reich tried to get beyond words and to treat a patient's problems on the body or energetic level alone. Why, then, did he fail? Because with due regard for their unreliability, words are indispensable to human functioning.

Words are the great storehouse of experience. They serve this function on a cultural level, in the stories we are told and in the books we read. They are not the sole storehouse, but they are by far the most important. History is not recorded only in words—there are the artifacts we discover or retain from past times—but to study history without recourse to words, written and spoken, would be a superhuman task.

Words serve the same function for an individual as they do for society. The living history of a person's life is in his body, but the conscious history of his life is in his words. If he lacks the memory of his experiences, he will lack the words to describe them. If he has the memory, it will be translated into words he will frame for himself, speak out or write. In any case, once a memory is translated into words, it takes on an objective reality, more so when the words are expressed. In my own therapy when I saw the image of my mother's face looking angrily at me for having disturbed her with my crying, I said out loud, "Why are you angry with me? I am only crying because I want you." I experienced the feeling as a child but spoke with the words of an adult. In doing so, I became acutely conscious of both the sense of hurt and shock at her reaction. Knowing this, I could understand why I have reacted in later life with similar feelings of shock and hurt when I encountered the same response to my reaching out to someone.

In speaking out, I objectified the experience for both myself and my listener, Reich. He, too, understood the experience and shared it with me. Sharing it made it even more real, for if I forgot, he might remember.

This is an isolated example. In the course of therapy one

discovers and relates many lost experiences that are hidden parts of the self. Reliving the experience on the body level provides a sense of conviction that can be attained in no other way. But talking about them to another person gives them a sense of reality only words can offer. This attaches to the part of the self or body involved in the experience, promoting its integration into the personality.

Feeling and experiencing are important, for without them the words are empty. But experiencing alone is not enough. One needs to talk about the experience repeatedly, to plumb all its nuances and meanings and to make it become objectively real in one's consciousness. If one does this, one doesn't have to relive the experience itself again and again to make it an effective agent for change. In this case the words evoke the feelings and become appropriate substitutes for action.

I believe talking is so important in the therapeutic process that I allow about half of all the time for talking with my patients. Sometimes whole sessions are spent discussing behavior and attitudes and seeking their connection with past experience. And some talk always accompanies the body work. There are times, however, when I sense that the discussion is repetitious and leads nowhere. When this happens, we get into the exercises, designed to provide the experiences about which we talk.

Readers who are familiar with my repeated emphasis on the direct connection between reality and the body may be surprised and confused when I now speak of the reality of words. This confusion is inevitable if we ignore the fact that modern man has a dual consciousness, as I pointed out in the preceding section. Words do not have the same sense of immediate reality as a bodily experience; their reality is mediated through the feelings they express or evoke. Words can, therefore, be unreal when they are completely dissociated from any feeling. But for many people, especially children, words can have a more powerful impact than a blow.

Children are not the only ones who can be deeply hurt by words. I think we all are aware of this fact. A highly conscious person chooses his words carefully when communicating a criticism or negative response, to avoid injuring another person's self-esteem.

Just as words can injure so they can have a very positive effect. A word of commendation or praise is deeply appreciated. It is one thing to sense your effort is recognized; it is another to hear that recognition expressed in words. Even when one senses he is loved, to hear the other person say, "I love you," is exciting, gratifying and enriching. I could give many such examples. "You are beautiful." "You are a dear." And so on.

I can only speculate on why words have such power. Feelings are subjective; words, however, have an objective quality. They are out there to be heard or seen. They also endure. We all know it is not easy to erase the effect of a spoken word. Once said, words seem to last. Some may ring through eternity. Patrick Henry's "Give me liberty or give me death" has persisted as a monument to the human spirit long after the man and the situation have faded from memory. Shakespeare's words have a similar immortal quality.

Since words are the repository of experience, they also serve to mold and shape future experience. When a mother tells her daughter, "Men are selfish. Don't trust them," she is first communicating her own experience and secondly structuring her daughter's future experiences with men. But it is not necessary to add the injunction. Simply saying either "Men are selfish" or "Men are not to be trusted," has the same effect. This is what we call schooling. The purpose of a school is to communicate past experience to a child mostly in the form of words and, in the same process, to structure the child's future relationship to the world in line with that experience.

I cannot go into the question of the values or the handicaps created by the process of schooling children. The institution of schools was necessary to the development of our present culture. The issue in any school program is whether the experience communicated was accurately perceived and is honestly reported. Certainly, in the matter of teaching history, distortions are not uncommon.

We are concerned with the power of words to shape experience. Consider the child who is told by a parent, "You never do anything right." This child will suffer throughout life to some degree from the sense that he can never do anything right. This feeling of incompetence will persist regardless of how well he actually performs in life. The words have become imprinted on the child's mind, and their erasure is no easy task.

In most cases I have treated I have found some evidence of imprinting often of a negative character. One patient reported she was told by her mother, "No man will ever want you," and these words were like a curse laid upon her. Here is another example. A patient told me, "I can't have friends. I expect and want too much." I knew this was true of him, but I didn't know why he persisted in making what he knew were unreasonable demands. We had discovered that his mother had been hostile to him in many ways. So I asked him, "Is it too much to ask for a mother who isn't hostile?" He immediately replied, "Yes, it is too much." When I asked, "Why?" he said he couldn't have one. I pointed out that my question dealt with *asking*, not *getting* . "Is it too much to ask?" He answered, "It wasn't for others; it was for me." And then, "My mother always said I asked too much."

A child never asks for "too much." It asks for what it wants. The "too much" is an adult evaluation that serves to make the child feel guilty just for *wanting.* The effect of the guilt is to cause the person to ask for too much so he can be rejected. The rejection supports his guilt and closes the circle in which he is trapped.

The power of words can only be countered with other words. The new words must have a ring of truth, must strike a bell within the patient if they are to free him from the bind of words. This is what we do when we work through a problem, analytically elucidating its what, how and why. This process leads to what the analysts call insight, which may be defined as "seeing the distortion in the imprint."

I am not arguing that analysis and insight alone will change a personality. There is another important factor, the energetic factor, that must be dealt with on the body level. What I am arguing is that a change in personality can be sustained only if there is sufficient insight as a result of a thorough working through of the problems.

The quick "cure" Reich was able to achieve could be called a magical transformation or a transcendental experience. It happened to the patient as a result of who Reich was and what he did. I have done similar "magic" for patients, but I know, too, such changes do not hold up. Just as the change can happen in one set of circumstances, so it can be lost in another. When it is lost, the patient doesn't know the way to his liberated state. He needs a map, just as Conway did when he was searching for Shangri-La.

One of the purposes of the analysis is to create that map in the patient's mind. It is a map of words, made up of memories, and is therefore the full history of the person's life. When it all comes together like the pieces of a jigsaw puzzle, it finally makes sense, and the person sees who he is and how he is in the world, as well as knows the why of his character. The result is a heightened consciousness of himself, of his life and of the world. All through my therapy with patients I alternate between expanding consciousness on the body level and heightening consciousness on a verbal level.

One of my patients expressed this idea succinctly. She said, "If you don't verbalize your feelings, it doesn't work in the end. It's the final clincher. It's the thing that sets the picture." I understood immediately. Words set the picture for better or worse. I would go further and say that words create the picture in our minds of the world around us. Without it we are lost, which is one reason why the schizophrenic *is* lost. He has no complete picture of the world or himself, but only dissociated fragments he cannot piece together. If the picture is seemingly complete but inaccurate because of illusions, we have a neurotic situation. As therapy progresses, one gets an increasingly clear and true picture of what one's life has been and who one is. No therapy is finished until the picture is complete. But, I must say again, the picture is a verbal one, not a visual one. Through the right words we see and know ourselves. We can consequently fully express ourselves.

Using the right words is an energetic function because it is a function of consciousness. It is the awareness of the exact fit between a word (or sentence) and a feeling, between an idea and a sentiment. When words and feeling connect or dovetail, the energetic flow that ensues increases the state of excitation in the mind and body raising the level of consciousness and sharpening its focus. But making the contact is not a conscious operation. We make a conscious effort to find the right words to fit our feelings—every writer does this—but the fit itself happens spontaneously. The right words slip into place, sometimes unexpectedly when we are open to our feelings and allow them to flow. I believe that the energetic charge associated with the feeling excites and activates the neurons of the brain involved with word formation. When these neurons respond appropriately to the sense of the feeling, the proper fit occurs, and a light seems to flash in one's head.

People somes use words that are not connected with feelings. In that case we say of the person that he speaks off the top of his head or out of his hat. These expressions can also mean that the words are unrelated to the reality of the situation. I am interested in the expression itself, for it is the language of the body and denotes some awareness of the dynamic processes involved in verbal communication. This becomes clear when we contrast these expressions with their opposite, "He speaks from his heart," or "His words come directly from his heart." Speaking from the heart is manifested in the tone of the voice and in the use of words that simply and directly express the speaker's heartfelt sentiment. When a person speaks from his heart, we are immediately impressed with his integrity and with the integrity of his statements.

When a person's words come only from his head, they lack this simplicity and immediacy. They are either technical or intellectual and reflect the speaker's primary concern with the idea rather than the feeling. I am not criticizing such speech when it is appropriate. But even in this situation most good speakers infuse their discourse with the language of the body and of feeling. They do this because they cannot fully dissociate their ideas from their feelings.

The dissociation of the two leads to a sterile intellectualism which some people mistake for erudition. Regardless of what the person says, one finds his remarks unexciting and leading nowhere. Recently on public TV I saw an interview between William Buckley, Jr., and Malcolm Muggeridge. The contrast in the speech of the two was striking. Muggeridge expressed his ideas in fairly simple language and with feeling. Buckley, on the other hand, used words generally found only in philosophic treatises. Muggeridge was interesting, Buckley was dull, and this difference was apparent in their bodies. Muggeridge, the older man, had clear, bright eyes and a lively, easy manner. Buckley was stiff, restrained, and his eyes looked washed out.

Words are the language of the ego in the same way that movement is the language of the body. Ego psychology is therefore concerned with the words a person uses. No serious study of the human personality can ignore the importance of the ego and its psychology, but neither can it be limited to that aspect of the personality. The ego is not the person and does not function independently of the body. A dissociated ego and a dissociated intellectuality represent a loss of integrity in the personality. Ego psychology is impotent to overcome this problem, for its exclusive focus on the ego furthers this dissociation. One has to approach the problem from the side of the body and its feelings to institute a healing process. But this approach must take cognizance of the fact that it is also one-sided.

Only through words can we bring a conflict to a head and resolve it. I use the word "head" in the literal sense of the head of the body. All organisms move headfirst through life, as they came headfirst into life. The head with its ego functions is the spearpoint of the body. Imagine an arrow without an arrowhead, and you have the picture of a body with its feelings but without a head to translate those feelings into effective action in the world. But let us not forget that an arrowhead without a shaft, or an ego without a body, is a relic of what once was a life-force.

Principles and Character

The failure of ego psychology to resolve the problem of the dissociated intellect has led in recent years to the development of techniques that emphasize regression as a means of helping a person reach a deeper feeling state. In many cases these regressive techniques expand consciousness by getting a person in touch with suppressed infantile feelings. Bioenergetics uses such techniques and has used them for many years. But regression and expanding consciousness are not ends in themselves or valid therapeutic goals. What every patient wants is to be able to function in the world as a fully integrated and effective human being. This can be achieved only if regression is balanced by progression, an expanded consciousness by a heightened consciousness, the movement downward by an equivalent move upward toward the head. One goes backward in time to move forward in the present.

Balance is an important quality of healthy living. This statement is so obvious it needs no support. We speak of a balanced diet, a proper balance between play and work, between mental activity and physical activity and so on. We are ordinarily not aware, however, how deeply the principle of balance operates within our bodies and in nature, although there we have become increasingly conscious of its critical importance. We have taken nature for granted and exploited it, upsetting the very fine ecological balance on which our survival depends. Now that our survival is threatened, we are beginning to realize the dangers of our ignorance and greed. And we have done the same with our bodies.

The principle of balance as it operates in the living organism is best exemplified by what is known as the homeostatic mechanisms of the body. The chemical processes of the body require the maintenance of a sharp balance between the hydrogen and hydroxyl ions in the blood and other fluids of the body. The optimal proportion is represented by an acidity of 7.4. Too many hydrogen ions create a condition of acidosis; too few result in an alkalosis. Either can lead to coma and death. Since life is not a static condition, but a process involving a continual interaction and exchange with the environment, the acidity of the blood is not constant. It fluctuates between narrow limits, 7.38 to 7.42, controlled by a feedback system that regulates acidity through respiration.

When the balance shifts to the acid side too much, an increased respiration blows off carbon dioxide, reducing the hydrogen ion concentration. When it shifts to the alkaline side, a decreased respiration leads to the retention of carbon dioxide and to an increase of hydrogen ions in the blood.

We know that our internal body temperature should hold fairly steady at 98.6 °F. We are not conscious, however, of the subtle mechanisms that stabilize our temperature. When we are cold, we shiver. Shivering is not a purposeless reaction. The hyperactivity of the muscles in shivering produces the heat needed to maintain body temperature. The shivering stimulates respiration, adding more oxygen for the metabolic fires. The involuntary tremors of the muscles in bioenergetic therapy have a similar effect. Increased body heat is automatically discharged by increased sweating and diminished by a reduced muscular activity.

Consider our fluid state, which has to be maintained at an optimum level so we do not become either dehydrated or waterlogged. On an unconscious level the body balances fluid intake with fluid discharge. The conscious mind plays a small role in this process, limited to finding and drinking water when the body sends it a signal of need. The body "knows" what it needs and what to do. So amazing is this "knowledge" that W. B. Cannon, who investigated these processes, entitled his study, *The Wisdom of the Body*.

Man intervenes consciously in these processes when the homeostatic mechanisms break down as a result of illness. His intervention is designed to restore the balance so the body can heal itself and maintain its life function. Balance is the important principle.

In terms of our larger activities, balance is equally essential. This is clearly illustrated in our stance and in our walking. We stand on two feet, and only when we stand on two feet are we properly balanced. One can disrupt a person's equilibrium by requiring him to stand on only one leg. This is what we do with our falling exercises. We walk or run on two legs, and we maintain our balance beautifully by shifting from one leg to the other. We don't do this consciously. If we intrude our consciousness too strongly into this activity, we would not go far. The story of the centipede that tried to decide consciously which leg to move and in what order is to the point. The poor creature couldn't move at all.

Balance implies duality—like having two legs—or polarity like the north and south poles of a magnet. It is represented in the blood by the balance between H^+ and OH^- ions. But balance is not a static phenomenon, for if it were, no movement would be possible. It would be impossible to walk if both legs were similarly and simultaneously activated. One would jump not walk. Life is movement and balance at the same time, or balance in movement. This balance in movement is achieved by a shift in charge, an alternation of excitation from one pole to the other, from left foot to right and back again, from breathing in to breathing out, from expansion to contraction, from the consciousness of the day to the unconsciousness of sleep. This rhythmic activity of the body is the *unity* underlying all the dualities we are conscious of.

There is no duality in life without an underlying unity. And there is no unity without its corresponding dualities. This concept of the duality and unity of all living processes I inherited from Wilhelm Reich. I regard it as his greatest contribution to the understanding of both the human personality and life. He postulated it as the principle of unity and antithesis in all natural functions. The dualities are always antithetical.

Our logical minds see things only as dualities—as cause and effect. This is the mechanistic attitude. Our spiritual minds, if I may use that term, see only the underlying unity. This gives rise to a mystical attitude. To comprehend the paradox of unity *and* duality is the province of functional thinking. That requires a new consciousness neither mystical nor mechanistic. And life is a paradox. It is a fire that burns in water, not on water, like an oil fire, but as part of the water. The amazing thing is that we are not consumed by the fire or drowned and lost in the water. There is a mystery here I believe will never be resolved or, at least, I hope it won't. Mysteries are essential to human beings, for without them we would lose our sense of awe and finally our respect and reverence for life itself.

Functional thinking is dialectic, and I have used dialectic diagrams throughout my work to explain relationships. I will use one now to show the relationship between the two modes of consciousness.

From the point of view of consciousness all one can be aware of is dualities, head consciousness or body consciousness, thinking or feeling. The unity exists only on the level of the unconscious or in the body processes beyond perception. How can we know that unity exists if we do not perceive it? We can deduce it, we can intuit the relationship, and we can vaguely sense the unity since the boundary between consciousness and the unconscious is not a wall but a twilight zone. On our diurnal passage through this zone we get many intimations of the underlying unity. Mystics whose consciousness extends more easily into this twilight zone are more aware than others of the unity.

There is another way to sense the unity. Head or mind consciousness and body consciousness not only interact with each

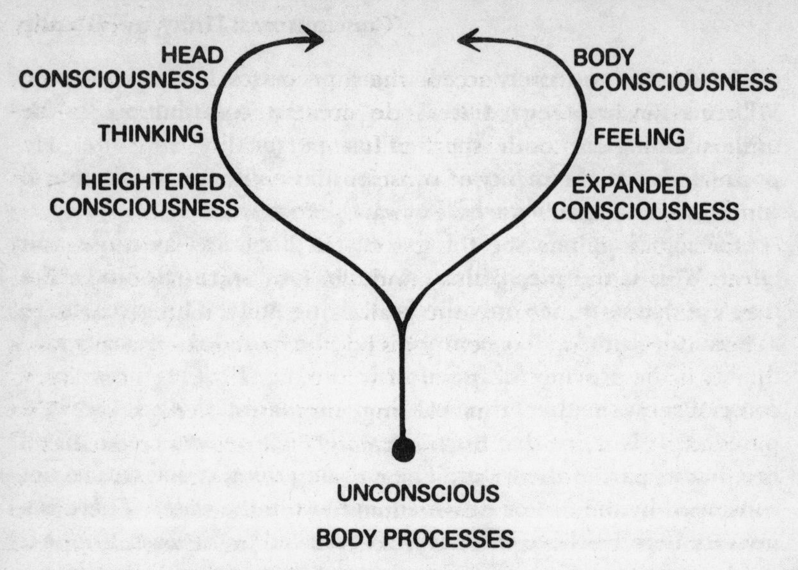

other, but touch and occasionally fuse. In the heat and excitement of the fusion they are sublimated and become a unitary consciousness that is both conscious and unconscious at the same time (another paradox). I experienced a number of such fusions in my life. As a child I become so excited watching a game that I couldn't tell for a moment whether I was dreaming or awake. I had to pinch myself to find out. And in sex I experienced an orgasm that sent me flying, extinguished my boundaries and made me conscious of my unconscious. These are ecstatic experiences. They have happened to many people. When it happens, the person "knows" and feels the unity of life.

Most of the time, though, we function with a dual consciousness. And that is normal, for ecstasy can only be an extraordinary experience if it is a true ecstasy. However, we are closer to that state when consciousness is both heightened and expanded. The two arrows of the dialectic diagram approach closer to each other.

To do this, we must accept the dual nature of consciousness. There is no ecstasy on either side alone, it is the meeting of the opposites that creates the spark of fusion.

If we accept the duality of consciousness, we must accept that on the conscious level we are aware of a dual nature to our personalities. When one focuses on thinking, as I am doing as I write, one is conscious of his mind and its mental processes. Since one's thinking is unique, one realizes he has a mind of his own. Then, if the person focuses on his body, he becomes aware it has a life of its own. From the point of view of consciousness one has to ask: "Who am I? Am I this thinking mind or this living body?" The obvious answer is both, but we cannot ordinarily be conscious of both at once. It is impossible for consciousness to focus on two distinct operations at the same time. Imagine two planes flying in two different quadrants of the sky and one searchlight trying to encompass both in its light; it is impossible. But this problem of man's duality does not ordinarily trouble us. The searchlight of consciousness is on a revolving table that turns quickly and easily. It can swing between quadrants so quickly that it can maintain both perspectives within the normal span of attention.

I can illustrate this concept since I use this facility consciously in public speaking. Over the years I have learned that an effective public speaker never loses touch with his audience. In lecturing I have made it a practice, which has now become a habit, to look at the people in the audience, to sense them and to talk to them. I might add that this habit has made it more difficult for me to talk to a microphone without an audience. But there is another problem in this habit or practice. If one focuses too strongly on the audience, one can lose touch with one's self, who one is, where one stands and what one has to say. And one can't be in both places at the same time.

All speakers face this problem. When reading from a prepared text, it is easy to lose touch with the audience. It is necessary then to look up and at them and make contact with them from time to time. What I do is swing my attention from the audience to myself and back again, in a smooth, rhythmical pattern so that there seems no break in contact on either side. This is the principle underlying the alternating motor. It is, the principle of rhythmicity which operates in us all the time, though most of us may not be conscious of its activity. It is like walking, which is possible only by alternately moving one leg after the other.

I believe in the value of duality on a conscious level. Without it, we could not move as smoothly and as effectively as we do to meet the various contingencies of life. Bioenergetics works on this basis. It alternates the focus from the body to the mind and back again, aiming to develop the patient's consciousness to the point where he can encompass both aspects of his conscious being in the span of his attention.

Of course this duality exists only on a conscious level. Below the level of consciousness there is unity; one is not a thinking mind or a feeling body, but a living organism. But since most of our life is spent in the state of consciousness, we have to be able to function with dualities. The whole theory of gestalt psychology is based on this fact—namely, that there is no foreground without its background, no figure without the field in which it exists, no quality without its opposite.

In the personality this means there is no thought without the framework of feeling in which it occurs. But focusing the light of consciousness on the thought plunges the rest of the field into darkness, and we often lose sight of the feeling that motivated the thought. We can, of course, check out our feeling and confirm that it harmonizes with our thinking. However, not infrequently, thinking and feeling conflict. I shall forgo any attempt to explain why this is so. The experience of this conflict is very common. I want to buy a bigger boat, but I think of the cost and the upkeep, and I am in conflict. Or I want to indulge myself by eating a delicious dessert, but I think of the weight I might gain, and there is conflict.

All therapists deal with conflicts not like the ones described above but similar in that there is a conflict between a feeling or desire one would like to express and the fear of the consequences. Since the consequences have not happened, the fear is present as a mental percept—that is, a thought associated with a bodily response. I am not saying the fear is imaginary because it is mental. It is physically experienced as fear, though it stems from a mental activity. Therapy deals with intense conflicts where the feelings seeking expression are important to the integrity of the personality and the consequences threaten that integrity. When one cannot resolve an intense conflict, the only solution is to suppress the desire or feeling that eliminates the fear and results eventually in the repression of the conflict. One removes the whole situation from consciousness, and in one sense, then, it doesn't exist. However, the conflict doesn't disappear. It becomes structured in the body on an unconscious level. It merely vanishes from view.

This manner of handling conflict creates the various character structures I have described. We consider such adaptations neurotic because they seriously disturb the person's ability to function as a fully integrated and effective individual.

But how do relatively unneurotic people handle the innumerable conflicts that arise in their lives between thinking and feeling? My answer is that they develop *consciously* accepted codes of behavior which are the opposite of unconsciously structured patterns of behavior. These codes of behavior take the form of principles.

It is interesting that while we use the word "character" in a negative sense, it has not always had that implication. In fact, "character" has often been used to designate certain virtues in which case it is coupled with the word "good" as in a "person of good character," while other people have "bad characters." The word "character" is related to "characteristic" and implies that an individual behaves in a typical or predictable manner whether good or bad. Predictability also means dependability; you could depend on a person with a good character to be virtuous and on a person with a bad character to be immoral or unprincipled.

But if a person's behavior is not structured or patterned, where does its predictability come from? In other words, how can a person who is relatively healthy, spontaneous and fully capable of self-expression have a character? First, we must recognize the difference between character and character structure. Adding the word "structure" denotes that the pattern of behavior is not consciously determined, but that it has become unconsciously fixed and rigidified on the body level. When a person's behavior is governed by conscious guidelines or principles, he will behave characteristically as long as those principles further his well-being.

The concept of principle is rarely mentioned in personality theory. We have almost reached the point in our culture where any principle is bad because it sets limits and determines responses. It is related to moral principles which so many people see as a restriction on their freedom or right to self-expression. This is an unfortunate development, for principles are the mark of a person who has achieved a higher level of consciousness. I am speaking, of course, of principles one consciously evolves, although they may be the same that society upholds and promotes.

Consciousness, we saw, begins with the perception of sensation. Sensations are generally localized or vague. In his respect they contrast with feelings that are more pervasive and more definite. When feelings become stronger and more sharply defined, we call them emotions. Thus, one could speak of feeling blue or low, but one would generally call sadness an emotion. The trouble is that we use the word "feeling" to include all body perceptions. Now, when our emotions become integrated with our thinking, we can speak of a principle. The order of development is as follows:

1.—Sensation
2.—Feeling
3.—Emotion
4.—Principle

On the level of principle, ego and body, thinking and feeling are integrated into a conscious unity.

One of the principles many people subscribe to is truthfulness. A person can be a truth teller because of fear of punishment by an all-seeing God, as a compulsive procedure or out of the *inner* conviction that it is the right way to behave. But to arrive at this conviction, one has had to have a choice between the truth and a lie. The conviction then arises out of the experience of telling the truth and telling a lie. In the former one senses the harmony between the feeling and the statement and perceives the pleasure resulting from that harmony. In the latter this harmony is lacking, and one can actually sense the painfulness of the conflict. One can then make a conscious choice based on body feeling.

All children lie at some time or other in their lives. They do it to explore the role of deceit and to sense the power it carries. Children will lie to test their ability to deceive their parents. It gives them a feeling of control if they get away with it. But they will also lie if they are frightened of the consequences truth may bring. In both cases they have gained something and lost something. The gain was in the sense of power and control or in the avoidance of punishment. But the loss is in the pleasure of being straightforward. If the loss is greater than the gain, the child will know that lying, except under unusual circumstances, doesn't pay for him. He will know that a lie is costly in terms of his good feelings, and he will develop the conviction that lying is wrong. His body and his mind will tell him so, and he will believe it not only with his head, but also with his heart. His conviction rests on two legs: knowing and feeling. In time and with further experience, truthfulness will become a matter of principle with him. He will avoid the conflict and the waste of energy in having to decide in the many situations that will confront him in life whether to tell the truth or a lie.

A principle operates like the balance wheel of a clock that maintains the mechanism's regular rhythm. The principle maintains the balance between thinking and feeling, so that both are harmonized without having to check each against the other constantly and consciously. Principles promote an ordered life; without them, I am convinced, there could be nothing but disorder and chaos.

It seems to me that in the absence of principles there can be no balance in one's life. It becomes easy to go to extremes, to justify the means by the ends and to follow the whim of the moment. One can get into the absurd position that every feeling is to be acted on since one doesn't know where to draw the line or, equally absurd, that all behavior is to be logically controlled. In the latter case we have an extreme rigidity, in the former no structure at all. People with principles avoid these extremes because the principle itself represents the harmony of opposites, the integration of thinking and feeling, the balance so essential to the smooth flow of life.

It is important to recognize that true moral principles cannot be inculcated by preaching, threats or punishment. These may make a person hesitant to tell a lie out of fear, but the decision will have to be made anew in each situation. This is not the same as having a principle that spares one the conflict. Further, the imposition of an outside force, whether as preachment or threat, disrupts the inner harmony and makes it more difficult to develop the inner conviction necessary for a principle. Let me put it this way: Principles are not commandments but convictions.

Here is an example of how a principle becomes established. I treated a young man who was heavily involved in the drug scene, although he hadn't fallen victim to heroin. Working with his body and expressing his feelings (hitting the couch in anger, for example) brought him to the state where he had good feelings in his body. Then one day he came into my office and told me he had smoked marijuana at a friend's house the preceding evening. "I lost all the good feelings I had worked so hard to get," he said. "I know now that marijuana is not right for me." Thinking and feeling had come together to create this conviction. It was the first statement of a principle that would become stronger as his good feelings increased, for he knew what he had to lose by using drugs.

It is impossible to develop principles if one has nothing to lose. Without good feelings there is no motivation to protect the integrity of the personality. The question of principles never enters into therapy until the body has been restored to a state of pleasure by a substantial reduction of its muscular tensions and blocks. Then the matter of principles arises spontaneously, as the patient strives to understand why he loses these feelings in the course of his daily activities. In the end, he develops his own principles of conduct to guide him in maintaining the state of pleasure or good feelings that is so important to his sense of himself and to his functioning as an integrated human being.

I don't think society is wrong to attempt to inculcate moral principles into young people. Each generation tries to pass its experience on to the next to facilitate their journey through life. Principles such as the Ten Commandments grew out of the accumulated experience of the race. But teaching principles is only effective when the preceptors' belief stems from their own inner conviction or feeling. In that case one would expect them to follow their own principles with pleasure. The absence of pleasure and good feelings in an older generation makes the young question their principles. Similarly, it makes no sense to proffer principles to bodies in pain. A principle is not designed to reconcile a person to his suffering, but to provide the inner harmony that makes possible a balanced and joyful life. Principles are not survival techniques. When the focus is on survival, principles are irrelevant. Before we talk of principles, we must be sure the young feel good in their bodies and about themselves. Principles make it easier for them to protect their good feelings.

There are many principles that people have discovered to govern their conduct in the interest of feeling good. Truthfulness is one; respect for the person or property of others is another. Several years ago my wife and I spent a week in Guadaloupe at the Club Mediterranée. My wife made the acquaintance of a local resident who was working on the grounds. In the course of their conversations she remarked that she had never tasted sugarcane. He offered to provide some, and they arranged to meet and go to a field of sugarcane. When they met, the man said it was a little distance from the hotel. On the way they passed several fields of cane, and my wife turned expectantly to the first one. Seeing her movement, the man said, simply, "Oh! But that is not mine." And he led her on to the field he owned, where he gathered some sugarcane for her. It would have been so easy to take a few stalks from any of the fields, but it was against his principles to take what didn't belong to him. I need not tell you what respect my wife felt for the integrity of this human being.

Bioenergetically, a principle is a flow of excitation or energy that unites head, heart, genitals and feet in one uninterrupted movement. There is a feeling of rightness about it, for the person feels connected, unified and whole. He needs no one to affirm its validity, and it is not subject to dispute. But it is a *personal* conviction, and he imposes it on no one.

Perhaps the biggest problem our society faces is the lack of moral principles in so many of its members. But I don't believe an imposed morality can work. It might keep a few people in line if it had the support of the majority, but it could never control the majority. I don't believe an imposed morality has ever really worked. The moral codes of the past were not imposed despite all evidence to the contrary. Moses brought the Ten Commandments to his people, but if these had not been in accord with their own inner convictions of right and wrong, they would have soon been discarded.

Moral principles are not absolutes, though some are close to being so. They develop to help people feel good and function effectively in a given cultural situation, and they become invalid when they fail to perform that function. Truthfulness may seem a natural moral principle, but there are conditions where telling the truth may be an act of weakness or cowardice. One doesn't tell the truth to an enemy when the truth would betray one's friends. A deeper principle of loyalty is involved here. But whatever the cultural situation, people need moral principles to guide and govern their behavior. Without them society would disintegrate into a state of chaos and people become alienated. If people develop their own principles, I am sure they will prove to be the same in a given cultural setting since human nature is the same.

In 1944 I wrote an article on adolescent sexuality for Reich's journal, *Sex Economy and Orgone Research.* At that time the advocacy of the right of adolescents to sexual fulfillment was considered dangerous. Discussing the matter with me, Reich said, "Lowen, it is not always advisable to tell the truth. But if you can't say the truth, don't say anything." Reich was a man of principles. He lived by them and died for them. One may disagree with his principles, but one cannot question the integrity they represented.

The underlying principle of bioenergetics is the simultaneous duality and unity of the human personality. Man is a creative thinker and a feeling animal—and he is just a man or a woman. He is a rational mind and a nonrational body—and he is just a living organism. He must live on all levels at once, and that is no easy task. To be an integrated individual, he must be identified with his body and with his word. We say that a man is as good as his word. With respect we describe him as a man of his word. To achieve this integration, one must start with being the body—You are your body. But it does not stop there. One must end with being the word—You are your word. But the word must come from the heart.

Index